PSYCHOLOGY AND TEACHING
OF READING

Psychology and Teaching of Reading

BY

EDWARD WILLIAM DOLCH, Ph.D.

Professor of Education, University of Illinois

AUTHOR OF

TEACHING PRIMARY READING
A MANUAL FOR REMEDIAL READING
PROBLEMS IN READING
BETTER SPELLING
HELPING HANDICAPPED CHILDREN IN SCHOOL

SECOND EDITION

THE GARRARD PRESS
CHAMPAIGN, ILLINOIS
1951

PREFACE

During the twenty years since the first edition of the Psychology and Teaching of Reading was published, much has been thought and learned about reading. Thousands of research studies have been made, and dozens of books have been written concerning reading. Much more improved practices have also become general in the teaching of reading in the schools.

Yet most of the published material on reading has dealt with circumstances surrounding reading rather than with the reading process itself. Many persons have studied the materials of reading, the eye movements used in reading, tests used to evaluate reading, what the teacher does about reading, and so on. We have very little scientific information concerning what the reader himself does when he reads.

Reading is after all a mental process. What does the mind do in reading? That is, of course, a psychological question. In teaching reading, as in all teaching, our methods and materials must be suited to the psychology of learning and of the particular kind of learning we are dealing with.

This book is frankly an attempt to explore the psychology of reading. We can study the mind in reading through all the evidences of its activity. Therefore our explanation of the psychology of reading must be based on all we know of reading and of how it is learned.

In seeking this explanation of what the reading process is, we try to use all the evidence available. Some evidence is given us by adults who study how they themselves read. Some evidence is given us by children who tell us how they read. Some evidence comes from what many children do or say as they read or after they have read. And some evidence is given us by results from clinics and laboratories. From the vast array of such evidence, we have tried to infer facts about the reading process.

The fundamental point of view of this book is that reading is a developmental process, a part of the general development of human beings. Therefore to round out the picture, we try to use in our explanations all that is known about human development. We try to show that reading is a growth, and to show how that growth takes place.

Since we, as teachers, are interested in the development of children and since we influence that development through the school, this book deals continually with school practices in the teaching of reading. Good teaching, as we have said, must be based upon how the child learns. If we can surmise how a child learns to read, we can tell how to help him develop in reading. This book therefore tries to put together what development in reading is with what the school can do about it.

Many thanks are due to thousands of teachers who have shared their experiences with the author. Teachers who know children can tell us a great deal about children and also about reading. The author has tried to consolidate the knowledge contributed by many such teachers, together with the results of all available experimental studies and also his own continued observation of children who are learning to read.

E. W. Dolch

Urbana, Ill.

CONTENTS

CHAPTER I

What is Reading?

To the skilled reader, the reading process may seem very simple. That is because the expert is largely unconscious of what he is doing as he reads and also because he has never thought of what reading really is. But teachers of reading must think of what the reading process really is, since they are to guide children in their efforts to acquire the many skills that we include under the one word, reading. Let us begin, therefore, by asking the question, What is Reading?

The Everyday Definition

If one were to ask the average citizen, "What is Reading?" he would doubtless say, "Why, reading is getting ideas from books." To him that is what reading seems to be. He is largely unconscious of what he does when he reads, and he has never thought about it. But a little thought will show the great inadequacy of this everyday definition.

READING AND IDEAS

In the first place, books contain the 26 letters of the alphabet in many different arrangements. These letter arrangements we call "words." Is a word an idea? No, a word is just a symbol for an idea. The

1

idea must be in the mind of the person looking at the word. If the person does not have the idea, the word means nothing. For instance, few persons looking at the word *"excoriate"* can "get" any idea because they do not have the idea that the symbol stands for. The idea is just in the mind of the reader. It is not in the book.

If anyone wishes to realize how he can be reading symbols and not "getting any ideas at all," let him take up a book on higher mathematics. He may be able to "read" or "say" every word, but his mind may be a complete blank. Similarly, if the average person tries to read a medical magazine announcing new discoveries to doctors, about all he will get is that "the something of the something does the something to something." The doctor may say that he gets ideas, but the ideas are certainly not in the magazine because the reader without the ideas gets no ideas.

If we use "idea" in a wider sense, however, we *can* get ideas *as a result* of reading. First, when ideas are relationships between things, the book can "put two and two together," as we say. The book can say, "The restless ocean," and we can suddenly recognize that we have never before put together the two ideas we have of "restless" and "ocean." We may say, "That's a fine new idea." We mean that we have put together two old ideas and made a new one. But the new one was not in the book. The book caused the reader to make the new idea in his own mind.

Likewise, we can get *new thoughts* from the suggestion of the book. If the book says, "Education makes life more interesting," we may get a new thought. We have the idea of education, and we had ideas about an interesting life. Suddenly we see that the two things go together, and we feel we have a new thought. But we had the "parts" of the thought before. The book just helped us put the parts together and we got the new thought "suggested" by the new words in the book.

It can rightly be said that reading means "meeting old words in new arrangements." In short, reading "shuffles" the ideas we have, and new *ideas* and *thoughts* result. Reading does this by bringing old ideas to mind in a new order or arrangement. If we have the ideas corresponding to the old words, we get the idea or thought corresponding to the new arrangement. The everyday definition of reading does not make this clear.

READING AND REACTION

The everyday definition of reading is inadequate in still another way. It seems to assume that the reader merely "takes" new ideas just as he would pick up coins that he finds on the street and put them into his pocket. It seems to say that reading is just "getting," and not "doing" anything. Our illustration of the coins will show the falseness of this conception of reading. Suppose you did see some coins on the street. Would you just pick them up, put them in your pocket and go on without a thought? To do so would be very unnatural. Almost certainly you would immediately begin to think about these coins. Where did they come from? How did they get there? Ought I to report finding them? And so on. The same would be true if you notice almost anything new in your surroundings. Suppose you saw a tree with yellow leaves. Would you just say, "Well, that's something new. A tree with yellow leaves. I will remember that." Almost certainly you would instantly begin to think, "Is that color natural? Or is the tree dying? What kind of a tree is it? How can a tree have yellow leaves?"

These illustrations and any others you may think of will surely indicate that the mind of a human being does not just "get ideas." If that human being is normal, he will immediately begin to "handle" those "ideas," to look at them from different angles, to question them; in other words, to think about them. Reading almost certainly includes thinking. If anyone reads without thinking, (1) he may be too stupid to think, (2) he may be too tired to think, (3) he may have his thinking blocked by resentment against being forced to read, or (4) he may have been taught "just to read."

It is to be feared that children in school are often taught "just to read." If one watches normal children in the early school years, one sees that they do not "just read." If they know the words they are reading, they immediately begin to think about the story. They ask questions. They add to the story. They applaud or condemn. They cannot help thinking about the ideas suggested to them. This is a carrying over into reading of their normal habit regarding language. In talking, if they hear a strange word, they instantly ask, "What is that?" If one watches their eyes, he sees the wondering activity there. To children, living is active, and language is living, and reading is language. It is to be feared that mass education has at times a sadly deadening effect upon this natural "thinking" about everything. Because in school most of the children must keep still most of the time, because they often must follow ideas they know little of or care little about, children all too soon develop a most dangerous passivity. As a result, very many of them *can* "read without thinking." But let us not call that situation normal. Let us not call it real reading.

Reading and Feeling

The everyday definition of reading, "getting ideas from books," also forgets completely the *feeling* side of life. Could we call the reading of poetry, just "getting ideas?" Would reading a prayer, such as Kipling's "Lord, God of Hosts, be with us yet, Lest we forget, Lest we forget," be merely getting ideas? Of course the man who gives us the everyday definition is not thinking of such reading. He is thinking perhaps of such reading as "Colorado is the seventh state in the Union for size, and the thirty-third in population." He does not see that there is any feeling about such reading. But let us consider that anyone who is from Colorado would certainly have feeling about that statement. He might think it incorrect and be angry. He might think it a fine showing, and feel proud. Or he might just feel happier to see any mention of his beloved state of Colorado.

The average man might be right in omitting feeling from reading in the sense that when he was in school most of the reading was about things he did not care about and could not care about; hence he came to believe that "you don't care about what you read." But if he would look at his present reading, he would not think so. He picks up the newspaper and skims over the headlines until he finds something he wants to read about. And why does he want to read about it? It is because it arouses his feelings. It may be a sad accident. It may be a horrible murder. It may be news that tells of harm approaching him or of something he has other interest in. In fact, his reading of the newspaper is almost entirely dictated by feeling. Even if he reads the ads, he is guided by his desires for a new car or a power lawnmower, or what not. The same is true of his magazine reading. Why does he get one mag-

azine rather than another? Because he likes and
wants the one and not the other. When he opens
the magazine, what does he read? He reads what he
wants to read, that is, what will give him feeling of
some kind. And when this same man goes to a library or bookstore, he is guided by feeling as well
as thinking. He is attracted or repelled by the covers
of books, by the illustrations, and by what is said in
the books.

We are conscious of feelings when they are strong,
but we are not usually aware of them when they are
mild or weak. Yet psychologists point out that we
are in some state of feeling all the time, including
when we are asleep. Even at times when we say
we have no feeling, we usually mean that we feel
depressed. So we must agree that the reading process is always a feeling process, as well as a thinking
process. Even the man doing mathematical or scientific reading is feeling. He is feeling a challenge and
stimulation if he is understanding, and a resentment
and concern if he is not. The boy in school is also
feeling a satisfaction if he is reading well, and a
worry if he is not; a drive of interest if the material
attracts him, and a sense of repulsion or annoyance
if it seems to him hard and uninteresting. All this
is in addition to his feeling about the ideas that are
being suggested to him, such as recollections of his
own puppy, or of a night in the woods or of helping
another fellow who was hurt, and so on.

The Everyday Definition and the School

Many of the failures of the school, and failures in the teaching of reading especially, have been due to a confusion with regard to the definition of reading. In the middle grades and in high school and college, far too many teachers are thinking that the everyday definition of reading is the right one. They have the common man's belief that "Reading is getting ideas from printed matter." Therefore they select the book or books which "contain the ideas" of their special subject, such as science, history, or what not. They then hand the books to the student and say, "Get the ideas from the books," meaning, in effect, "Get the words from the books." Then they give examinations in which the student is required to hand back the right words. If the student is good at memorizing words and is good at guessing just which words the teacher wants, he may rate as a brilliant student, even though he does little thinking or feeling during what he calls reading.

We have seen that the everyday definition of reading (1) ignores the fact that meaning comes from the reader's past experience, (2) seems to assume mere "getting," (3) omits any *thinking,* and (4) leaves out the *feeling* element entirely. Let us then try to frame a definition of reading that will be more satisfactory.

The Expert's Definition of Reading

Since we have just tried to point out what really goes on in the mind of the skilled reader during the process we have called reading, we can now frame a definition to include the various aspects of the process. Let us therefore say that for the expert reader, *"Reading is imagining, thinking and feeling about ideas and thoughts made from past experiences that are suggested by perception of printed words,"* (remembering of course, that we also read material in handwriting of all kinds).

In this definition, we have it definitely stated that reading is something that goes on in the mind. That is a fact never to be forgotten. Reading uses the eyes. It uses printed matter. But *the reading is done by the mind and is a process of the mind.*

Inevitably reading uses all of the capacities of the mind. For the mind does act as a unit, even though we think of its operations separately. For instance, we can discuss memory, but the mind never merely remembers without doing other things at the same time. The same is true of thinking or feeling or perceiving or imagining or what not. No process ever goes on singly and alone. Probably all of them are in operation at all times. Therefore, in all real reading, all the mental processes are involved.

READING AND GOOD TEACHING

Interestingly enough, good teachers have always known that many mental processes go on at once.

In preparing for a lesson in beginning reading, the good teacher "arouses past experience." She gets the children to *remember* experiences that are related to the reading lesson, and at the same time, she is arousing *feelings* of interest and pleasure, and she is getting *thinking* about those past experiences. Inevitably also, *imagination* begins to work on the materials thought of and presented.

Soon the class looks at the pictures for the story, and *perception* is added. Immediately, *memory* of more past experience is stimulated; *thinking* about what is in the pictures goes on; pleasant *feelings* spring up, aided by the skill of the artist in his use of form, composition, and color; and *imagination* runs ahead trying to make up stories about the pictures.

Then *perception* of words is begun as the children look below the pictures. But the teacher never thinks of reading as merely perception of words. Her questions and comments, the comments of the children that she encourages or asks for, all assume *remembering, imagining, feeling* and *thinking*. We may say "the teacher combines language with reading," but she is just encouraging all the mental processes in order to get greater and fuller understanding of what is read.

READING BY ADULTS

To see how reading operates at our own adult level, let us make an experiment that illustrates how all or most of the mind and its abilities operate in reading. Let us "perceive" some reading matter a part at a time just as we are bound to perceive it in reading. We shall give the parts, one at a time, and see what happens in our minds as we "read."

"The tired teacher . . ."

This unit of three words of the reading matter has just been perceived. What happens? Perhaps two things happen at once. There may be the thought, "Yes, teachers do get tired." There may at the same time be a real sympathy for "the tired teacher" since memory tells us we have also been just that "tired teacher" many and many a time. But notice that we do not know what teacher we are talking about. No explanation went before, and therefore memory cannot help us to understand why she is tired. But imagination is running ahead, and we wonder what this tired teacher looks like and what she is going to do.

". . . smiled kindly at the timid little boy . . ."

Now we know what she is doing. We remember that we have just read that she is tired, but she still smiles. We like her for it. We would also smile kindly at a timid little boy, for that is the way we feel toward timid little children. We remember many of them. And we think that of course if the boy is timid the only approach is to smile to encourage him. But what does the little boy want? asks our imagination. We have perceived this section of the sentence and have worked on it with memory, imagination, thought and feeling. So we go on.

". . . and said, "I will help you find your pencil.""

Here our thinking is rounded out and we can consider if the teacher is right in helping the little fellow or whether she should suggest he find it himself. But we do share her sympathy with the timid child, and we know from memory of our own experiences that we would be likely to help him ourselves. At the same time, we smile in appreciation that the pencil is a big loss to him but a rather ridiculous thing to worry about from our point of view. Where is the pencil? Where was it lost? Is this the schoolroom after school? We "think so," meaning "we imagine so."

This illustration can be multiplied every time we pick up a book. In reading we "perceive old words in new arrangements," but we do not and cannot use perception alone. We *remember* what has gone before in the sentence, story, or what not. We may remember illustrations above the type or on a previous page. We remember our own experiences. As we *think* of the meaning of our perceptions, in the light of our memory, we instantly cast ahead in *imagination* to what is coming, either in the sentence or in the story. And the ideas suggested have for us at once some *feeling* tone, even though it may be slight and not consciously noted. And if we are normal persons, we have questions, comments and *other thoughts* along with all the mental activity. All of this is reading.

The Time Element in Reading

One may immediately question whether any reader would do all the things we have suggested in the time it would take to read this simple sentence about the tired teacher and the timid little boy. Some readers would, and some would not, depending on many circumstances.

All of this feeling, thinking and imagining would be done if this sentence were part of an absorbing story which we were living along with the author. If the schoolroom and the tired teacher are real and vivid to us, it would be almost as though we were watching a play. The teacher acts very tired. The timid little boy opens the door and comes slowly in. The teacher looks at him. The child does not speak for a moment. If we were seeing the scene like this, we would be reading it very slowly so as to live the scene fully. Then we would think, feel and imagine just as we do in the theatre. Reading about the scene would be living the scene.

If, instead, we were glancing along "to see what happens," as we so often do in reading, all the mental processes would be shortened or made more or less unconscious. We might not even take time to "see" the teacher and the little boy, but merely get the word meanings as "some teacher" talking to "some boy," but not any visualized individuals. If we were in a hurry, as we have said, we might not care about either teacher or boy, and so would feel very little about them and perhaps not think at all. It is true that we all read that way sometimes and perhaps some persons read that way all the time. But is that real reading?

TIME ELEMENT IN PLAYS AND MOVIES

Here we have part of the explanation of why we find more pleasure in plays we see on the stage than when we read them in a book. The tempo of the play is slower and we have time for much thinking and feeling about what is going on. Likewise, we see the players and the scene, while in reading we must imagine them if we are to see them—and perhaps we do not take time to imagine in reading.

A similar example is the way people enjoy reading a book much more after they have seen the movie which was made from the book. It has been found, as a matter of fact, that when a movie is made of a book, either modern or classic, immediately there is a great demand for the book, and people report they read it with great pleasure. No doubt the explanation is that, having seen the movie, the reader imagines as he reads or he remembers the movie. He "sees" the people and places, and he therefore feels and thinks more as he reads about them. He would say they "mean" more to him.

Perhaps a similar illustration lies in the way we enjoy a good book more and more as we read and reread it. Each time, we "see" the action better, and each time we feel it more, and have more thoughts about it. This is perhaps the truest test of a "classic," or "book that lasts," that we can read it over and over and enjoy it more and more. Surely this is a case of giving more time to the reading, in the sense of doing more of imagining, thinking and feeling as we read.

TIME ELEMENT AND ORAL READING

We may say right here that this time element is a very important part of the problem of silent or oral reading. Children like to be read to orally. They can "see" and enjoy stories better that way. This may be because they do not have the distraction of word perception, but it is also a matter of timing. A "dramatic" reader reads more slowly than the inexperienced oral reader. But children also like to read stories orally themselves. They say they get more meaning that way. They obviously get more pleasure that way. It may be that they do so because the slower oral reading gives more chance for all the mental processes that give meaning. Finally, it is found that when one tries to read hard material, he gets more meaning if he reads it more slowly. Somehow the slow reading seems to enable the mind to do the things necessary for understanding. It is a matter of time needed for the mental operations.

This problem of the "time element in reading" will need to be remembered throughout all our considerations in this book. We shall call attention to it at the proper time, but the reader should realize that the time element underlies all the problems of word recognition, of word attack, of meaning, of sentence and larger unit comprehension, and the like.

The Expert's Definition and Beginning Reading

We have pointed out how true for the expert is the definition of reading, *"Reading is imagining, thinking and feeling about ideas and thoughts made from past experiences suggested by perception of printed words."* But this psychologically correct definition of reading must be used with caution in the schools, or it may cause much trouble. The teacher or the reading specialist may try to apply this expert's definition to the work being done by the learner in the beginning stages of reading. He would then be assuming that the expert's method of doing a thing is also the method of the beginner. That is a fallacy which misleads many persons with regard to methods in teaching beginning reading.

Many persons are mislead by their observing the performance of certain children. For instance, many children seem to "burst into reading," and obviously think and feel about the ideas and thoughts suggested by it. But such persons were not noticing the piecemeal, gradual, trial and error process that the children were going through before they had the complete reading process.

So also teachers who have classes of superior children make sweeping statements about how children "just read" if they are only motivated and then surrounded with books. What the teacher sees is the complete reading process *after* it has been built up. She does not see what these children have been doing to build up this skill. In the past, those children have been figuring out signs, they have been struggling with the newspaper and with magazines. They have developed by an irregular, piecemeal process that adults seldom see.

Let us therefore not assume that experience with children of superior background and superior mental age shows us that all we need to do in school is to motivate children and surround them with books. The expert's definition of reading is for expert adults and for the superior child. It may also apply to the average child if we give him material of *high* interest and *low* reading level. But it does not apply to the normal "teaching of reading" that we must carry on with the usual reading books in our reading lessons in the schools day by day.

The Learner's Definition of Reading

We have pointed out, and doubtless the reader has verified from his own experience, that many mental processes go on in reading, in fact, that reading actually includes all of them. It even includes motor reaction, for if one is reading about violent physical activities, he will find that his own muscles are responding. He will be unconsciously taking part in the fights, the flights, the tremendous physical efforts of the people he is reading about.

We have also stated that the methods and processes of the expert are not the same as those of the beginner. This fact is shown in the learning of almost any skill. There we find that the beginner has to think of one thing at a time, and cannot do the complete act smoothly and efficiently. In swimming, for instance, the beginner finds himself concentrating on arms or legs or breathing, and so cannot do the smooth coordinated act as the expert does. In handwriting, the beginner has to pay attention to one thing at a time until he can build up the whole smooth process. In almost any activity the beginner must pay attention to parts while the expert performs the act as a unit.

In addition, we must emphasize that in his reading the beginner is tremendously handicapped by lack of life experience. Consider the mere time of living, the child's six to ten years perhaps against our twenty, thirty or more. That comparison says we have many times the life experience the child has. But we can put it much more strongly: The child knows only his home, a few playmates, and his neighborhood. We know many cities, stores, shops, industries, and life of many kinds. We know classmates of school, high school and college, and friends of many neighborhoods, churches, clubs and so on. We have seen hundreds of movies, and have read thousands of books and magazines. The child has read a few school textbooks.

For the child, then, we will not at once use the expert's definition of reading, ''Reading is imagining, thinking and feeling about ideas and thoughts made from past experiences suggested by perception of printed words.'' We must have a simpler definition that will describe better what reading is to the typical school child.

Note d

What Is the Learner's Definition?

For the *learner's definition* of reading, then, we suggest the following:

''Reading is (1) recognizing most of the words, (2) guessing or working out the others, (3) getting the meaning and (4) then discussing the meaning in a class situation.''

We should note that this ''pupil's or learner's definition'' assumes several things. First, it assumes that the reading matter has difficulties. This is the normal situation for school reading. For the normal child, the textbook is never just ''easy reading.'' Second, our definition assumes a class reading situation. That is, it assumes the class is reading and discussing what is read. That is the normal situation in textbook reading.

The Learner and Easy Reading

In a good school, we do have, parallel to the text-book reading, a "wide reading" program which is very different from text book reading and which is more like normal adult reading. An adult normally reads material that is much easier than the limit of his capacity. For instance, the newspaper, which may be of about sixth grade level, is read by college graduates. All popular reading matter is of a level that is very easy for the educated adult, since mass publication must remember that the average schooling in the United States is not much beyond the eighth grade. So the adult reads "very easy" material most of the time.

In the "wide reading" period, we give the child also material that is "very easy" for him. If then we do give a child material that is within his experience and that is several grades below his maximum reading ability, he can read such material much as an adult reads the newspaper. Then he would be following the expert's definition, or "imagining and thinking and feeling about ideas and thoughts made from past experiences suggested by perception of printed words." But such reading is not typical "school reading." For most "school reading" we must use the learner's definition,

"Reading is (1) recognizing most of the words, (2) guessing or working out the others, (3) getting the meaning, and (4) discussing it with the class."

The Learner's Definition and the School

Even the learner's definition, true as it is, requires careful application to the teaching of reading. This definition has four parts, "Reading is (1) knowing most of the words, (2) guessing or working out the others, (3) getting the meaning, and (4) discussing it with the class." The great problem is the balancing and coordinating of these parts.

This definition tells us first that the child must know most of the words. Do we in our reading work, teach the right words, in the best way, and at the right time?

Second, the definition says the child must guess or work out the others. Do we help in this guessing, do we teach how to work out words and do we cause these two processes to work together to best advantage? And do we time correctly our teaching of methods of "working out"?

Third, the definition says "getting the meaning," but it does not intend that comprehension should wait until the third step. Comprehension may begin through imagination just as the child begins to read, and it then goes on during all the steps of perceiving some words and working out others. Comprehension also goes on during the last step of discussing. Getting the meaning is a gradual and continuing process. Meaning "grows on us." So the teacher must pay attention to the step of getting meaning at all times during the teaching of reading.

The fourth or last step of "discussing" may in part precede the reading, continue with it, and follow it. It may be a large part or a small part of the whole process, depending on the material. "Discussing" is a real and essential part of the learner's definition, however. The children discuss pictures and share experience and "dig up" experience as they read and after they read. Discussion "develops" meaning, through memory, imagining, thinking and feeling.

Since there are these different aspects of the learner's reading process, it is easy to see that we may over-emphasize one part and under-emphasize another. One of the frequent criticisms of the teaching of reading is "too much of this and too little of that." Such a condition may often exist. It is very hard for anyone to keep four things in attention at once. Just as soon as we begin to put more attention on one thing, the others tend to be lost sight of. So even the learner's definition of reading must be used wisely — differently with different children, with different material and at different times.

A Child's Mistaken Definition of Reading

We must admit that there is another definition of reading that is very common in the minds of children. It is an entirely mistaken definition, but one they have been led to build up from their school experience with reading. This mistaken definition is that "Reading is saying what is in the book."

We find this definition in the mind of the child who, when asked to read a selection for someone, said, "Are you going to ask questions, or should I just read it?" This definition is in the mind of the child who reads smoothly aloud and then cannot tell a thing he has read. It is in the mind of the child who repeats exactly what the book says and, when asked to explain, says frankly he has no idea what it is all about. Obviously, all such children,—and their number is enormous,—believe that "Reading is saying what is in the book."

Causes of the Mistaken Definition

How does this mistaken definition of reading arise? There are several possibilities. One may be that teachers accept smooth oral reading as satisfactory and go on just as if the child understood. The child may thus discover that he should put his efforts on smooth oral reading and that he need not bother to think of the meaning. You will note that in the Learner's definition of reading, "getting the meaning" tends to be a separate additional step with the child and not an immediate, integral part of the reading process as it is with an expert. The child may not take that added step because he has no incentive to do so and because we do not see that he does.

Another possibility is that some teachers so often accept the words of the book in answer to their questions that children think "getting the words of the book" is the proper objective. In the past, such has been exactly the objective of many schools and teachers. The book "had the facts" and if one could repeat the book, one "knew the facts." It seems strange to us now that at any time intelligent people could have so neglected meaning and failed to understand that meaning depends on experience. But there are still remnants of the old point-of-view with us. If we give a "question on the book," and the child gives us "the answer in the book," and we accept that answer without question, the child is certain to believe that "reading means saying what is in the book."

A third important cause of the situation is that so much of school reading matter is beyond the experience of the children. It is true that we begin with the home and the school, but very quickly we go on to the community and to adult interests and concerns. Even their own community is foreign to a great many children, whose world is the back yard, their toys and their close friends. These children are not now typical perhaps, because most children listen to adults and to the radio and go places with their parents, but there are still many children with such starved environments that they just do not know what much of the material in readers is about. If the child does not easily and naturally get meaning, he is not likely to ask about it or to struggle to get meaning for himself. It is much easier just to say the words.

In the middle and upper grades there is an even more serious situation as a result of our going beyond children's experience. Our traditional curriculum in geography, for instance, takes the children all over the world before they are fourteen years old. This might be all right if it were done largely in pictures, but instead it is done chiefly with words. It is impossible for a vast number of those words to have any real meaning to most children. So the reading becomes "saying what is in the book." The teacher may not like the situation but there will be examinations with questions which the children must answer. So if she just sees that the children have the right words, they may "pass." Thus, many teachers who know better go ahead letting the children think, as a practical matter, that "Reading is saying what is in the book."

Teaching the Right Definition

We trust that this situation may not long continue. *First* of all, we hope that every plan of the curriculum and every word of every textbook may take into strict account the actual background of the children reading and, when background is lacking, that it will be supplied. This is a great deal to hope for, but the movement for visual and auditory education is in this direction. So also is the movement for more understanding of child development and child psychology. *Second,* individual school systems are making great strides in making all reading a real experience for the children and not just "saying what is in the book." Individual schools under the leadership of wise principals are doing much in this direction. Individual teachers are attacking the problem by trying to make teaching more vital and meaningful.

Third, another way in which we can dispel this mistaken definition of reading from children's minds is to have every day the *wide reading period* already mentioned. In that period, the books will be easy and the material close to child life and interests. In that period, everybody will be "imagining, thinking and feeling about ideas and thoughts made from past experiences suggested by perception of printed words." This will be true because there will be no struggle with words; they will be perceived so easily and unconsciously that the child will not be aware of them as words. The reader will immediately get the ideas and thoughts, and they will be so interesting that he will be bound to think and feel about them. In this period, the children will be "lost in their reading," so that any noise or disturbance will

go unnoticed. When the period comes to an end, the
teacher will have to insist that the books be closed.
If this kind of reading is done every day, even fifteen to twenty minutes of it, the children will never
get the idea that "Reading is saying what is in the
book." They will be so accustomed to understanding what they read that when they do not they will
demand explanation. They themselves will say,
"Yes, that is what the book says. But what does it
mean?"

The Child's Mistaken Definition and the School

There has been in the schools some misunder-
standing of the child's mistaken definition of reading, that "reading is saying what is in the book."
Teachers and writers on reading have found out
that many children have this definition. College
teachers have discovered that even students in their
college classes may have it. When they ask such
students, even those in teacher training, for the
meaning of a reply to a question, the student may
say, "I don't know, but that's what it says in the
book."

In a sort of horror at this situation, some well-
meaning people have rushed to the conclusion that a
child should never "say what is in the book." They
have declared there should be an eternal ban on
any reading aloud of what is in a book, because if
anyone says what is in the book, he is bound to be-

come a "word-caller," a person who never understands what he reads.

Right Use of Oral Reading

This is a well-meaning but very strange attitude.
First of all, all the good readers now living started
by saying what was in the book. In their time in
school, oral reading in practically every grade was
universal. And here they are, skilled readers. *Second,* oral reading is the method in almost all schools
in the country right now, in spite of all efforts to
ban it in certain localities. The children want to
read aloud and the teachers feel they must have the
children read aloud if they are to know what the
children are doing. So the children are saying what
is in the book and still becoming expert readers.

Third, these well-meaning persons have reversed
cause and effect. "Saying what is in the book"
does not make meaningless reading. It is meaningless reading that makes children *merely* say what
is in the book, without thought of feeling. It is true
some children read only words, without meaning.
But that is a symptom. Let us not try to suppress
symptoms. Let us stop the causes. If the reading
is about things which children know and are interested in, and if the children discuss what they read
(which is the fourth step in the learner's definition)
they will read with meaning and thought. Then
none of them will think that merely saying what is
in the book is reading.

Remedial Reading

This book deals, from time to time, with prevention of reading difficulties, but it makes no attempt to cover the intricate field of remedial reading. All the problems in that field are dealt with in the author's Manual for Remedial Reading (Garrard Press, Champaign, Ill.).

Summary

What is reading? The average citizen would say, "Reading is getting ideas from books." (1) The *first* difficulty with that definition is that books contain only symbols for ideas. The meaning or idea is in the reader's mind. (2) The reading process is active, and is not mere "getting." This everyday definition of reading also neglects the fact that (3) we normally think about new ideas suggested, and (4) also feel about them.

The school has too often accepted the everyday definition of reading and put a premium upon getting words from books.

The expert's definition of reading describes what really happens when the capable adult reads, "Reading is imagining, thinking and feeling about ideas and thoughts made from past experiences suggested by perception of printed words." This definition emphasizes that reading goes on in the mind, and involves all the capacities of the mind. The good teacher knows this, and she therefore arouses memory of past experiences, gets perception of pictures and words, and stimulates thinking, feeling, and imagining. If we, as adults, watch our own reading process, we find that we also use all these capacities of the mind in reading.

The time element in reading is important, since time is needed if all these mental activities are to be part of the reading process. We use them all when we wish to get the most from our reading, though we may go more rapidly at times and neglect some or many of them. In school, the time element is important in audience reading, in oral reading, and in study.

The description of the expert's reading process must not mislead us with regard to typical school reading. Exceptional children may read in the expert's manner, but they learned their reading by an entirely different process which adults seldom see.

The learner's definition of reading is that "Reading is (1) recognizing most of the words, (2) guessing or working out the others, (3) getting the meaning, and (4) then discussing the meaning in a class situation." The school may provide a wide reading period where the reading is so easy and so interesting that the child may use the adult expert's method, but that is not the typical method of the class group reading lesson.

The school must carefully consider the learner's definition of reading and its implications. Each of the four parts must be studied and integrated with the others. (1) We must see that the child knows most of the words, (2) we must help him to guess or work out the others, (3) we must assist him all during the process in getting the meaning, and (4) we must see that discussion broadens and enlarges meaning and gets thinking, feeling, and imagining.

Unfortunately, the child often has the definition that "Reading means saying what is in the book." He may have this idea all through school and college. He learns it through our acceptance of smooth oral reading as sufficient or through our acceptance of the words of the book as answers to questions. An important cause of the situation is that so much of our school subject matter is beyond the experience of the children, and the child, and often the teacher, gives up trying to put meaning into the hard reading materials. Three remedies are: (1) in all planning, taking into account the children's background or lack of background, (2) making all reading work more vital and meaningful and (3) providing wide reading periods when the material is so easy and interesting that getting meaning is bound to result.

This mistaken idea that reading means repeating of what the book says does not mean that the book should never be read orally for fear of producing word callers.

CHAPTER II

Development in Reading

The traditional view of the child seemed to consider him as the sum of all his experiences, and then seemed to consider that learning to read was just another set of experiences that were to be added to the total. In other words, both the child and learning to read were thought of in a rather mechanical way. Therefore it was felt that if we could only discover which were the proper learning experiences, we could "give them" to every child and therefore every child would inevitably learn to read.

The modern view of child nature and of learning is quite different. The child is conceived of as a growing thing, just as every other living organism in the world is a growing thing. Every growing thing develops from its beginnings to maturity by a continuous process which is organic and not mechanical. A growing organism does not just add up experiences as with an adding machine. It somehow makes those experiences part of itself. After any experience, there is not just the old self plus the new experience; it is somehow a new self.

Taking this developmental view of child nature and of learning, we have two things to consider. One is the fundamental nature of the child who is growing. The other is the nature of the experiences that will help him grow in the direction in which we wish him to grow. The fundamental nature of the child will be found to underlie all we have to say in the following chapters. We will always be referring to child nature, to natural interests, and so on. All of the time, we shall be keeping in mind what the best thought tells us is the fundamental character of a growing individual in the early years.

INDIVIDUAL DIFFERENCES

At the same time, we will have constantly in mind the fact that individual children undoubtedly differ from one another in many fundamental ways. This may not mean that what is natural for one child is entirely unnatural or lacking in another. Such cases may occur or seem to occur. Rather, we will be thinking that children may have the same fundamental characteristics but may vary greatly in the strength of the different ones or in the way they interact. For instance, everyone seems agreed that curiosity about the new and strange is a fundamental characteristic of child nature, but we do become conscious in our dealings with children that they differ very greatly in the strength of this curiosity or in the direction this curiosity takes. Much of that difference may be explained by differences in training or experience, but, making all allowances for different training, there still seem to be fundamental differences in strength or direction of curiosity. Similarly with all the other qualities which we say are "natural" to children. We will expect to find different children differing with regard to them.

In our discussions of educational practice, it will be necessary to refer constantly to classroom allowances for such differences.

Child Experiences and the Beginning of Reading

It is perfectly obvious that school life follows some kind of preschool life. We must therefore make some assumptions or have some idea of what kind of preschool life children have. Here our emphasis on individual differences is very important. It may well be that children do have much the same experiences when in the cradle or in the play pen. The possibilities in such an environment are limited. But as soon as a child is allowed to crawl about the floor of the room or of the house, startling differences in experiences appear. At one extreme, the crawling child may be almost entirely alone. He may be an only child; his mother may be busy elsewhere in the house; he may have little to handle or play with. At the other extreme, there may be small brothers and sisters playing in the room. There may be a kitten or puppy. There may be a great variety of objects, from kitchen pans to sofa pillows. And the mother may be nearby and may often come in to speak to him or to stimulate or guide him in many ways.

The great differences in experiences that we have mentioned at the crawling period become even greater when walking is achieved and the child may go about more easily and may go farther afield. With each increase in age and in motor and speech development, the variety of kinds of experience increases, and the differences between children's opportunities to grow increase. In our discussion of reading readiness (Chapters III, IV, and V) much attention is given to this period of child development which precedes the school years. In all this discussion, the great emphasis is upon the differences in the development of individual children up to the period when reading is supposed to be begun.

The emphasis of all these chapters is upon the rather obvious point that reading has a natural place in child development and that it should be handled as a phase of that development. It is not just given to a child or "put on him" as you would put a coat about him. He grows into reading as he grows into everything else. The problem for the school administration and for the teacher of the first grade is to study how child experiences may be so managed as to lead naturally from preschool development and into reading development.

The Developmental Nature of Reading

Having developed the children up to the time for beginning reading, and having "grafted" the reading activity on to the natural growth of each individual, we must then consider that "learning to read" is a development in itself. Again, it is not just an adding of one thing to another, making a sum total called a skilled reader. The concept of learning as growth points out that children must grow into reading skill just as they grow into any other kind of achievement; and experience with the teaching of reading tells us the same thing.

Our failure to teach certain children how to read is the most striking proof that learning to read is a growth process. Our fundamental failure, perhaps, at all grade levels is to fail to get the child to want to work at learning to read. This failure is at all times and at all levels a failure to follow the fundamental growth formula, that the new desire must be "grafted on" to an old one. All desires go back to fundamental root desires in the human being, and every new desire must get its force ultimately from some such root desire. But it does not do so in any mystical way. Instead, the new must be so associated with or "grafted on" the old that the old drive sends its force into the new activity or in the new direction.

Those children in our schools who are eager to learn to read are showing in this new form their eagerness to learn that has previously gone in other directions. The children who continue to attack reading with enthusiasm are showing in this new way their old eagerness to attack and achieve. It is up to the school and to the teacher so to manage affairs that each and every child has his former drives channeled into the reading activity. If we do not manage this, the child does not have any drive in reading. And without drive, little is accomplished.

With later reading experiences we have the same difficulty. Our chief failure is in trying to give children experiences for which they are not ready and into which they therefore cannot enter with enthusiasm and success. Far too often, our material is unsuited either to the child's drives or to his stage of development. Very often the exercises we assign are not at all suited to the learner and therefore do not become part of him and are only gone through mechanically and without definite benefit. Reading is a growth for each and every child, and he incorporates into himself only that which is fitted to his stage of growth at the moment. All else does him no good.

Stages in Reading Development

It is dangerous to try to point out "stages" in any growth process because to do so may give a false idea of the situation. Growth is continuous and may be going on in many different ways at the same time.

Yet to guide our thinking and to guide also our help to the child, we must pick out different stages for our thought and study. In our further discussion of such stages in the development of reading, it must always be remembered that they are not distinct, they are not separate, they do not have definite beginnings and endings. If we can remember this, we will not falsify the situation.

The stages in reading development that we have identified constitute the chapters of this book. Though the chapters are self-explanatory, it will be helpful to make an overview of the whole at this time. Thus the reader may better see the interrelationships between the discussions and the reason for their arrangement. The three chapters on Reading Readiness deal with the pre-reading situation and therefore do not deal directly with the actual reading development.

1. BUILDING SIGHT VOCABULARY

The child naturally becomes aware of reading by becoming aware of words. He sees words on signs all about him. He sees words under the pictures in books. Other people look at those words and say something which the words somehow seem to tell them. Very soon, these adults tell the child that a certain set of marks says "garage" or some other word. Then when the child sees that same sign, he thinks or says "garage." He sees the same sign elsewhere and again thinks or says "garage." He is approaching reading by means of sight recognition of words.

When we say the child naturally learns words first, we do not mean that school teaching of reading should use the word method. That is an entirely different matter. We are just pointing out the first step in reading development as it occurs before the school begins its work.

In some cases the child's introduction to reading is quite different because the parents teach him the alphabet and teach him to recognize individual letters. Then the child sees about him what seems to be strings of letters rather than word units. He would not see "garage" perhaps, but six letters beginning with a "g." The parent might say the word "garage" but the child at first might not see the word as a whole. Ultimately, of course, he will see words as words, but we do not know how long it would be before he progressed from seeing letters to seeing words.

The sight method of learning words as wholes is the one universally used by the standard basic readers. They may introduce the words by means of the story or the sentence, but finally they would come to sight recognition of individual words. This method of sight recognition is challenged at times by those who believe that phonics is the right method to use in beginning reading, but the sight method is still the dominant one and for many reasons will probably remain so.

Learning of sight words is put first because it is the child's first introduction to reading. But sight learning continues to be a major factor in learning to read at all levels. At all times, in all subjects, the teacher or the other pupils tell what certain words "say," and the child remembers, thus adding to his sight reading vocabulary. In fact, when the child learns to help himself at word recognition by sounding, he does so in order that he may add the words which he sounds to his sight vocabulary for reading.

We shall see, when we discuss further the building of sight vocabulary, that we shall regard it as a natural growth process to be aided by the best motivation and the best techniques of teaching.

2. INDEPENDENT WORD ATTACK

In the beginning, the child usually reads in a class under the constant supervision of the teacher. This continues for some time, but then we wish gradually to lead the child to become an independent reader. Some children grow in that direction rapidly and others largely fail to do so. We can help children to become independent readers by motivating them as strongly as possible, and also by providing them with interesting and easy materials. But we must also help them to develop independent word attack.

Of the various methods of independent word attack, an important one is guessing from context.

This is a kind of growth that comes to some children very rapidly. If they have the interest in reading and are exposed to reading matter that is not too hard, they develop very rapidly real skill at using context. Other children do not develop use of context unless they are especially taught to do so. They seem to be hindered by the fear of failure or by past experience in which unpleasant consequences followed wrong guesses.

The chief method of independent word attack is, of course, sounding. The printed words represent sound words, and the child wishes to find out what they "say." He can do so by using the principles of sounding attack. Here, however, we certainly have a problem of growth rather than mere "learning" in the sense of memorizing. The growth has at least three steps: 1. the acquiring of knowledge of sounding principles. 2. the developing of habits of sounding attack, and 3. the developing of sounding skill.

Growth in sounding does not come for a child, however, unless we begin at the right time and in the right way. If we begin to teach sounding too soon, the child will meet with failure and will develop fear and antagonism. We must begin only when a state of "sounding readiness" is reached, and that varies with different children. Then, after growth in sounding has really begun, we must not try to push it faster than it can go. To do so again brings failure and stops growth. Developing sounding requires great skill on the part of the teacher. Heretofore we have been far from successful in securing growth in sounding by all children.

3. Developing Meaning Vocabulary

The development of meaning vocabulary begins with the very beginning of language, in the first years of life. It is a kind of growth that precedes all contacts with reading. But in our study of development of reading, we have put meaning vocabulary in third place. We have done so for purely practical reasons.

In the first step in reading, the building of a sight vocabulary, word meaning is not a problem. The teacher in the classroom uses only words of which the children already know the meaning. The first reading books carefully keep within the meaning vocabulary of the child. From time to time, the teacher may have to explain some word she uses or that appears in a book, but ordinarily, she would not devote much time or thought to meaning vocabulary.

Sight vocabulary is the chief concern of the primary grades, and at the same time, independent word attack is being developed. By the middle grades, there is presumed to be enough word attack for the children to begin wide reading in many fields. At once, the problem of word meanings becomes a

very important one. The teacher must give constant
attention to the new meanings. She should give
thought to methods of extending meaning vocabulary. She should develop in the children curiosity
about words. She should give them a desire to find
out about words and methods of finding out.

Our placing of Developing Meaning Vocabulary
in the process of growth in reading is therefore a
matter of emphasis. Its gets its great emphasis after
methods of independent word attack have been developed. From that time on it continues to be most
important in all growth in reading.

4. FLUENCY AT SOME USEFUL LEVEL

Fluency in reading is a kind of development that
is going on all the time. Naturally there is fluency
in recognition of basic sight vocabulary. There is
fluency involved in rapid independent word attack.
Fluency is affected by size of meaning vocabulary
and by its progressive development. All these kinds
of fluency combine to give fluency in getting meaning during the process we call reading.

The reason for giving special recognition to fluency in a study of reading development is that continued pressure for more and more development
along all the other lines is likely to hinder the development of fluency. We know that in the development
of every skill there are always two elements, (1)
ease or fluency at one level of difficulty, and (2) ad-

vancing to higher levels of difficulty. If all the thought and pressure on the part of the teacher and the school is to advance the child to ever higher levels in reading, there will not be either the time or the desire to develop fluency at any particular level of reading difficulty. Hence we have to "take time out" as it were, to look seriously at the problem of developing fluency, even though we may slow up development in other directions.

Our heading specifies fluency at "some useful level" because we must not think only of school uses for reading. All levels of reading ability have use in school, but outside of school, only certain levels of achievement are useful. When children get to the upper grades or higher, and as they approach the leaving age, we must begin to think of reading as playing an important part in their recreational or vocational life. The child must have some fluency in reading at a level that will be useful in that recreational or vocational life. In the past not enough thought has been given to this future use of reading. Now we are much concerned with guidance of children, and therefore are looking toward their future. That is why attention is here given to *fluency at some useful level*, meaning useful for the practical purposes of later life.

5. STUDY, OR GETTING MORE FROM READING

So far, we have been thinking of reading development as growth in the use of reading for the routine purposes of living, in school and out, those purposes being to expand experience in the many directions made possible by newspapers, magazines, and books. But the school is also thinking of carrying development of reading into more technical fields, into content subjects where the reading material is more difficult and where the purposes are not attained just by ordinary reading. Instead, the student must "get more from reading" than he will if he "just reads" the material. In other words, this section deals with the development of study.

We shall see that "getting more from reading" may mean growth in either or both of two directions. (1) There may be growth in methods of covering much material in a short time. This has been called "extensive reading," and is very important at certain times and for certain purposes. (2) There is also growth possible in what may be called "intensive reading," where more time is taken to get more from the reading matter than would result from ordinary reading. Various habits and skills may be developed with this purpose in view.

These two developments in reading should go on side by side, and the student must learn when to use each of the different kinds of reading at the proper time. The work of the school should involve many kinds of study, and the well equipped reader should have learned habits and skills which aid him no matter what his purpose may be.

6. A Lifetime Reading Habit

Finally, development in reading during the school years should blossom out into life-uses for reading when school days are over. This may be called developing a life reading habit.

After his school days are over, the individual may have fifty years in which to use reading for his life purposes. Does he do so? He does if during the school years he has developed certain attitudes toward reading and certain habits about the use of reading matter. He may or may not have developed skills, but if he has the attitudes and habits, the skill will develop in time.

Though we have mentioned Lifetime Reading Habit as if it were the crown or end of the process of reading development, it is not so. As a matter of fact, life reading habits are being built from the first grade on. All of the time, the child is learning attitudes toward reading and its value to him in his life and his personality development. This development goes on year by year. It may go at times in one direction, at times in another. Its course is never finally set until the last teacher has had contact with the individual. We should all of the time be thinking of this life reading habit as part of the individual's reading development as it is a part of his personality development. Though we are putting it last, a consideration of the great importance to the individual of his after-school reading may help us in developing reading most effectively during all the school years.

Summary

The traditional view of learning was a mechanical one. Now we think of learning as growth and development. Growth depends on child nature and on experiences. Throughout this book we shall constantly keep child nature in mind, and especially the great differences between children. The child experiences that come before reading also differ enormously.

Reading is itself a development and growth, and our failures in teaching reading have been chiefly due to our failure to make full provision for the facts of child development.

Though it is dangerous to speak of stages in growth, for convenience we shall note in our discussion the following "Stages in Reading Development":

1. Building Sight Vocabulary.
2. Independent Word Attack.
3. Developing Meaning Vocabulary.
4. Fluency at Some Useful Level.
5. Study, or Getting More From Reading.
6. A Lifetime Reading Habit.

CHAPTER III

Readiness as Mental Age and Interest

Obviously, it is unwise for anyone to attempt to learn a skill unless he is ready to learn it. There are always conditions that should precede or accompany efficient, wholesome learning. This is naturally true of learning to read. Hence, before we begin to consider the learning of reading itself, we need to ask ourselves about this state of readiness for the learning.

READINESS AT ALL LEVELS

The term "readiness" is often applied to readiness for reading at all levels; that is, at fourth grade level, or eighth grade level and the like. Usually, of course, the readiness needed for fourth grade is efficient learning in third grade and readiness for eighth grade usually means successful work in the seventh grade. In that sense, there is no problem as to the meaning of readiness for reading at the grade levels beyond the first.

In another sense, there is real "readiness" for each and all of the grade levels. That is, we may mean, not just "enough skill to take the next step," but conditions that will make the next step success-

48

ful. Here readiness would not merely mean previously acquired skill but also the conditions that are necessary for successful progress in learning. One kind of condition includes the setting in which the progress is to take place. For instance, a pleasant emotional atmosphere in the fourth grade room can be considered necessary readiness for the learning of reading in fourth grade. Another kind of condition implies knowledge necessary for progress. For example, some knowledge of Switzerland could be considered necessary readiness for reading about and learning more about Switzerland. These two factors, (1) "previously acquired skill," and (2) "conditions that are necessary," are factors at every grade level. However, it confuses teachers to use the word *readiness* in this broader sense. It is much more advisable to restrict "reading readiness" to mean preparation for beginning reading, that is, readiness *before reading is begun*. We shall hereafter use it in that sense.

It will be noted as we go on, however, that some of the things we discuss as conditions to successful *beginning* reading are also necessary conditions for success at all levels.

EMOTIONAL ADJUSTMENT

Much of the literature on readiness discusses *emotional adjustment* as a prerequisite for reading. It is true that we find many emotionally unstable and emotionally disturbed children in first grade and later, and we could consider them as a group. But a study of these cases shows that the emotional disturbance comes from many different causes and situations. These different causes and situations should be dealt with on their own merits. Therefore, we shall not have a separate heading of "emotional adjustment" but shall find the problem of emotional adjustment appearing in a number of different school situations. After all, the teacher deals with the child in a situation and must think in terms of the situation. If emotional maladjustment might arise, she will look out for it. But she can act much more intelligently if she is thinking of the actual child-life or school situation and sees directly how the emotional problem arises from it. Therefore, look for emotional maladjustment under all of the factors in reading readiness.

Readiness for Beginning Reading

A very practical approach to the problem of reading readiness is to observe groups of children who are supposed to be beginning the learning of reading. If one sits in a room with beginners, very soon one sees children who are not learning. Let us suppose that the teacher is doing the most efficient job possible; hence we cannot blame this failure to learn on the teaching. At once we must ask, "Why are these children not learning while the others are?"

They have the same favorable conditions that the others have, but they must be lacking somewhere. In other words, they must somehow lack "readiness" for the learning. If we study the individual cases, we will come to the conclusion that there are a number of different kinds of readiness which may be lacking.

Readiness as Mental Age

If we study the children in the beginning group who are not learning to read as the others are, we will find some who are definitely "too young" for the work. They are definitely immature. The teachers often call them their "babies." These children play rather aimlessly. They pay little attention to what is going on. They may even wander about the room. The teacher tells the others not to mind what they do as they are "too little" to learn with the others. And so they spend more or less of their time in the first grade room just "growing up."

This immaturity or "youngness" is very clear when the child is an extreme case. Some, for instance, have mental ages of four years when they enter first grade. Obviously, the job of learning to read is beyond them. School systems which have kindergartens try to keep these children in kindergarten longer, or sometimes they get the parents to retain them at home for a while. These clear cases of immaturity are recognized by all concerned, even by the parent if she comes to school and sees the situation.

The real problem of "mental immaturity" comes when there is a child not too greatly different from the others in this respect. This child is kept at his work with difficulty, but the teacher struggles to get him to concentrate on it. This child pays attention part of the time, but not long enough to learn as the others do. This child does learn some words, but he confuses them in a way the others do not. He is a "borderline case," as we say. He illustrates a real problem, which is to decide just where to draw the line between the mature enough and the too immature.

READINESS UNDER DIFFERENT CONDITIONS

If we ask just when a child is mentally mature enough to begin to learn to read, we must ask what conditions of teaching we are thinking of. Are we thinking of *individual teaching?* If so, it is obvious that we can get results with a younger child if we teach him individually. We can sit down beside him and direct his attention constantly. We can adapt immediately to his changes of interest and mood. We can deal directly with his individual past experience, and so on. A single teacher tutoring a single child can get results that are impossible in a group. She can get some reading done before six years mental age.

If, however, we ask when a child is mature enough to learn to read under group teaching conditions, then we must ask (1) what size of group? and (2) what kind of teacher are we thinking of? Suppose we have a school with *a group of fifteen beginners and a highly skilled teacher*. Under such conditions, relatively immature children may learn to read just because they actually get a great deal of individual attention. The teacher-pupil contacts are many. Usually in such a set-up there are many children of superior ability who actually take care of themselves, freeing the teacher to give more time to the slow. Finally, the superior teacher knows just what to do and how to do it and makes her contacts doubly effective. She can usually get reading done at six years mental age.

Here we must give the caution that even if this favored set-up makes learning to read possible by more immature children, we should not be too ready to take advantage of this possibility. Parents who find their children not learning in the public school often send them to a private school where they have these favored conditions. Then the children begin to learn to read. But should they do so? Immature children need general child development much more than they need reading. An immature child needs to become mature, not to become a "reader." It is usually very inadvisable to use special or artificial means to "force the growth" of a child in one spe-

cial direction. So, admitting the possibility that a
favored environment may permit reading at an
earlier mental age than otherwise possible, we do
not recommend that solution.

READINESS FOR THE PUBLIC SCHOOL

Ordinarily, of course, learning to read means
learning to read in the usual public school. In such
a school we practically always find thirty or more
children in the room. We very often find teachers
without special or extraordinary ability—just good
teachers. We find a shortage of materials of all
kinds. In other words, we find just "an ordinary
school." That is the only kind of school the admin-
istrator can calculate on. He has some superior first
grades; he hopes for more; but he has what he has.
What level of mental maturity is required for learning to read in this "ordinary school" situation?

After much experience, schools generally have
about decided on 6½ years mental age as a requirement for beginning reading in the first grade. This
does not mean that all children below 6½ mental
age fail to learn to read and that all children of 6½
mental age do learn. It only means that with large
numbers of children, *most* of them below 6½ mental
age fail and *most* of them at 6½ mental age and
above succeed. "Most" is all we can say. There are
no fixed percentages. And we must note that there
are always exceptions. Some mentally younger children learn and some mentally older children fail.

READINESS AND SCHOOL LAWS

Here the school must deal with laws and board rulings with regard to chronological age for entrance. Children are traditionally admitted to school on chronological age, with the added traditional assumption that all children are about alike. All people know that children are not alike, but our society is based on the tradition of equality, and the same entrance age for school is considered one of the requirements of equality. This "equality" varies, of course, from place to place. Some state laws say the child must be admitted at 7 years and the local school board can keep to that age or lower it. Some states say the child must be admitted at 5, and the school board cannot raise the figure.

But *no state law or local school board regulation says children must be taught to read at any certain age*. School boards and superintendents should make this fully clear to their patrons. "Admitted to school" means "admitted to school," and that is all. The time at which reading is to be taught is a psychological and technical matter that people without technical experience should not pretend to know about. For the person without special training to tell the school when to teach reading is like the city man trying to tell the farmer when to plant his corn. Yet deferring the teaching of reading after children enter school must be explained to parents, and here is one of the important areas of public relations.

Parent education should begin at this point, if not before, and much time and expense should be devoted to getting parents to understand the reasons for delaying reading, if it is to be delayed.[1]

A very successful method for a school board to use is to announce that they are following the best scientific advice and are admitting children to the teaching of reading at the mental age of 6½. The board can then specify that they will assume that a chronological age of 6½ means a mental age of 6½. That is reasonable. But the board should say they can admit other children to reading who are *proved to be 6½ mental age by an intelligence test.*

Most parents will be entirely satisfied to have their children begin the usual reading at 6½ years of age, but certain parents will want their children tested. They will be the parents belonging to the professional and managerial class, a very small number indeed, but a number to be reckoned with. Most of the time their children, when given a psychological test, will be found to be 6½ years mental age when they are 6 years physically. If the school is to deal with entering mental age at all, this is a good way to do so. Instead of putting the burden of proof on the school to show a child is *not* ready, the burden of proof is on the parent to prove that he *is.*

---

[1] See Chapter X Teaching Primary Reading, E. W. Dolch (Garrard Press, Champaign, Ill.), for full discussion.

Experience Rather Than Reading

Having discussed mental age from a "practical" point of view, let us consider the much more important problem of mental age, child development, and reading. Let us admit frankly, that "reading is a substitute for living." It is much better for children to visit a farm than it is for them to read about visiting a farm. It is much better for them to make toys and play with toys than for them to read about making toys or playing with them. It is much better for children to be part of a group and work and play together than it is for them to read about such a group. Let us frankly admit that children need experience more than they need reading. They need to live rather than to read.

Naturally, good teachers everywhere use the beginning reading book and the reading lesson as a stimulant to fuller living. They try to give experiences and to have activities related to the reading. That is, they use the reading as a guide to child development. A good series of readers is planned for this purpose. It tries to lead the children into fuller living by the topics and pictures presented. Perhaps this guidance furnished by the basic reading materials is necessary in most schools.

The very best kind of school, however, would not need the basic book and its stories for fuller living in the beginning grades. It would discover and capitalize on the children's interests. Such a school would have a program of individual and group living that began where the children were and led them out into wider fields, using books as an aid rather than a guide. We know, of course, that such a plan is very difficult because of the strain put upon the teacher. She must be very skillful at knowing children and their motives, and she must be very skillful at group guidance. In addition, she must have a philosophy of education that will enable her to make a plan for her particular group of children. She would then use the children's developmental program to make their own reading matter in the form of charts. Thus, the reading done by the group would follow their living and be a result of it. The teacher would not have to try to make the living follow the reading as she often does when using a basic series of readers.

PRACTICAL VALUES

Such a plan of "Living rather than reading" would have the great advantage of not being tied to the necessity for learning sight recognition of a certain series of words. Those who were immature in word recognition would just go on living and learning. Later on, the necessity for word recognition would come up, but by that time the children would be older and the recognition would present fewer difficulties. This freedom from having to "cover" so many pages a day in the reading book is a very great boon indeed. It liberates the children and the teacher. Theoretically, at least, it is the ideal plan for child development.

Such a plan would also result in rapid growth in reading later on. As the children developed experience and capability they would be getting more and more ready for the reading experience. They would not become just barely capable of reading but amply and fully capable. They would not be so liable to confuse words because they had had much practice in distinguishing things from one another. They would not be just barely capable of sitting still for fifteen minutes but would have become able to sit still for much longer. Consequently, when reading was finally presented, these children would go ahead at a very rapid pace. They would have complete confidence and immediate success. The result would be happiness for all concerned.

AN EXPERIMENT IN DELAYED READING [2]

The method of "Experience rather than reading" has actually been tried in many places. One such place kept records so that we know very *definitely what happened*. A group of 25 children was chosen at random for the experiment. Each child's parents agreed to leave the child in the group for two years and also not to discuss with him or let anyone else

---

[2] Reported in Proceedings of the American Educational Research Association for 1940 by Morphett and Washburne of Winnetka, Ill.

discuss with him the problem of when to begin reading. Then each child was matched by many tests with two or more other children who were to begin reading in the usual way.

The experimental group was given every opportunity for activity, materials, games, pets, a garden outside, trips planned, etc. After these activities, experience charts were made and the children were allowed to read them if they wished to do so. The children liked to tell of their experiences and to make the charts, but they had little interest in struggling to remember lines or words exactly. So they were not pressed to remember. This went on and on, with great interest in activity of all kinds and little interest in words. For the first year, there was no reading. During the second year more and more children became curious about words. By the middle of the second year, the group wanted to settle down and learn which words were which. They immediately had success. In fact, by the end of the third year, the group had learned almost as much as the control children who had begun a year and a half sooner.

Then a strange thing appeared. By the end of the fourth year, the slow-beginning group was *half a grade ahead* of the early-beginners. Each year, the children who had had "living rather than reading" got further ahead in reading than the exactly matched control children. At the end of the seventh year, they were a full grade ahead. This was not because of special teaching, since after the first two years, the children were all put in the same group. But the children who began later seemed to have a great enthusiasm for reading, they seemed to have a different attitude. And this attitude resulted in the greater learning. That is the only explanation possible, but it is enough. To delay learning a skill until it is learned easily and with enthusiasm is always good psychology. It seems to have worked with reading.

SUCCESS OF DELAYED READING

The experiment in delayed reading we have just described, and many other similar experiences, have led many persons to say, "Yes, children *can* learn to read at 6½ years mental age, but *should* they?" That is a most important question. Children can learn foreign language in the grade school, but should they? Children can learn arithmetic many years before they have any need for it, but should they? Mere ability to learn does not mean we should immediately rush off and learn. Would it not be better to learn a little later on, and meantime learn something more important for the child at the time?

Schools at different places throughout the country are trying out this plan of delaying reading. Some of these are private schools whose patrons believe in the philosophy of "experience rather than reading." Others are public schools in enlightened communities. Two things are necessary before any school can try the plan, however. The first is community understanding. If, to a certain community, school means reading, and progress means getting into the next book, delay in beginning reading is hardly possible without first a great deal of community education. And we do not yet have a procedure for such community education that is sure to get the desired result.

The second thing necessary for a program of "experience rather than reading": is a corps of teachers who know *how to conduct such a program* and the building and other arrangements that make it possible for children to "live" in school rather than just to sit in seats with a book. Such buildings and programs are developing in many places. Teachers of beginners are more and more learning how to conduct this group living that should precede reading. Let us hope that the development of this philosophy continues rapidly, for the sake of the children coming on in our schools.

Readiness as Interest

Modern education places a great stress on motivation. It views learning as an active, creative process. It believes that we must somehow cause children to "go after" something if they are to learn it, and not merely sit passive and wait for the teacher to "hand it" to them. Therefore, there has been an ever-increasing emphasis upon arousing interest in reading before we begin the teaching of reading.

This very emphasis upon "getting interest" in learning how to read leads to a question which appears very strange if we consider it for a moment. Do we have to arouse children's interest in ice cream or candy? Do we have to arouse interest in picnics or the circus? Do we struggle to get children interested in a pet dog or cat? Obviously not. Then why is it that we seem to have to work to "get interest" in learning how to read?

We should add to this question a second one, why is it that some children are fascinated by reading from their earliest years? These children pore over books long before they can possibly know one word from another. These children are hungry to hold and to own books. These children ask us about the signs all around them. Whenever they see a word they ask us what it says. They seem more eager to read than to take part in almost any other activity we can bring to their attention.

DIFFERENT KINDS OF CHILDREN

When so many children do not turn naturally to books and some others do, we are forced to the conclusion either that children are born different in some way that causes this difference or that they are made different by training. Many persons are sure the whole thing is a matter of training. They tell how the child who wants to read has been surrounded by books, has been read to, has been thrilled by the world of imagination, and so on. They conclude that if every child were surrounded by books, were read to, and so on, he too would be thrilled by the world of imagination and be eager to learn to read. But is this so?

Many parents have tried to develop in their children this eagerness to read and have miserably failed. They have bought books, they have read at meal time and at bedtime and in between. By their reading they have held the attention of the child for the time. But when the reading was over, the child dashed out to play with other children or turned to his toys. The books lay all about him, but he did not open them. Somewhere or somehow the method failed. And this in spite of the fact that perhaps an older brother or sister "went for books" with the greatest eagerness. Why did not the same recipe work on both children?

When we use the same treatment on many children (actually use it and do not merely think we use it), and some react one way and some another, obviously there is some difference in the children. Observers of children are sure there are such differences. And those differences have a very direct relation to readiness for learning to read.

Roughly speaking, we can see in children three different kinds of dominant interests, and each of these affects their learning how to read. All children have all three interests, and in many children they are equally balanced. In some children, however, one of the interests is very strong and tends to dominate. Let us point out these cases of dominant interest, with the understanding that in individual children the differences are, of course, a matter of degree.

THING-MINDED CHILDREN

The usual psychological term for the children we have called "thing minded" is "concrete minded." This means that these children are dominated by their perception of and interest in the world of things, including pets and animals of all kinds. These children are always making things. They collect. They handle. They build. All children have this tendency to handle and make, but with these children, this tendency is very strong, stronger in fact than many others. Of course the tendency to be interested in and work with things may be encouraged by parents who buy toys that go and tools and clay and other materials, or who get and keep pets, and so on.

Parents have often tried very hard to develop this interest in a child by getting him all the things and animals he could want, but he just didn't respond.

He would not be interested. Often fathers who are "thing minded" try to get their boys to follow in their footsteps but fail utterly. The father gets the electric train, but the boy ignores it. The father fits out the workshop, and the boy does not work in it. So there is strong evidence of the presence of this "thing minded" tendency in some children and also evidence of its lack in others.

People-Minded Children

All children are interested in people but some children are most intensely interested in them. These children want to sit with the adults and listen by the hour. These children are never seen alone. Always there is a playmate. If you want to find these children, ask where the crowd is; that is where they will be. Of course these children are not all the same. Some want to be with the crowd to dominate it; others are perfectly content to be with the crowd as a follower or hanger-on. But they must be with the crowd. Sometimes such a child is an only child, and the parents are driven wild by his refusal to "stay at home and play." He cannot stand being alone. He must have someone to talk to or listen to. He may hang around his mother constantly until she tries to drive him away. Such a child is just socially sensitive to an abnormal degree. All children are more or less socially sensitive, but some are more so than usual.

As we have suggested above, some parents try everything to get a socially minded, or "people minded" child to do something by himself, to work alone, to be happy in some job. He does not respond. Similarly, parents often try desperately to get a "thing minded" child to be more with people. The child just wants to be let alone with his play, but the parents insist he go play with Jimmy or Mary. He doesn't want to. He doesn't care for companions. He is interested in his toys and tools of all kinds. The parent then has parties to "socialize" the child, and he has little pleasure in them. The parents try to get him to join the Cubs or Scouts or special clubs, but he is not interested. Thus, as we have said, there is evidence of this socially-minded tendency both from those who have it and from those who do not.

Verbally-Minded Children

The two types of children we have described, the concrete minded and the socially minded, do not naturally take to reading books. How can a book be as interesting as a toy truck or a person? It is unnatural for such children to sit and look at pictures too long or for them to be interested at all in the printed matter that adults are so concerned about. To them, there is just nothing of interest there.

But there is a type of child who is fascinated by the letters and print he sees all about. Those letters say words, and what are those words? Such a child is always asking, "What does that say?" Looking at a whole landscape, such children will center attention on a sign. In a room full of playthings, they will go toward a book on the table. There is for them a fascination about words. We do not know just what there is about language that attracts these children, but adults of the same type, when in a foreign section of a city, read the names on stores and wonder what the names mean. This interest in symbols shows itself clearly in high school when foreign languages are offered. Verbally-minded children take these languages with pleasure and continue fascinated with them. Other children "see no sense" in a foreign language and have no interest at all.

Types of Children and Interest Readiness

Having made this excursion into individual differences of children, we may return to our first problem, "getting interest in learning to read." It is at once evident that some children, when they come to school, will be already interested in learning to read even at a young age. Other children will not be naturally interested in reading even though several years older. Which children are to be the standard for our criterion of "having interest in reading" before we begin the teaching of reading?

It is to be feared that far too often we think of the verbally-minded child as the criterion for the time to begin the teaching of reading. That child is anxious to get hold of a book. We accept him as the "normal" and give all the children a book. One reason for our doing so may be that most teachers were at one time verbally-minded children. When they were little, they wanted to get hold of books, to own books, to read books. They now "expect" the children to be interested in reading. So they are likely to feel that something is wrong with the children who are not interested, who would rather do almost anything but sit down and look into a book.

Interest in Stories vs. Interest in Working

Teachers do find that almost all children like to hear stories. Therefore, it is a common practice for teachers to read stories to beginners several times a day. This is supposed to develop "interest in reading." Let us agree that reading to children gives pleasure through imagined action, and develops the children in many ways. We should read to children more than we do rather than less. But let us also agree that this is developing *interest in stories*. There is little evidence that it makes children anxious to work hard in order to learn words so that they can read.

We must here make a clear distinction between mere "interest," and a desire to work hard. We all "would like" to speak a foreign language but will we work hard to learn it? We all "would like" to be able to play an instrument, but will we work hard to learn it? Learning to read requires work. Children want to learn to read, but do they want to work? Here is the explanation of the experiment explained on page 59. Those children were not told they had to read. The school just gave experience and waited. By the middle of the second year, the children were old enough, and well enough trained so that they said, "we want to learn to read and let us get to work and learn."

This point must be forever kept in mind just because children will say so glibly, "I want to learn to read." Parents say so easily, "Why of course my child wants to learn to read." The answer is, "Does he want to *work* at reading? Does he *work* at anything at home? Does he have the determination and the habits *to work and learn?* Or does he just want to play at reading?" We must add at once the fact that much of reading *can* be learned through play.[3] Skilled teachers use play very successfully. But learning to read cannot *all* be play.

Play vs. Work in Learning

Because adults sometimes have a wrong idea of what play is, we need to explain at this point our meaning for *play* so that our use of the word

---

[3] See Games in Appendix C of Teaching Primary Reading.

throughout this book may be understood. We wish to avoid the idea some adults seem to have that what you get paid for is work and what you don't get paid for is play. That is only partly true and it is partly false.

Mentally speaking, *play is anything you do for the fun of doing* it. The reward of play is in the doing. If a teacher enjoys teaching, then teaching is play for her. If the doctor or lawyer enjoys his work, then it is play for him. If the ball player likes to play ball, then he is playing when he plays ball, even though he gets paid for it. One of the recipes for happiness is to choose a job that you like and then get paid for doing what you like. That is, get paid for playing.

Everyone will say at once that not all teaching is play, that at times you get tired and cease to enjoy it. The same is true of the ball player. Sometimes he does not want to play ball either, but he has to anyway. Here we see the difference between *play* and *work. If you do a thing not because you enjoy doing it but because it is a means to an end, then it is work.* The end may be a paycheck, or it may be prestige, or it may be benefit to humanity. But you are doing something for the end and not for the doing.

By this rule, much of teaching is work, and much of doctoring is work, and much of every profession is work, even though the person chose the

profession and likes it. He just does not enjoy it
all the time. Similarly, much of what a business man
does is play, even though he would say he did not
choose the job. The salesman likes to meet people
and to sell. So much of his selling is play, though
much of it is drudgery. The manager likes to manage, and is playing part of the time because he is
enjoying his work. Even the typist likes parts of her
work, and such parts of it are really play.

How Children Learn to Work

With children this distinction is very important.
The young child plays all the time. That is, he does
what he does because he likes to do it, and when he
no longer wants to do it, he stops doing it. He flits
from this to that, following his fancy and doing just
what he wants to do. Many children keep up this
play life for many years. They are encouraged in
it, or at least are permitted to play all the time.

But well-trained children soon learn that there is
adult approval to get. To get it, one does not just
play; one does things he doesn't want to do. Also
there are things one wants to have, and to get them
one has to do things he doesn't like to do. There
are things one wants to make, but soon the making
is not fun and you have to go on anyway if you want
to finish. So by gradual degrees, under expert guidance, the "play child" learns what work is, and
learns that work is good because it gets what one

wants. This lesson should be learned in the home but it often is not. Then it has to be learned in school. For it must be learned if the child is to be happy and successful in life.

PLAY AND WORK IN READING

Our question then becomes, "Is learning to read play or work?" The answer must recognize, *first,* different kinds of children. For verbally-minded children, learning to read is play. They like to do it, they easily succeed in doing it and they do not need to work. This does not mean that they do no work, but their work is done when they are trying to read material that is far ahead of them. When they are in the first grade class, they are playing. But at home or in other places they will pick up newspapers and magazines and work hard at reading them. So these children are not to be considered typical or to determine our ideas of typical first grade reading.

For the average child, learning to read should be play, with just a touch of work constantly included. We have the children look at the pictures, and they like to look at pictures. Then we push them just a little to notice things they do not easily notice or think things they did not immediately think. Later, we have them look at a page of familiar words. They find it play to recognize what the words say. But on the page there are two or three strange words. We ask them to work at recognizing those words.

The same thing occurs with charts. It is play to say what you think should be on the chart, but the teacher asks you to say it a little differently and the effort to do so may be work. It is fun to remember most of the chart, but some parts are not remembered easily, and that is work. Even in coloring the workbook, there is this mixture. It is fun to spread colors, but it is work to stay within the lines. So in every phase of child living, play must dominate perhaps, but always there must be the little element of doing what you don't find such fun for the sake of some result you want. That is work and results in learning how to work.

Transferring Interest to Learning to Read

The basic principle for acquiring interest is that *new interests must be grafted upon old ones.* Teachers have always used this principle in trying to get children interested enough in learning how to read to put forth effort in that learning. We have already mentioned this principle indirectly many times.

First, we have said that games have interest, and if we use games that involve learning words and doing other reading, there is a tendency for the game interest to add some interest to learning to read. This is the more true when success in the game involves success in doing some reading. The pleasure of success is transferred to the idea of learning how to read.

Second, we have pointed out that experiences and trips and the like have interest. We try to attach this interest to learning how to read by making an experience chart and having the children "read it." Of course when the children are "reading" an experience chart they are largely reciting from memory, but there is some attention to words and there is some recognition of the characteristics of reading matter. This attention and recognition is part of learning to read.

Third, incidental use of words and sentences is also a case of "transferring interest" to learning how to read. We put labels on things which have interest. We write announcements on the board, and those announcements have interest. We make a weekly or monthly calendar, we put news items on the board, we give assignments in writing, and the like. All of these devices deal with things that interest the children, and all of them try to transfer some of that interest to the process of learning to read.

Fourth, the pictures in the book have interest, and we try to transfer that interest to the effort to read the lines under the picture. That is why the artist tries to tie picture to text, and then the teacher also tries to join the two. She may think chiefly of teaching certain words, but she is also getting some interest for the work of learning to read. That is, she is getting the children to know that if they try to read what is under the picture, they will find out more about what the picture means or tells.

Finally, as we have mentioned, the interest of stories read to the children and also of the stories they read is intended to transfer to the process of learning how to read.

DIFFERENT MEANINGS FOR "LACK OF INTEREST READINESS"

From all these considerations, we find that "lack of interest readiness" may mean different things in different school situations.

1. The children may have little interest in the school because the school room may be lacking in interesting things, activities or stories.

2. If the teacher gets the children interested in stories, they may still be interested only in play and be unable to do the work connected with learning to read.

3. The children may be willing to work at reading, but the learning tasks put before them may include too much work, and thus the interest readiness which existed may be destroyed.

4. If any single child lacks interest readiness, we must study that particular child to find out if he is or is not the verbal minded type. Then we must consider his previous training at home or school to see if work habits have or have not been produced (see further discussion in Chapter IV). Finally,

we need to know his individual interests and drives to see if the school has made contact with them or if it possibly can do so.

We may say definitely, however, that nothing is of more importance than the child's interest in learning to read. For such learning, effort will be required of the child, and the child alone can put forth that effort. If he is driven to put forth effort, he will also be made to dislike reading. Instead, he must be gradually brought to the point where the effort is natural to him in his situation. If there is enough interest, many of the other requirements for readiness can be met. The child who is immature will "stretch" his maturity if his interest is strong enough. The child with handicaps will overcome those handicaps. The child undeveloped in any particular will rapidly develop as needed. Let us have, above all, interest in learning how to "read," meaning a determination to read in spite of obstacles. Then we will get results.[4]

Summary

Readiness means the conditions which should precede or accompany efficient, wholesome learning.

Readiness for all grades means both previously acquired skill and also conditions that are necessary

---

[4] See Chapters IV to IX in Teaching Primary Reading (Garrard Press, Champaign, Ill.) for classroom methods.

for progress. We shall use "readiness for reading" to refer only to readiness for beginning reading.

No special discussion of emotional adjustment will appear since cases of emotional maladjustment are discussed under the conditions which may produce that maladjustment.

Readiness is often interpreted as a certain level of mental age. But the level of mental maturity needed to learn to read depends upon the conditions of that learning. If the teaching is to be individual, a younger child can learn to read, even before six years' mental age. If the teaching is to be in a group, we must ask what size group and what kind of teaching? A very small group, with skilled teaching, permits learning to read at about six years of mental age, but we should not push children in reading by securing such special conditions since children need to develop rather than just to become readers.

For learning to read in the usual public school, six and a half years' mental age is a safer criterion, but this is only a general principle. Many learn to read before six and a half years' mental age and many do not learn to read at that mental age. The school board may set six and a half mental age as the minimum, and assume that six and a half chronological will give that mental age, permitting the parent to prove by mental test when a child has reached the minimum mental age of six and a half years.

After all, reading is a substitute for living, and the children need experience in rich living more than they need to read about it. The school may use the basic reader as a guide to a program of all-around child development, or it may devise its own program for child development. In that case, reading would be introduced by experience charts based upon the program of living, and the teacher would not be tied to coverage of certain textbooks. As a result, formal reading would be delayed until such time as the children would be fully ready for it, and greater final progress would result.

A very careful experiment in a school system has shown that children who begin formal reading later than the usual time may after several years be ahead of those who followed the more usual program.

Much has been made of interest as a requisite for readiness for reading. In study of children, we find some eager to read at an early age, and others who at the usual beginning age are quite indifferent. This fact leads us to ask whether we do not have here a fundamental difference in the children. A study of them would lead us to identify three types of interest which children manifest, most children having some of all three types and other children showing one or another very strongly. Some children may thus be called "thing minded" because they are predominately interested in objects, materials, pets, and the like, and not at all interested in books. Other children may be called "people minded" because they want always to be with people and to talk to people, and are not interested in toys or pets or in books. Still other children may be called "verbal-minded" because very early they show an interest in printed words and in books, and they eagerly go to books, both before entering school and all during the school years. Not only do these different types of children show strong interest in one direction only, but they resist all our efforts to get them interested in other things. It is understood of course that these interests are usually mixed in individual children to a greater or less degree.

It is to be feared that our plans for the teaching of reading are too often based upon the interests of the verbal-minded children.

We read to children to develop their interest in reading, but we can be sure only that this arouses their interests in stories, and not an interest in working hard to learn to read. We must distinguish between work and play in learning. Play is what we do because we like to do it; work is what we do for some end and not for itself. Children naturally play and they have to learn to work. That is, they have to learn that some things have to be attained by doing what they do not at the moment want to do. Well-trained children have gradually discovered the need for work and have gradually come to accept a certain amount of work willingly. Now reading cannot be all play, though we use play motives and methods a great deal. Children do not have a genuine interest in learning to read until they have the desire to work to learn to read. That is real interest readiness.

In practice, we try to transfer interest to reading from other activities already interesting. Some of these are games, activities and experiences, interesting objects, pictures, and hearing and reading stories.

CHAPTER IV

Readiness as Physical Fitness

We often hear it said that certain children are not ready to learn to read because of some physical weakness or defect. Such a statement is not clear because throughout the country there are children learning to read successfully who have all the possible physical handicaps and defects that are usually thought of as barriers to learning. Children are learning who have only partial sight, who have ill health, who have poor hearing, who have speech defects and who are crippled in other ways. If physical handicaps may block reading, how are these children reading?

THE CHILD COMPENSATING FOR LACK OF PHYSICAL READINESS

Perhaps the chief factors which make it possible to learn to read in spite of physical defect are *intelligence* and *interest*. The very bright child may be half sick, but with only partial attention he can learn as much or more than the more fit children. The child who is very eager to learn to read may not be able to see the blackboard but he may "listen so hard" and watch what the teacher does so well that he learns to identify words in spite of his handicap. The child who can hardly hear what is going on may concentrate on his book and workbook and figure things out for himself without hearing what the teacher is saying.

Many handicapped children have help at home and though learning little at school may learn enough outside to "keep up with their class." This situation of *the child compensating for physical handicap* is so common that many persons are not at all aware of the amount of physical handicap among beginning children. Surveys tell us that there are millions of children who are malnourished and other millions with impaired sight or hearing or with defective speech, that there are many thousands with all the other defects. The percentages given lately by an authority are:

TABLE I

Percentage of the Children in the Population With the Chief Types of Handicap

Eye Defects of all kinds	20%
Impaired Hearing	14%
Defective Speech	7%
Crippled	3%
Heart Cases	1%
Malnourished	20%

As given by Harry J. Baker in *Introduction to Exceptional Children*, Macmillan Co., New York, 1944, and quoted in *Helping Handicapped Children in School*, E. W. Dolch, Garrard Press, Champaign, Ill., 1948.

The School Compensating for Physical Handicap

We have noted that children with high intelligence and interest and with home advantages may compensate for a physical handicap so that they do not lack readiness for reading because of it. But such children are not in the majority. A very large number of children will be prevented by physical handicap from learning to read unless the school does something to compensate for the handicap.

In the case of physical handicap, we do not have the simple solution of "just wait until they grow up." Delay in beginning reading or nonpromotion may solve some of the other deficiencies in reading readiness, but they will not solve lack of physical fitness. Nonpromotion may seem at times to compensate for a physical defect but it does so in a way that is not desirable. It often happens that if a malnourished and listless child is retained in first grade, he may have enough maturity and experience the second year to compensate for his lack of energy. The extra year of mental age may be enough to permit him to learn in spite of his ill health.

The same thing may happen with other defects. An added year may permit the child to learn anyway in spite of sight or hearing defect, even though no one has tried to help him or to correct his handicap. But is this a humane way to solve the difficulty? The child may learn to read the second year, but his handicap still persists and he is working under it all the time. Likewise, his failure is certain to have left some emotional mark upon him.

Rather than resort to such a crude and inhumane solution for lack of physical readiness, we should know just what the situation is with each child and do something about it. We shall therefore discuss separately the various physical handicaps, with the question in mind, "just how does the physical defect handicap the child and how can the school compensate for it?"

We shall not here go into complete detail concerning physical handicaps. Instead we shall simply sketch the situation, emphasizing the psychological aspects of the handicap and its treatment. For more complete consideration of physical handicaps and of school methods, see the book, Helping Handicapped Children in School. (E. W. Dolch, Garrard Press, Champaign, Ill.) In that book, a chapter of over thirty pages is devoted to each single kind of handicap, giving all its characteristics, and what the school can do about it.

HEARING DEFECT

Children who are totally deaf, or too deaf to be dealt with in school, are not here being considered. Their problems are special indeed and require specially trained teachers. The children we shall here think of are the millions who have poor hearing. Their defect ranges from a slight dullness of hearing down to the point where, to be heard, the teacher has to speak loudly close to the better ear.

The situation of the hard-of-hearing child is that he does not know or has only a vague idea of what is going on. We ourselves have this same sense of bafflement if we are trying to get a story or speech over the radio when it is confused or indistinct. As we know, in such a case we do one of two things. We either struggle harder to hear or we just ignore the sounds and shut the radio off. In the schoolroom some children struggle to hear, and even with incomplete hearing can follow the lesson. These children are compensating themselves. But all too many children just cease the struggle and let the vague and indistinct sound go on without paying any more attention to it. When children do this, they sometimes become quite content to look around or just amuse themselves at their seats. At other times these children are emotionally disturbed and show frustration or resentment. Thus they are not only discouraged by their failure to learn to read but they are made unhappy by not being part of the group and its activity.

We need not emphasize here the duty of the school to find out which children are hard-of-hearing and to secure help for them from specialists. But for those who cannot be helped, and for those who are not being helped, what can we do?

First, the teacher should give special attention to the hard-of-hearing child to give him emotional security. She should smile at him and speak to him when he passes near. Also to give him security, she should see that he has things to do at which he succeeds. These may be jobs about the room, or work at his seat. This work must be adapted to the child so that he is happy and successful in doing it.

Second, seating will often take care of hearing defect. The child must be seated so that he can hear to best advantage. If possible, his seat should be in the center of the room so that he can hear the other children from all directions. If this puts him too far from the teacher, he must sit close to her, and she can then often repeat what other children have said if it is something for the hard-of-hearing child to know or to answer.

Finally, the teacher must take care of the attitude of the other children. There must be no making fun of the handicap. This is a chance for the others to show helpfulness and they must see their opportunity. If the child should wear a hearing aid, this attitude is especially important. Most children are very timid about wearing a hearing aid because they feel it makes them different and an object of ridicule. The teacher must get all to ignore the aid altogether and act as if it were not there. She can best do this by explaining all about the hearing aid and how it works so that all curiosity is satisfied. The teacher may insist that the child wear the hearing aid during a discussion period and let him take it off if he wishes at other times, hoping that pretty soon he would rather just keep it on. The attitude of the other children will control the matter.

Especially during playtime is the hard-of-hearing child a problem. In some games, he will not be handicapped, but he will be left out of others. The leaders among the children should understand this and try to get the child into their games. The teacher will have conferences with them about it. The whole purpose will be to build up the handicapped child's security, to keep him interested in school and in learning, and to help him more and more to do his own compensating for the handicap. For in later life he will have to do just that.

SPEECH DEFECT

The case of the speech defective is very like that of the hearing defective child. Both types tend to play naturally with others when they are very young, since the other children get used to the handicap. Then as they get older, these types of handicapped children tend more and more to withdraw into themselves and refuse to participate. In both cases, the reason is the same, fear of ridicule. In both cases, the teacher must strive to maintain the child's security and self-confidence, both by seeing that the child has success, and also that the others have an understanding attitude. Even children are touched by the inquiry, "How would you like to have something wrong with your mouth so that you couldn't talk plainly?" Young children will show sympathy, and the handicapped child will not object at first. It is only older handicapped people who fiercely object to sympathy, because they feel that it is condescending and suggests inferiority.

Speech defects should have the immediate attention of speech specialists if possible, but the teacher can do something about them. In fact, she must do something because the child is in her room every day. Here we must make a sharp distinction between stuttering or stammering and the other kinds of defect shown by mispronouncing.

STUTTERING

In stuttering or stammering, there is usually nothing at all wrong with the speech organs. In fact, there is nothing wrong with the child's ability to pronounce. He can usually pronounce anything if he is relaxed, as, for instance, he is in singing. No one stutters in singing. But during ordinary speech, the child is blocked by certain letters or certain words. Why this should be is a matter of some dispute. The best opinion seems to be that the stutterer is seized with a fear that he will not be able to say the troublesome letter. It is claimed that if the stutterer could be entirely confident, he would not stutter. At least he can say lines in a play without stuttering. Sometimes, if he becomes greatly interested and forgets himself, he does not stutter. The teacher need not go into all the circumstances, but should only understand something of the stutterer's predicament.

It appears that stuttering begins in a child's life at a time of emotional stress and strain, usually before school or at the beginning of school. It is thought to continue as a symptom of inner emotional difficulty. Therefore the treatment is to develop confidence, assure relaxation, and get happiness and success in the work being done. There are devices to help one overcome stuttering, but a teacher need not deal with these. They should be prescribed by a speech specialist. But the teacher can help adjust the daily school life of the individual.

To help the stutterer through school work is a peculiar problem. If the child talks and stutters, he is becoming more in the habit of stuttering. If the child does not talk, he is not learning to overcome stuttering. So he must somehow talk and he must also talk without stuttering. How is this to be achieved? One device is to have the child volunteer on subjects on which he is fully confident. This sometimes gets talk without stuttering. Another plan is to have the child rehearse his talking, such as rehearsing a part of the reading lesson beforehand or rehearsing a talk that is to be given to the class. In many cases, this will get talking without stuttering. At any rate, we can say, negatively, that the teacher should not excite the child. She should not allow a class to laugh at him. She should not surprise him with questions. She should not demand that he say things when and as she wants them. All such measures increase tension and fear, and they increase stuttering.

MISPRONUNCIATION

The other type of speech defect is wrong pronunciation of words or parts of words. This may be due to malformations of the speech organs or just to poor use of those organs. In either case, the teacher must realize that in all probability the child is unaware of his errors. The chances are that he thinks everyone pronounces words just as he does. This belief is common with small children who use baby talk or who lisp. They are unaware that they speak differently, largely perhaps because the home does not call their attention to the difference. But when these children come to school, the other children are prompt to tell them their mistakes. Most of these children very rapidly lose their wrong speech habits. They want to talk like others, they hear how others talk, and they imitate. Some children do not do this, however. The reason seems to be either that malformation of the mouth makes it hard for them to say things the right way, or that these children do not hear the difference.

With speech cases which do not correct themselves, the teacher needs to find out if the child actually can say the word in question the right way. Can he actually say "little" instead of "ittle." Can he say "mother" instead of "muvver"? The teacher may first listen to see if there is some other word in which the child gives the correct sound. If he says "this," he could say "mother," because both have the sound of "th." The other plan is to have the child listen to someone say the word right and then to have him say the word correctly. That is, to have him imitate. If he can imitate correctly when he listens, he could say the word correctly at other times.

We have here the process of change of a habit. The *first* step is wanting to change. Does the child want to speak the words correctly? The *second* step is being able to do the thing right, and we have previously assured ourselves that the child can pronounce the word correctly. The third step is *becoming aware of* the old habit. This is an important step because the old habit is unconscious, and the person does it without knowing that he does. The child does not hear himself say "muvver." So someone must remind him again and again. Each time he is reminded he becomes more likely to catch himself without reminding.

The *last* step is *continued repetition* until the right thing is done unconsciously instead of the wrong. It may take a year or two for the child to get the new habit unconsciously, but he will if the other steps are continued.

If there is a malformation of the mouth, the child will have to use special effort to make the sound right in spite of it. For instance, if the teeth have grown in wrong, some special manipulation of the tongue may be necessary to compensate for the malformation. If the child is motivated, he will make this compensation if possible. Sometimes, of course, it is not possible, and surgery or other help may be needed.

Some children with speech defects learn to read readily, because the child compensates for the defect. Sufficient intelligence or interest may do the trick. When the child cannot compensate, the school must aid. It may do so by causing the parents or some welfare agency to have dentistry or surgery performed that will correct the defect.

General Health

Doctors are placing more and more emphasis upon general bodily condition and health as affecting everyone's happiness and ability to work. This is in direct contrast to the old Spartan tradition that we should urge children to plug ahead regardless of how they feel. Many parents and some teachers still follow that tradition however. It may work with adults, but it surely does not with children. If a child is not in good physical health, he does not feel well, and he is usually not going to work well.

The effect of poor bodily condition is both mental and emotional. The mind is more sluggish, and, in effect, the mental age is lowered. One who does not feel well is not as bright as he usually is. One who knows a child well can immediately see in him this kind of temporary dullness due to a cold, to a head-ache, to stomach upset, or to other ill health. Like-wise, poor bodily condition causes a general state of emotional depression, and easily results in irrita-tion, resentment, and the like. Teachers know this from their own experience. Children also are de-pressed and irritable if they are not well.

As suggested, if we know a child we can see changes in him caused by poor bodily condition. But suppose a child has all along been in a chronic state of malnutrition, throat irritation, infection, or so on. In such a case, we can only compare him with other children of his age and say that he must be ill because he acts so differently from the others. The teacher can observe some conditions such as temper-ature, appearance of eyes and throat and so on, but she should have a health inspection made by a school nurse or doctor. Fortunately it is becoming more and more common for the schools to have children inspected every morning, especially the young children.

Many school programs now admit the presence of poor health conditions among beginners, as well as other school children, and make plans for correction. The drinking of milk at recess time is good if the milk goes to the children who need it most rather than to those who need it least. The school should provide milk for all. A program of hot lunches is also a part of a nutrition plan for all. Many schools use sets of health readers to ensure that every teacher will stress good eating habits, good sleeping habits, care of teeth, avoidance of harmful foods or drinks, prevention of infection, and the like. Sometimes special lessons are given to the children by doctors or nurses. These health classes may be conducted after school for both parents and children to attend, in an attempt to improve health conditions in the homes.

Nervous Condition

One of the results of our speeded up tempo of living is its effect on the nervous condition of children. Nature seems to have intended that we go to bed at sunset and get up at sunrise, but many adults insist upon using electric lights to push the day into the night. Naturally enough, this night life of adults, which they now seem to consider so "natural," interferes with the sleep of children, who, incidentally, need many more hours of sleep than their parents. There are physical results, such as children yawning in school or falling asleep at their tables, but there are also nervous results. Some children develop a constant state of nervous tiredness. They do not have the drive they should. They do not show in school the attention to work of which they are really capable. They are in a state of partial nervous exhaustion.

Another cause of nervous exhaustion is worry and a feeling of insecurity on the part of the child. Many children live in homes where there is constant bickering between adults. Sometimes they live with one parent who constantly says evil things of the other parent. Or they live with grandparents who criticize the parents in the child's hearing. Sometimes the parents are in constant fear of loss of jobs or of eviction or of other calamities, and they communicate their state of nervous tension to the children. In short, modern civilization is full of difficulties for adults, and the children living with those adults may be kept in such an emotional state that they reach a condition of nervous debility or exhaustion.

The time may come when family welfare societies or other public agencies will send visitors into homes to try to improve the conditions which cause children insecurity and worry. In the meantime, all the teacher can do is to give the child her friendship and affection and to make school a haven of security. She must combat the home conditions by school conditions. For instance, many teachers believe that in first grade at least there must be daily relaxation periods. Each child has a rug or mat of his own, or even a clean newspaper, and at a regular time lies down on the floor and relaxes. The teacher goes about quietly testing the "rag dolls" by lifting a hand and dropping it or otherwise teaching what relaxation means. Many children will go right off to sleep as soon as they relax, and teachers feel that there is nothing better these children can be doing than relieving themselves of the ill effects of our present artificial life.

A few cases of nervous condition that have become actual mental disease will come to school. Some children, for instance, refuse in school to say a single word. They are called "mutes." This is a form of resistance they have taken to adult aggression and attack upon them. Some children are victims of hallucinations, being convinced that they are being pursued by enemies or other danger. A much more common type is the advanced tantrum case, who drops on the floor and screams and thrashes about when crossed. Such a child has consciously or unconsciously adopted that method of attacking adults who stand in his way.

The tantrum case is usually solved by ignoring. If everyone else goes about his business and lets the child scream, he soon gets tired of screaming for nothing. But the case of the mute or of the child who is haunted by fears and hallucinations is much more difficult. All the teacher can do is to give friendship and security and a chance for self expression through some kind of play. Usually the help of a specialist is needed for these children. But if the teacher does not understand the situation and tries to force the child into another kind of conduct, she is just driving the child farther and farther into mental disease.

CRIPPLED CHILDREN

Crippled children are of many kinds. Some children have lost an arm or leg but are otherwise just like other children. Some children are twisted into awkward and often unpleasant forms and postures by crippling accident or disease. Other children have heart defects and do not appear crippled at all, though they are as effectively prevented from playing tag as if they had lost both legs. But does crippling affect learning how to read?

First, if crippling affects a child's *status in his group,* it very much affects his learning how to read. If the defect sets the child apart, keeps him from playing with the others, and makes him the object of ridicule, he is prevented from entering properly into the social side of learning how to read from the chart or the basic reading book. So the teacher's first concern is to keep the crippled child an accepted member of his group. She does this in several ways. One way is to show her friendship for the child, the tendency being for the others to imitate her in this. Another way is to praise the work of the crippled child so that he will have prominence in the room. Also, she may so manage appointment of committees and group plans as to give the crippled child a chance to lead where he has special abilities. For instance, if he can draw well, he can be the chairman of the committee to illustrate the daily class newspaper that is to be put on the board. All these ways are intended to build the child some prestige in the group.

At times, it may be necessary, however, for the teacher to give the class some training in consideration. In the absence of the crippled child, she may talk with them of his difficulty and how anyone would feel about being in such a situation. So the group can enter into a benevolent conspiracy not to notice the defect and to treat the handicapped child just as one of the others. They can even plan to give him a chance to take part in play as scorekeeper, or the like. This means developing group feeling. Of course the teacher cannot develop it unless the group accepts her as a leader and wishes to go along with her suggestions.

Second, the crippling may actually affect the child's individual *efforts in learning* to read. Suppose that because of the crippling he is babied at home and allowed to do as he pleases. Then in school he may not try to read but may assume that there also he can do as he pleases all the time. Sometimes the crippling requires braces or otherwise makes the child uncomfortable in school seats. In that case, paying attention is difficult. Sometimes heart cases and others are required to rest on a cot a certain part of the time each day. That necessity may hinder the child from taking part in the regular reading work. Sometimes the child may be a spastic and unable to hold his book or to write in the workbook. Sometimes a spastic may also be a speech defect and thus have that handicap too. The question we must ask ourselves always is, how is the child hindered in doing the regular reading work, and how can we help him?

We must mention again that of course some children do their own compensating for a crippling defect. If they have intelligence enough and interest enough, they may learn to read in spite of everything. But we are here thinking of children in whose case the school must do the compensating.

Eye Defects

The most common of all physical defects affecting reading is eye defect. As already mentioned, some children have serious eye defects and still compensate for them and learn to read as well or better than others. Other children do not or are not able to compensate, and therefore do not learn to read.

Eye defects hinder learning to read in two ways. *First,* and most prevalent, is the nearsightedness that keeps the child from seeing what the teacher puts on the chart or on the blackboard. Nearsightedness is relative. Some children cannot see the board at all. Others can see vague forms instead of words. Others can see the words, but the individual letters are not clear. Also the result varies with the position in the room of the child's seat. Many nearsighted children succeed because the teacher happened to put them in front of the room, and others fail because they were seated at the back. The result also varies with the teacher's method, as nearsightedness does not make so much difference in work with the book or in seatwork but makes a great deal of difference if there is much use of the blackboard or chart.

Teachers and other adults must understand that few children know they are nearsighted. They think everyone sees things as they see them. They see peoples faces as blurs and think they are blurs for everyone. To them, street signs are confused marks, and they think that is how others see them too. So one cannot expect the child to tell you he cannot see. He thinks he is seeing as well as anyone. Instead, one watches for the signs of straining to see, and one also watches responses when children are asked to read what is on the blackboard. Many children will shake their heads, meaning they cannot see, and the teacher may assume it means they do not know the words.

Careful observation will very often show which children are nearsighted except that some clever children may compensate for the difficulty by excellent guessing. They can tell what is on the board because they remember what the teacher said when she wrote it. By certain signs they recognize things and persons which actually appear to them just as blurs. The eye defects of such children may go unrecognized for years, unless there is a vision examination.

The *other way* in which eye defect hinders reading is by making close work unpleasant whether it be reading or fine drawing or anything of the kind. There are a group of defects which have this result, and the teacher can hardly discover them by observation. There is *astigmatism,* which twists the shapes of letters and is said to cause nervous fatigue as a result. There is *slow accommodation* of the lens, which makes it hard to shift from near vision to far vision and back. There is *far sightedness* which makes near-seeing a strain. And there is *muscle imbalance* which causes fatigue when the eyes are forced to work together at close range. Much is known about all of these defects and they are discussed at length in *Helping Handicapped Children in School.* The important point is that they can usually be discovered only by a vision examination and should be corrected with the advice of a specialist.

Vision Testing

Here we must emphasize that we speak of *vision* examination, and not *eye* examination. The eye specialist examines eyes. The teacher can certainly tell if the child can see. Anyone can by the use of very simple devices. So the school tests vision and then sends the child to the eye specialist for him to examine the eyes.

We must also add that we should test vision *under reading conditions.* The Snellen chart, which tests vision of one eye at a time at twenty feet, is certainly not testing reading vision which is done with two eyes at 14 to 16 inches. The Snellen chart is valuable chiefly to discover nearsightedness. It is not very good even at detecting nearsightedness, as any nearsighted person knows. The nearsighted person is very skillful at guessing. If he sees a round blur on the chart, he knows it is an *O,* a *C* or a *G.* If he can detect a break in the blur at the right, he knows it is not an O but is either a C or a G, and he can score 50 per cent by a pure guess. If he sees a long rectangle, it is either an M or a W. If it is fuzzy at the top, it is a W. If at the bottom, it is an M. Now this kind of guessing may give a correct score on the chart, but it is not reading. Clinics know all this because every day they receive children with defective vision who have been declared to have 100 per cent perfect vision by the Snellen chart.[1]

There is another point which teachers need to know about vision testing. They often find children deficient in vision according to a screening test, send them to a specialist, and the specialist says, "No glasses." Is the vision test wrong? Not necessarily. The eye specialist is accustomed to finding imperfect eyes. There are few perfect ones. But he does not want to put pieces of glass in front of a

---

[1] The most widely used vision test is the Betts telebinocular made by the Keystone View Co., Meadville, Pa. The Massachusetts Vision test is also practicable in the schools.

child's eyes if he can help it. Those glasses may break and put out an eye. So the eye specialist asks the child or parents how the child is getting along in school. If the child says all right, the chances are the specialist will not prescribe glasses. He will expect the child to get them later, when he is older and when he needs to read more. But the question is, does the child know if he is getting along all right in school? The eye specialist and the teacher should get together on this point even if only over the telephone. Otherwise, the specialist may not report that there is any difficulty and the teacher may not get a chance to ask for advice.

PSYCHOLOGICAL CONDITIONS

Some other psychological conditions about eyes and sight need to be mentioned. For one thing, if a parent gets the idea that something is wrong with a child's eyes, she will tell the child and he may at once use that as an excuse for not trying to learn to read. He may even invent headaches and other troubles when asked to read. This situation happens far too often and needs an examination by an eye specialist to straighten it out.

Many eye specialists believe that we should not teach reading at all at six years of age because the child's eyes are growing until seven or eight. One answer to this view might be that the reading we do in first grade is very little, but this suggestion of the eye specialists should be taken seriously and might reduce our emphasis on close work in first grade.

CROSS-EYEDNESS

Finally, a situation that needs immediate attention is the cross-eyed child, that is, the child who is using only one eye and may be losing the sight in the other. Crosseyedness can generally be corrected if attacked early enough, and therefore every cross-eyed adult is a monument to our neglect of a child. We must get professional attention to a cross-eyed child just as early as possible, preferably in the preschool years. Or we should educate mothers so that they will take such children to specialists long before preschool.

Summary

It is often said that lack of reading readiness may be due to physical weakness or defect. Yet many children with physical weakness or defect do learn to read with the others.

The child may compensate for lack of physical readiness by employing more intelligence or showing more interest than the others. But the school should compensate in some way. Non-promotion the first year may adjust some of these children by giving them time in which to compensate themselves. But such a solution is a poor one.

The hard-of-hearing child may not be ready for reading just because he does not know what is going on. He should be (1) given emotional security, (2) seated to best advantage, and (3) protected from the criticism of the rest of the class, and made a part of the group as much as possible.

Speech defect cases should also be protected from ridicule and given as much security as possible. They should be given attention of specialists if possible. Stutterers must be enabled in some way to "talk without stuttering," since to talk with stuttering increases the habit problem, and not to talk does not help it. Mispronunciation cases often solve themselves, but when they do not, the teacher works on change of habit of speech. She finds if the child can possibly pronounce the difficult sound right, and then helps him hear the mistake and change over to the right pronunciation. Some cases require dental or surgical attention.

Poor general health does a great deal to slow up or prevent school work by children. A teacher should become skilled in detecting bad physical condition, even though we are now more and more having daily inspection by nurses. School programs now contain both provision for feeding children and attempts to better home health conditions, as well as planned instruction in health through health readers.

Nervous tension is very common in children, due both to our tempo of life and also to feelings of fear and insecurity. The teacher tries to combat over-nervousness by giving security, and also by providing relaxation at regular periods during the day. Extreme cases of nervous difficulty require the help of a specialist.

Crippled children may or may not have difficulty with reading because of their condition. The teacher should try to secure for each crippled child status in his group, sometimes having also to develop consideration of his condition. She must sometimes develop in the child an effort to learn that is lacking because of home mismanagement.

Eye defects very often affect readiness for reading. They may keep a child from seeing the board, or they may make close work unpleasant. The teacher should conduct some kind of vision examination to discover each child's situation. Every cross-eyed child should receive immediate expert attention.

CHAPTER V

School Adjustment, Experience, Perception

Readiness as School Adjustment

Learning to read implies first going to school, and going to school implies very fundamental changes in the lives of many children. Three of these changes may be definitely pointed out, though there are a host of others which are also important. For instance, the separation from mother is at the time a major tragedy for many children, but this is an experience we do not think of very often because our gaze is centered in the new situation of the child in school, rather than on the tearing away from the old situation at home.

Social Adjustment to a Large Group

In a child's normal social development, he becomes adjusted to his role as a member of the family, and then gradually becomes adjusted to some group of children in the neighborhood. This process varies greatly with different children, but it is usually a change from individual play in the home, or play with a brother or sister, to play with a group in the yard or in the lot next door, or on the street. For any child, this adjustment to a gradually larger and more varied group goes on until he is six years old, or whatever the entering age is for kindergarten or school.

Then, with no preparation, the child is sent blocks away from home and put into a large group of strange children of his own age. This is a startling and shaking experience for most children. For some children, of course, it may be only a natural development because they have been getting along successfully with many people, and the large group in school is just a further opportunity for happy self-expansion. But to most children the change is a sudden and tremendous one, coupled as it is both with separation from the familiar adults and the introduction of an entirely new adult as the one in power and control.

What Social Adjustment Demands

We have here the problem of "social adjustment" of the individual child to the large school group, and we need to state definitely what is implied so that the teacher can use definite means and methods to further this adjustment.

First of all, adjustment here means a *lessening of the fear* that is certain to be caused by the strangeness and by the large numbers of competitors in play. (1) Mere "getting used" to the situation lessens this fear, unless some unhappy experience occurs to increase it. So ordinarily, the fear lessens with time. (2) But the teacher also lessens it by developing in the children friendliness toward herself as a natural and instinctive response to her real affection for them. That is why no teacher without real affection for children should ever be allowed in the first grade or kindergarten. A teacher may pretend affection, but the children know the difference. (3) To lessen fear, the teacher provides play materials that the child is used to or that he can take up easily, and this playing with things gives renewed confidence. (4) *Finally*, the teacher directs games in which all the children take part as directed, and each child feels that he knows what to do and is doing the right thing; hence he still further gains self confidence.

Free play is made much of in preschool and kindergarten work and also in first grade, but its effects upon the fear-confidence adjustment has to be carefully watched. The larger, self-confident, socially capable children have a fine time with free play, and are said to be more "adjusted by it." The submissive children, who are accustomed to having things taken away from them by the stronger children and who are used to being shoved aside, may seem to be "adjusted," if we assume such habitual submission to be a satisfactory adjustment. But for many children the rough and tumble of free play is a harrowing experience that leaves permanent scars on the personality.

Many children are raised by their parents in a general atmosphere of courtesy and sharing. They are taught that "please" is a magic word which causes people to do things for you. They assume that people take turns and respect property. Then to be thrown into the jungle law of free play with ordinary children is terrifying. All their acquired values of social contact are violated. They are pushed around in a way they have never known or dreamed of before. To them, free play time is a time of fear and frustration. To these children, only directed play, where rules are given and everyone compelled to follow them, gives confidence.

Second, after a lessening of the fear natural to the strange situation, the beginner must *learn the "give and take"* of large group activities. Here we have the strange necessity of teaching one child to "fight for his rights," and to teach another to stop fighting, or to teach one to stop shoving and to encourage another to shove at the proper time. It is remarkable that children ever make sense out of adult direction in this situation. We adults understand that there is a system of property rights, and precedence rights, and inviolability of personality rights, and so on. We cannot explain this system to children; instead, in particular situations we say do this or don't do that. Strangely enough, most of the children do gradually build up an understanding of when it is right to take something and when it is not right. Often it will help the children if the teacher has a list of rules to repeat to the children as the occasion comes up. For instance, one such rule is, "Whoever gets a toy first in the play period can keep it as long as he actually plays with it. If he puts it down, the next one who gets it has the right to keep it as long as *he* actually plays with it." A set of such rules for conduct is very much needed whenever children are "playing together." We put "playing together" in quotes because if there are no rules the phrase might often be "fighting together."

In practice, the teacher of beginners spots the children who push themselves forward too much, and in them encourages more mildness and consideration. She also spots the children who do not push themselves forward, and protects them to some extent until they can develop more confidence. To the child who obviously does not know what to do in a social situation, she suggests, "Why not do so and so." Here is the fine art of guiding child development. We all try our hand at it, and none of us is satisfied with the result. But we have to do our best in this situation of the gradual arising of social law and custom out of the jungle of instinct.

To repeat, the child has to learn the "know how" of social contact with strangers, for the other children are mostly strangers to him. He has to become acquainted with these strangers and learn what to expect from each of them. With some he can share, and with others no one can share. Some will play fair and others will not. All this, with thirty in the group, is a bewildering situation. Until a child has mastered the situation to some extent, we cannot expect him to be so emotionally settled as to be able to direct his attention to reading.

DOING AS THE TEACHER DIRECTS

It should be realized by all persons concerned, teachers or parents, that it is necessary for a child to do just *what* the teacher tells him *when* she tells him if he is to learn to read. We hear about and see many apparent violations of this rule. We see individual children doing in school just what they please and still learning how to read; but such children are not being taught reading by the teacher. They are learning by themselves or are being taught at home by parents and brothers and sisters. There are whole schools with little discipline or control by the teacher where the children learn to read, but those schools have higher mental age than the normal and more favored homes than the normal. The average child in the average school will not learn as those children learn.

The child must do as the teacher directs because otherwise he will not *look* where the teacher tells him to look, *say* what the teacher tells him to say, and *think* what the teacher wants him to think. Reading is learning to match sight and sound, to match the visual word that is before the child with the sound word that is already in his mind. If the child matches, he learns to read; if he does not, he does not learn. And he will seldom match correctly and often if he does not do just as directed.

Since "doing as directed" is so essential for readiness for reading, a great problem arises in many schools because so many children have the definite habit of *not* doing as directed. Directions have been showered upon them by parents and nurses, and they have learned to ignore those directions or sometimes even to do the opposite out of a felt need for self assertion.

In saying this we are not claiming that there is a "breakdown of the home" but merely pointing out that there has been a great social change. A generation or two ago, the typical American home was a common enterprise for all persons in it, parents and children alike. If it was on a farm, everybody took part in farming or gardening or caring for chickens or housecleaning and the like. When the parents wanted something done they told the child to do it, and he did it at once or else. No one could stand for foolishness. If the home were in a city, it took all hands to prepare food, to do the washing, to sweep and dust, to make clothes, and so on. To run any household took much labor, and the labor was done by children as well as adults. And the parents who headed the work would not tolerate shirking or loafing just because if the child did not do the job the mother had to do it herself, and she already had too much to do. Work for all was the rule except in the very few homes that had servants.

Nowadays, we have most of the work of living done for us by machines. Mother drives to the supermarket instead of sending Jimmy to the corner grocery. Electricity makes the toast instead of having Susie stand with the toaster over the coal range or the gas stove. Mother brushes over the floors with the vacuum cleaner where formerly Susie and Milly and mother altogether, with broom and dustpan and dustrag, could barely get things straight. Nowadays, there is practically no work for children. If there is a job it is easier to shoo the children outside and do everything yourself. So there is little training in work habits, which includes "doing as directed."

Parents are struggling with this situation as best they can. They divide what jobs there are. They invent chores. They give children definite directions for eating, for caring for the child's own room and clothes, for managing the radio and television set, and so on, and make those directions stick. But after all, the "discipline of work" is largely lacking.

The school recognizes that the lack of the habit of doing as directed is not a sign of depravity in the children but the result of a difficulty that is understandable. So the teacher begins at once to see that her directions are followed and that the habit of following directions is built up. Here the teacher's great difficulty is due to her having too large classes. With too many children, the teacher often cannot enforce her directions and thus build habits. Some children persist in their disregard of directions, and the teacher cannot get around to all individuals to remedy the situation. Therefore many children fail to do as they are told, to look where they should, to repeat as they should, to mark as they should, and so on, and thus fail to match sight words and sound words. They fail to learn to read because they were not ready in this basic school adjustment of doing as the teacher directs.

PAYING CONTINUED ATTENTION

Following directions means that the child *tries* to pay attention as the teacher requests. But *can* he pay attention? Here also we have a matter of habit. For attention cannot be got by main force. We can force the outward appearance of attention, but that is all. All teachers know how children look at them as if they were paying attention but instead think of something else. Real attention of the mind is a habit that must be acquired.

We would understand attention much better if we realized that it is really the *ignoring of distractions*. It is natural for the attention to wander to every little thing that calls to our eyes and ears. It is natural to hear every sound, follow every moving object, and the like. That is what the small child does. But as we grow older, we learn to ignore sights and sounds and thereby to keep the mind on one topic. We even get to the point where we can be reading a book while all about us people are talking or the radio is going or things are moving, but we never notice them at all. We have learned the habit of ignoring distractions or the habit of attention.

The way to learn to pay attention is by paying attention. That is, the child must learn to ignore distractions by ignoring distraction, since you learn to do a thing by doing it and not by doing something else. This training begins normally at home and continues naturally into school. The very young child for instance, likes to play in the sand. His sand digging and building holds his attention. Other children may be near. Other children may say things about him or to him. But he goes right on digging, ignoring the distractions. In so far, he has learned to hold his attention to what he is doing.

In the same way, the child pays attention while someone is reading to him. He thinks of getting a drink, but goes on listening. His foot itches, but he is too busy listening to scratch it. So gradually, listening to the story develops the ability to let other appeals go by and keep on paying attention to the story. So we may well say, ''Whenever you see a child busy with something, try to let him stay busy and do not interrupt him.'' He is learning to pay continued attention, an ability that will be very necessary for his further development.

In the first grade or kindergarten, however, there are children who do not seem to have learned how to ignore any stimulus at all. At every sound, they turn their head. Every idea they have takes them out of their seats to look or to go somewhere else. They seem unable to keep their attention on anything. They flit about, as it were, from one thing to another. We say they have flighty attention.

Of course all paying attention or ignoring distractions is relative. It is a continual competition between the distraction and the work at hand. If the work at hand is interesting, other things can be ignored. If, however, the work loses interest, or the distraction becomes stronger, the habit of paying attention may not be strong enough, and attention will wander. At times attention may wander and come back. A child may leave a toy for something else, but when the other thing palls, back he may come to the first toy. There is always a situation of competition between attractions. The stronger the habit of attention to the work in hand, the less flitting of attention there will be. We can, however, gradually get more and more stability, so that the child does not change so easily, and stays with one thing longer.

Following directions and *the habit of paying attention* naturally work together. The teacher tries to get attention to the reading and gives directions. The child tries to follow directions, but unless the material or his habit hold him, the teacher will again have to call on him to pay attention. She brings him back, as it were, time after time. The teacher of beginners needs endless patience for this never ending "bringing back" from excursions of attention to other things. She seats the children so that they will be distracted as little as possible. She tries to get as interesting pictures or stories as possible. But she is still competing with all the other things the children can see, hear, or think of.

Readiness as Experience and Language

EXPERIENCE AND THE FIRST BOOKS

For reading readiness, children need "experiential or experience background," as it is called. This is sometimes taken to mean that they need certain experiences in order to understand the beginning books in reading. If this were the only meaning, experience background would have little importance. Very little background is needed to understand the material in the beginning books. In those books, some small children play with one another or with toys or with pets. There are no objects or persons that a three or four year old does not know. Everything takes place in an average home that every young child presumably knows about. In fact, the authors of the beginning books are so anxious that every child understand the words and ideas that they purposely "go back" a year or two in child experience for their material. So much so that some sophisticated children rather scorn beginning reading books. In short, experience background is no problem if understanding the words of the first books is all we are thinking of.

EXPERIENCE BACKGROUND FOR FIRST GRADE LIVING

There is, however, a much truer and more vital conception of experience background. It is that for the child to live adequately in the first grade group, to take part in first grade activities, to grow along with the first graders, he must have had a certain background of living behind him. Otherwise, he is a baby and out of place, or a stranger or a misfit in the group, incapable of using the environment that the first grade puts about him.

Here we have a most interesting question to which there has not been as yet a satisfactory answer. What constitutes normal living experience for the first six years of a child's life?

Surely we should have some list of necessary or desirable experiences and be able to check against this list to find any particular child's deficiencies. However, lacking such a list, we do have some idea of what the average normal child has experienced, and with any particular child we can check to see whether he has "lived" richly or poorly during his first six years.

One careful attempt to check on child experience has been made by Dr. Paul Witty, who has devised an interest inventory that attempts to find out about experience background. We reproduce below the part of this inventory that applies to children entering school. You will note that certain definite topics are covered. One is leisure time occupations including toys and tools and their use. Another is family relationships and clubs. Spending money is an important item. Movies, radio and television are now an important part of a child life. Then there are types of excursions to different kinds of places and by different methods of travel. Finally there are future plans and the possession of pets and hobbies.

Inventory of Pupil Interests and Activities *

Name..Date of Birth.......................Age..........

Grade............ School.................... Teacher.................... Date....................

1. What do you usually do:
   (a) Directly after school:...
   (b) In the evening?...
   (c) On Saturdays?...
   (d) On Sundays?...
   At what time do you usually go to bed?........................ When do you get up?........................

2. In the space below write the full names and ages of your close friends...
   ....
   ....
   Do you have a nickname?................ What?.................... Do you like it?....................
   Would you rather play by yourself, with other boys, girls, or boys and girls? (Underline)
   Do you quarrel with your friends? Never, sometimes, often. (Underline one.)
   If you have any brothers or sisters, how old are they?....................
   Do you play with them?...
   Do you do things with your father or mother?..........What?............

* From Reading and the Educative Process, by Paul Witty (Ginn & Co., Boston).

3. To what club or organizations do you belong?.................................
What do you do in your club?..
How long have you been a member?............Are you an officer?........
Where do you meet?.......................................When?............................
Do you go to Sunday School?...

4. Do you take any kind of special lessons outside of school?.............
What kind?..Do you like them?...............
Is there another kind of lesson you would rather take?....................

5. What tools or play things (toys) do you have at home?.................
Which do you like best?...
Do you let other children use your toys?................If not, why?........
....
Is there any tool, toy, or equipment that you especially want?......
....

6. Do you receive spending money?............Regularly or occasionally?
....
Have you ever earned any money?.....................How?.......................
....Do you have chores or other regular
duties to do at home?............................What?.......................

7. How often do you go to the movies?............................With whom,
usually?...
What are the names of two good movies you have seen?
(a)..   (b)...
Underline the kinds of pictures you like best.
comedy   western   ''sad''   news   love   serial   mystery
gangster   educational   society   cartoons

8. Have you been to a farm?..............Circus?...............A Zoo?..............
Have you been to a museum?...
Have you been to an amusement park?...................Do you ever go
to concerts?............................ How often?..
Have you ever been to a picnic?.................Have you ever taken a
trip by boat?...............By train?...............By airplane?.................
By bus?...............By automobile?...............Where did you go?........
....

Where did you go during your last summer vacation?....................

....

To what other places would you like to go?..

9. What would you like to be when you are grown?..............................
   What would your father and mother like you to be?........................

10. What are your favorite radio or television programs? (First)......
    .... (Second)............................ (Third)........................
    To how many programs do you listen regularly? One, two, three,
    or more? (Underline)

11. Do you have a pet?....................What?..
    Are you making any collections?................Of what?........................
    Do you have a hobby?................What?..

To get honest answers to questions on such an
inventory, one must first make friends with the child
and gradually get him to tell about himself. After
one has the required information, there is still the
question of whether the child has had "average"
experiences. One cannot be too sure of this because
everyone has his own idea of what average experiences are. But one can tell pretty well which children are much deprived. For instance, there are
children who have never owned anything—pet, toy,
or what not. There are those who have been nowhere
at all, neither on a trip nor to a carnival nor to anything. Other children have had no social life whatever. They have been only children and have been
restricted from making friends with any other children. In these and in many other ways children have
been deprived of normal experiences. We say "deprived" not in the sense that anyone is necessarily

to blame but just that there is a great lack where experience should have been.

GIVING CHILDREN EXPERIENCES

The great problem for the school, of course, is how to help the child who is lacking in normal experience background. Actually, we try to help in three different fields. We try, *first,* to give "thing experience." For this reason the first grade has toys and tools, pets and materials of all kinds. Children do their cutting and pasting, their sawing, their coloring and painting, their putting together, their building and so on. This tends to make up somewhat for all the doing and making that should have gone on at home. *Second,* we try to give "people experience," providing guidance in all kinds of games and group activities. We have sandpiles, and swings and seesaws and jungle gyms and all kinds of possibilities for play by twos and threes or in groups. This helps make up for lack of large families and neighborhood playgrounds and play groups.

Third, we try to provide "place experiences." We try to take children to places that perhaps their parents should have taken them to. Giving this kind of experience is in its infancy at present. Soon each school will have a list of the possibilities of its neighborhood, whether they be dairies, parks, woods, factories, stores, theatres, radio studios, farms, markets, and what not and will definitely see that every child in the school gets to go to every one of them.

This means a "visiting program" that is begun in first grade and continued systematically and efficiently year by year. It is to give the children a basic background from which to think about their life in their neighborhood, home town, or state and country.

Not too far off is a "visiting program" for the nation, by which every child will see Yellowstone and Niagara and a steel mill and a coal mine and the National Capitol and Carlsbad Caverns, and so on. With cheap and efficient bus transportation, every school can manage its own "visiting program," and start that program early in the child's school life instead of delaying it to the end of high school as is sometimes done.

EXPERIENCE AND LANGUAGE

It is strange but true that experience alone does not educate. Many children have actually been to many places and seen many things, but they are no different than if they had never been anywhere. We see the same thing with wide travelers and with soldiers who have been to many places in the world. Somehow experience alone did not seem to take effect. We can see the same thing in our own experience if we will go through a fine museum, but agree not to look at the label on a single exhibit. We will come out with a confused lot of visual images. But what did we see? We cannot tell anyone. We cannot think very clearly about what we have seen either. The reason is, we have had experience, but no "labels." Without "labels," that is, without words to think with and talk with, our experience has not educated us.

The words in our minds are like labels on thousands of little drawers. Into each drawer we put experience from time to time. Some drawers have very little in them. The drawer labeled "cassowary" may contain only the meaning "some kind of animal." The drawer labeled "Jersey cow" may contain years of experience with a pet cow who was a Jersey. But living without labeling is not profitable. The experience goes by and we cannot file it away in the proper drawer so that it will be preserved. Without language, we cannot keep experience very well, and we can make little use of experience. What we need is not just experience, but *experience and language*.

This is the reason that children need guides on their trips. They need someone to name what they see, and then to put together the things they see. If the child sees at the dairy a sort of pot with hoses attached, the guide will say "That is a milking machine. See the cups at the ends of the hoses. Each cup is put over one of the teats on the cow's milk bag, called an udder, that you saw near the back legs. Then air sucks the milk out of the udder into the pot that you see." Thus five or six things that the child looked at were each named and then the names used to put them all together in an active relationship. This is the function of language in learning. All experience must be given symbols so that it fits into our thinking and talking and reading system, and then the symbols must be related to one another so that the things represented are related. Thus experience is unified and made more permanent.

We say all this just because many adults have failed to guide the child's experience in this way. The child may have traveled on a bus but never have become aware of the engine, the driver's controls, the light switches, the adjustable footrests, the baggage compartment, the schedule, and so on. No adult named these things and related them. So the child retained only a vague mixture of images, with some feeling tone, pleasant or unpleasant. The same is true if the child visited the ocean or the mountains, or the circus or the zoo. Unless some adult named what was seen and related what was seen by use of the names, little usable experience resulted.

If the child is deficient in this combination of experience and language, the school has to try to do what it can to remedy the situation. As above suggested, the very simple first books may be read with complete meaning, but unless the children have much more experience and language than these books require, the discussions that should result from that reading and that should result from the questions and the telling of activities will not be very interesting and meaningful to many children.

The teacher, therefore, watches her group to spot the children who do not respond with evidence of meaning in their minds as she or the other children talk. She spots those who do not "see much" in the pictures that are supplied. To help those children she herself names and relates the symbols, or she has other children do this. She constantly is aware that there is much of "typical living experience of the first six years" that is missing in her class. She keeps up the daily experiencing and tries to fill in the blanks that she finds. She is trying to get full readiness of "experience and language" for each of her children.

Readiness as Perceptual Ability

After all the other kinds of readiness are developed, we come to the fact that in order to get thought the child must read words. Therefore, the final problem is whether he has sufficient perceptual ability to do so.

Early Perceptual Development

It is well to recognize that the perceptual ability needed for reading is the culmination of a long development in perception. Though we are forced to speculate about much of this development, we can be sure that the child begins with the "blooming, buzzing confusion" that James speaks of. Out of this confused, largely meaningless situation surrounding him, the child must gradually separate certain elements, such as light and dark, hunger and satisfaction, rest and movement, and so on. Then gradually he finds elements that go together, such as those that make up a face above him, or his own hand before his face.

When the child is sitting up, and later when he is getting around under his own power, he keeps on separating parts of the environment and seeing those parts more clearly. For instance, he finds that the form of the dresser drawer is separate from the form of the whole dresser. He distinguishes the handle and the spout of a pitcher from the form of the whole. Naturally there is an accompanying process of relating these new elements to other things, since he sees that the drawer is part of the dresser, and the handle and spout are part of the pitcher.

Of course the process of attaching meaning to these new elements of the environment is going on all the time as we have considered under the heading, Experience and Language. At the moment, however, we are calling attention only to the process of "seeing differences more clearly." For instance, the child early sees the difference between a horse and a dog; he later sees the difference between a chow and a shepherd dog; then he sees the difference between a cocker spaniel and a springer spaniel; and his perception develops on and on until he can tell one particular cocker from another one of the same color.

This development of perception takes a special form when the child is given picture books. The things themselves are not in the picture books; there are only colors, shades and lines "representing" the things. We as adults understand these "representations" at once, but the process is not at first easy for the child. He must learn that certain lines represent a hen; that certain other lines represent a rabbit. After using many coloring books, the child becomes expert at understanding representations. But some children have few if any coloring books, and do not get this training.

When a child goes from natural forms to geometric forms, we see this development rather clearly. At first, every form may be seen as either a square or a circle, depending on whether the lines are straight or curved. Then some of the "squares" are seen as oblongs, since the width is greater than the height. In a similar development some of the "circles" are seen not to be circular enough and they are called ovals. Thus gradually more and more attention is paid to certain detail differences in what at first were very similar figures.

UNCONSCIOUS AWARENESS

Perception is usually defined as "awareness," and it is usually assumed that this means "consciousness of." [1] But we are forced to believe that much of this

---

[1] In this section, certain phychological terms are employed in their popular meaning and usage for the sake of understanding by a wider audience. Technical distinctions familiar to psychologists had to be for the moment ignored.

awareness of difference is an unconscious matter on the part of the child. When he tries, for instance, to put geometric pieces of wood into a form board, he discovers that some will fit and others will not. Does he say to himself, "Oh, this piece has straight sides and the hole has round sides"? At the age when a child can fit the forms into the holes, it seems very doubtful that he becomes conscious of the exact differences between the forms and the holes. He just knows some fit and some do not. Of course, he must be unconsciously aware, or he could never put the right one in the right hole except by chance.

We see this unconscious awareness in a child's dealing with people. Many times, after a visitor has gone, a child will say, "I don't like that man." If you ask why, the child will not have any idea. But he was aware of something about the man that caused him to be repelled. And this awareness was unconscious.

We shall see that in reading there is a great deal of this unconscious awareness in recognition of words. Children tell words apart in ways they cannot explain because they are not conscious of their reason or method. But they must have become aware of the differences somehow.

ALL PERCEPTION AS "READING"

It is common for us to use the word "reading" in a very wide sense. We speak of "reading faces." We say we "read the stars," or "read the signs of game" and so on. In every case, we are talking about attaching meaning to stimuli, and use the word "reading." But in our language, the word "reading" has almost universally come to mean attaching meaning to one kind of stimuli only, the words on the page. It makes for clearer understanding if we keep the word "reading" for this kind of perception alone. When we use it to speak of "reading" other things, let us consider that we are using a figure of speech, saying that our understanding of the signs of the weather, for instance, is "like" reading.

Delayed Perception. Very often a child will not recognize a word when he first looks at it, but after he has looked at it a while he will suddenly do so. He cannot tell us what happens because he just does not know. We have this same experience when we see someone who looks familiar but cannot think of who he is until hours or days afterwards. Delayed perception is common in reading, and the teacher should not hurry a child too much if she thinks delay will help him. And she should not lose patience with delayed perception. The child cannot hurry it.

What Is Perceptual Readiness?

TELLING ONE WORD FROM ANOTHER

After all, reading requires that the child "tell one word from another." That is, if the teacher points to one word and says "mother" and points to another and says "father," the child must see some difference between the words if he is to tell them apart later.

It is possible for a teacher to be deceived at this point if she is not careful. For instance, if "mother" is on the left and "father" is on the right, the child can call them correctly by remembering the place in which each is. The words can look entirely alike to the child, but he remembers that the left one is "mother" and the right one is "father."

One special phase of "recognizing by place" is in chart [1] reading. The teacher writes "We saw a big black cow," and asks the child to point to "big." Actually, both words "big" and "black" may look quite alike to the child, but he repeats the sentences a word at a time, finds which is "big" and thus may be able to point to the right word without any real recognition at all. Whenever a sentence has been memorized, or a list has been memorized, the only way we can check on real word recognition is to mix up the words in another order. Then and then only can we be sure the child can "tell one word from another."

It is very hard for an adult to realize that words look very much alike to the beginner. One way for the adult to realize this is to take up a book in Chinese or Greek or Arabic. The words do look very much alike. At least there are some that have

---

[1] See chapter on Charts in Teaching Primary Reading.

to be matched carefully to make sure they are not the same. Perhaps something of the child's confusion will be understood if the reader will read the following paragraph just as it is, *without turning it around*. Begin at the right end of the first line.

When any text in English is turned upside down, the reader at once has a feeling that the words are familiar, but he is not sure. He has to look at every word separately, and for some time. This experience gives some little idea of how hard the child must look at words and how confused he feels.

Does this little test give some sense of the difficulty of word recognition for a child? You can be sure that the child has even more difficulty than you have had. After all, you read the familiar in an unfamiliar position, but to the child, everything about words and reading is unfamiliar.

Perceptual Readiness Is Relative

We must admit at once that the ability to "tell one word from another" is relative, and develops gradually. Very young children can tell "mother" from "no," just because of the difference in length. Or they can tell "dog" from "man" because one has parts "sticking up or down" and the other does not. It is for this reason teachers find that beginners quickly learn the unusual-looking words and have difficulty with the little words that look much alike.

In the usual teaching of reading, beginning with a preprimer with fifty words and rapidly going to other books, the teacher finds that growth of perceptual readiness often does not keep pace with the word difficulties. Suppose she works on reading readiness until the children can tell apart a dozen words which may appear in the readiness book or that may be presented on labels, or the like. Then she starts the book. At first, all goes well, and the children tell which word is which. But very rapidly the book brings in words which look very much alike, such as "her" and "here" and "may" and "my." Immediately some of the children have trouble telling one word from the other. This is not to be wondered at. In fact, little attention seems to be paid to this problem, that perceptual readiness does not develop as fast as the word difficulties develop in the reading books. The only answer, for a large proportion of children, is to delay beginning a book until perceptual readiness is quite advanced. As it is, the teacher often gets perceptual readiness for the preprimer, and then does not have readiness for the primer which follows immediately.

DEVELOPING PERCEPTUAL READINESS

It is always a problem how far a native ability can be developed or how fast. Surely we can develop every ability we possess, but there are also limits to the rapidity of this development.

Here we run into the much discussed question of the relationship between maturation and learning. Without going into all of the problem, we can state the consensus of opinion on three points. *First,* learning cannot push maturation beyond its own rate of growth. *Second,* learning can, however, help a child to mature at his maximum rate. And *third,* learning can help a child to benefit by or use the maturation he has already attained.

Our aim, therefore, in giving training in perceptual readiness is (1) to be sure the children grow in perception as fast as they are capable of growing, and (2) to be sure that each child uses the perceptual ability he has attained.

We must also state two dangers in giving perceptual training. If we try to "push" a child beyond his maturing abilities, we will do one of two things. First, we may make him *immune to stimulus.* We see this when children are urged continually until they pay no further attention to urging. We see it when children are surrounded too early with things that we think should stimulate them but do not. They become "used" to the surrounding and there is no stimulation at a later time when they might react strongly. We do not want to "use up" our materials, our games and our workbooks too soon and thus make children indifferent to them.

Second, we may "push" a child into emotional resentment and frustration. Parents are especially guilty of this kind of pushing because they are so anxious for the child to "develop," and do not realize how much waiting there is to their job. The school finds some beginners antagonistic to the activities that are provided because parents have made those activities unpleasant by too much urging and pushing.

These basic considerations admitted, we may ask how perceptual ability or readiness is best developed. As explained earlier, this development of perception is a continuous one, going in general from perception of the large to perception of the small, from perception of the more obvious to perception of the less obvious. The fundamental principle to follow in trying to avoid pushing is to *stay at a lower level much longer than seems entirely "necessary,"* letting the child himself go on to more refined work. He will give the cue. For instance, large blocks are much used for perceptual training. The child must pick the block that fits his tower or wall or building. Children can continue this building for years without necessarily going to smaller blocks or interlocking blocks or other refined building materials. Two things are happening with the blocks, however. First, the child is building more and more exactly. Second, he is choosing blocks and fitting them more easily and automatically. He is benefiting at that level even though he seems to be "doing the same thing."

Similarly in discussion of pictures, the children will stay for a long time at the level of just telling what they see in the picture, without explaining or making up a story about it. There is the constant temptation to push by asking questions so as to get a higher level of perception or discrimination. We should be slow to do this. It is generally better to let the child react with his own perception and discrimination, leaving it to him to begin to perceive more accurately and discriminatingly.

Students of child nature have made much of this point. They say that we do much harm by "pushing." Just as soon as a child begins to be happy and confident at one level of activity, we break up his confidence by asking questions that put him again in a position of insecurity. He has an answer, and then we ask another question. He is satisfied with what he perceived, and then we put him again into doubt. Probably there is a great deal of truth in this view, and we should be careful not to be guilty of thus hampering a child's growth by trying to get him to grow faster than he naturally will.

READINESS MATERIAL FOR PERCEPTUAL DEVELOPMENT

With all these points in mind, we will look at many readiness materials with some doubt. Consider a typical "readiness book." It begins with a page or two of pictures of children or playthings. It goes on to a few pages picturing similar toys or similar animals. It has a few pages of geometric figures. It rapidly goes into fine discrimination of differences in clothing or expression or the like. And

by the end of 42 pages it is into discrimination of
words. This is a speed of progression entirely
beyond any possibility of natural perceptual growth.
If the first pages of the book fit the child's stage of
perceptual growth, the last pages are impossible.
And if the last pages are appropriate, the first pages
are too easy to be of much teaching value.

The natural conclusion must be that the typical
readiness book is not planned so much to develop
readiness as to be the final step or "topping off" of
the process of developing readiness. The readiness
book is taken up as a sort of "clincher" with the
understanding that most of the work on readiness
has been finished. There must be before that a long
period of games and handling of all kinds of materials. A whole chapter on materials and methods
for developing readiness will be found in Teaching
Primary Reading (Garrard Press, Champaign, Ill.).

Uneven Readiness

A study of children beginning school impresses
one very strongly with the conviction that children
are very uneven in their development of different
kinds of readiness. Some beginners are high in
mental age and very low on school adjustment.
Others have been to kindergarten and, as a result
of that training, may be excellent in school adjustment but be lacking somewhat in mental age. Children may even be well developed perceptually but be
short on interest or on school adjustment habits.

Other children are satisfactory on all counts except some physical condition, such as nearsightedness or nervousness.

WHICH ARE THE CRUCIAL FACTORS IN READINESS?

When we look back over the factors in readiness that we have discussed, we find that some do not make so much difference and others do. Of course any factor can be crucial if it is extreme, such as an extreme physical handicap. But ordinarily we can say that some factors are more to be looked for and required than others.

First of all, we may say that *perceptual development* is more crucial than any of the others since without perceptual ability, "telling one word from another," there is no reading. All the other kinds of readiness are useless without perceptual development. Therefore, though we work on all the other kinds of readiness, we must have an eye on this one kind of development as the deciding factor as to when reading is begun. This fact is behind the kind of test of reading readiness that was formulated by Stone and Grover. They call their test a Classification Test for Beginners, but one finds in the test just two parts, both of them comparing word forms to see if they are alike or different. Stone and Grover concluded that this perceptual discrimination between words is needed just before beginning to read. Therefore if you test this discrimination you have tested the final step in reading readiness.

Second, next to perceptual development, *School Adjustment* is the most crucial kind of readiness. The brightest children, it is true, can learn without school adjustment, for they actually teach themselves and are not dependent on the teacher and school. For all the other children, to lack *attention,* to lack *doing as directed,* and to lack *fitting into the group* means to fail in reading. Perceptual development may be there, but it will not be used.

The other factors in reading readiness all take their place at times as crucial but they are generally less important if the child has perceptual readiness and school readiness.

To the teacher the fact of uneven readiness presents a great challenge. Because of it, she cannot do her work merely by running all the children uniformly through certain exercises to get for all the same result. Some school administrations may think of the readiness period in those terms, but some persons think of the whole school as a sort of assembly line along which all children travel to get all the same attachments added or the same processes done. Instead, the teacher has every reason to remember that each child is different from every other child, and that each may need a different kind of readiness.

It will help the teacher if she makes a list of her beginning children and to the right of the list draws

five columns, headed Physical Readiness, Interest
Readiness, Experience and Language Readiness,
School Readiness, and Perceptual Readiness. Then
let her think of each child with reference to each of
these factors. Let her mark each child on each, putting in the right column after his name a minus sign
if he seems to be lacking, a check if he seems to be
satisfactory, and a plus if he is well along in readiness. She can then look at each child's marks and
see him both as a whole and as needing certain
things more than others. She can also look up and
down the columns and see which factors need to be
emphasized in the class as a whole. She will thus
have both a group and an individual guide for her
planning.

REMEDIAL READINESS WORK

After the teacher thinks her children have reached
readiness, and she begins the teaching of reading,
she will discover that she has been mistaken about
some of the children. She will then consult her check
list, just mentioned, or make another, and plan to
help certain children in certain ways. Some will
need special help in sticking to the job, as their *interest* has proven weaker than she expected. Others will
begin to display shortage in *experience and language* and will need more chances to talk to the
group and more explanation of ideas which she
thought they already had. Other children will be
weak in the *school habits* we have listed under school

readiness: doing as directed, paying attention, and fitting into the group. Still other children will persistently mistake one word for another and so suggest that they *do not yet perceive* differences clearly enough. These children will be given more opportunity to compare one word with another, as with flashcards, or to play readiness games that train in perceptual keenness. So the work in readiness does not end with the first lesson in reading. It continues until all are fully capable to hold their own in all the areas of readiness we have described.

ABSENCE AND READINESS

One of the most annoying experiences for a teacher is to see the children "go backward" after an absence, whether the result of sickness, traveling, or what not. The child in school gets habits that work in the school situation. When he is removed to a home situation that does not have the same pressures, he will lose his school habits. So the teacher may expect "going backward" whenever there is absence or other disturbing factors. Sometimes emotional upset at home will have the same effect, making the child more immature, less responsible, less developed apparently, than he was before. In growth in maturity, ground is gained slowly and lost easily.

Reading Readiness Tests

Testing for reading readiness is a practical expedient adopted by large school systems where children must be handled in large numbers by persons who have little chance to know them as individuals. These tests are a makeshift. The way to know a child is to have many contacts with him under many circumstances. Merely to ask him a series of questions at one sitting or to have him make some marks on paper is a very poor way to know him, and often is no way at all. It is used only as an expedient and should be thought of only as such.

The difficulties of the reading readiness tests are easily seen if we ask, "Which factors in Reading Readiness do they measure?" Our answer is bound to be that they test some poorly and others not at all. Physical handicap is being measured if the child cannot see or hear well enough to know what to do, but the child then merely fails the test and his score does not say "Lacking in physical fitness." Many children fail the reading readiness test through lack of interest or lack of attention, but there is no way of knowing if a low score means these things.

Low scores on a reading readiness test are assumed to mean lack of intelligence, lack of experience and language, or lack of perceptual ability. Yet even these are confused. If a child does not mark a triangle when told to mark one, we cannot tell whether he lacks experience with triangles, or cannot perceive the difference between geometric figures, or is too immature to follow directions. An especial danger is that many readiness tests are in parts, and one child may score high on one and low on another, while another child may reverse the situation. As the total score is usually recorded and used, the scores of these two children would say they did the same on the test, which would be far from true.

For instance, on some readiness tests, number is included, along with vocabulary and perception of differences. Children who have been given money to spend will usually score high on number, while others who have not handled money will be almost lacking in number knowledge. Some children with favored homes will score high on vocabulary, while other children, equally capable, will have been ignored by parents and not given language opportunities, and thus score low on this section. Hence one does not know what to do with a score on a readiness test unless he knows the scores on the different parts of the test and also something of the background of experience of the child taking the test.

Many psychologists prefer a beginner's intelligence test to a readiness test, believing that the intelligence test will give us a better idea of the child's general development, rather than weighing a few areas such as vocabulary or number. Until we have better readiness tests, this view is well founded. Other persons regard the intelligence test as too general, and want measures of special kinds of development. There is as yet, however, not sufficient evidence that any test is better in the long run than the general intelligence test.

How should readiness be measured then? First, we must take time to know the children. This can be done in Kindergarten or during an initial "Kindergarten period" in the first grade. The effort will richly repay us in avoiding the early frustration of childhood and "setting of children against school." Second, we can go slow in beginning reading so that there will be no doubt about there being sufficient readiness. This follows the general maxim for all education, "When in doubt, go slow." We can do much harm by pushing. We do little harm by waiting. After all, children need general development much more than they need reading. They so badly need self-confidence, self-control, knowledge of the world about them, skill in adjusting to others, physical skills, and much else. Time devoted to these things will pay much richer dividends than a premature start in reading.

Classroom Procedures

In Chapters III, IV, and V, we have repeatedly given illustrations from classroom practice to explain the points made concerning the process of developing readiness. It must be realized, however, that these illustrations are only a few from an enormous number that are possible. Anyone having to work with children in the development of readiness of any of the kinds described should be sure to have at her command a great diversity of classroom pro-

cedures for the purpose. Many of these will be found
in Chapters IV to IX of the author's Teaching Primary Reading (Garrard Press, Champaign, Ill.),
but others should be found in the many other books
on reading, in the magazines for teachers, and in
the manuals issued by publishers to accompany their
readiness programs.

Summary

Readiness as School Adjustment implies first the
social adjustment to a large group of children. This
adjustment requires (1) a lessening of the fear that
naturally arises in the circumstances, (2) learning
how to "give and take" with a group of children.

Then School Adjustment means *learning to do as
the teacher directs.* Many kinds of home conditions
not only fail to teach the following of directions but
cultivate antagonism to adults.

Finally, School Adjustment requires *learning to
pay continued attention.* Practically, this means acquiring the habit of ignoring distractions. It is
learned by being absorbed in activities.

Readiness is also conceived of as a certain preparation in *Experience and Language.* Here is meant
preparation for first grade living rather than for the
very simple reading material of first grade. A simple inventory of necessary child experiences may be
made. To children who lack normal experience, we
try to give "thing experiences," "people experiences," and "place experiences." But all experi-

ence, to be truly profitable, must be accompanied with language, so that the experience may be talked about and thought about.

Finally, readiness may be in terms of *Perceptual Ability*. Perceptual development starts from the early years and means learning to distinguish from one another similar things, people, etc. Most of this distinguishing is done by unconscious awareness. Ultimately, perceptual readiness means *telling one word from another*. This development is relative; that is, at first some words can be distinguished, but not others. Here we have the influence of maturation, but we can make sure that the child develops as fast as he is able to. Pushing will, however, do no good, but may do harm. Material for the development of readiness generally assumes that the development will go faster than it actually can.

Uneven Readiness is common. That is, a child becomes ready in some ways but is not in others. In that case, we must consider *perceptual development* as the deciding factor. Next to it, *school adjustment* is necessary. Remedial readiness work is often necessary; that is, training on the aspect of readiness that has not kept pace with the others.

Readiness tests obviously do not measure all aspects of readiness. Therefore, the teacher must determine readiness by her knowledge of the individual children.

CHAPTER VI.

Building a Sight Vocabulary

Building a Sight Vocabulary

When we who are expert readers look at reading matter, the words are known so quickly that we are unaware that we are recognizing them, and we are instantly conscious of meaning. We "see through the words to the meaning," just as we see clearly through a plate glass window. That is because the words we are looking at are in our "instant sight vocabulary."

Each one of us has, for use in reading, a "stock" of sight words which we recognize as immediately and unconsciously as we recognize the handle on a door we are about to open or the chair in which we are about to sit. All the familiar things about us are. recognized instantly but we are conscious only of their use or meaning. So with our stock of sight words. We get their meaning without hesitation whenever we see them because they are recognized instantly. Each person has such a stock of words that he uses in reading. One of the goals in reading is to increase that stock continually.

Size of the Expert's Sight Vocabulary

The instant sight vocabulary of the expert reader is enormous. Its size can be estimated in several ways. One way is to consider what type of materials the expert can read without ever hesitating in recognizing a word. Can he read the Sunday newspaper without hesitating at any time for word recognition? Then he must have an instant sight vocabulary of over 20,000 words, because the different words in newspapers have been counted and found to run to that figure.

Another rather easy way for anyone to determine his sight vocabulary is to sample the dictionary. Let him turn the pages of the large dictionary one at a time, glancing at the guide word at the top of the page (this is the first word defined on the page). Does he recognize it instantly, or does he have to look at its parts and think the sound of them? If he "gets the word" instantly, let him tally one for his sight vocabulary. After he has gone through the whole dictionary, he can figure what per cent of all the first words he recognized and then can claim (roughly) that he recognizes that per cent of all the words in the dictionary. Many educated persons find by this method that their sight vocabulary is over 100,000 words.

Let us emphasize that we are not speaking of meaning vocabulary. We all know vastly more words on careful consideration than we recognize instantly at a glance. Meaning vocabulary is considered in Chapter IX.

When Are We Using Sight Vocabulary Only?

The best proof of our use of sight vocabulary only is the regularity of our eye movements. The good reader's eyes "stride" across the page, seeing regular, equal sections of the line, and spending about the same fraction of a second on each fixation. The eyes go across-back, across-back, across-back, and so on in regular rhythmic fashion. There are no regressions, no hesitations, no irregularities. That kind of reading proves the use of sight recognition, for if any words were not recognized at sight, the eyes could not go regularly ahead. Therefore if one wishes to see how difficult material he can read at sight, let him have his eye movements photographed and let the eye movement record prove his regular instant recognition.

With children, we can make this same test, or we can use instead the flashing of words. If children can call words instantly, without hesitation, as they are rapidly flashed, those words are obviously part of their instant sight vocabulary. Sometimes we have a child read a word list (not in alphabetical order) to determine sight recognition. If he can say the words rapidly, one after another, he is probably recognizing them immediately.

Speed of Recognition Is Relative

When one recognizes words easily as he reads aloud, he may be recognizing them only at the rate at which he speaks, which may be 120 to 135 words per minute. But suppose as he reads aloud, he looks up at his audience half the time. Then he is speaking at 120 words per minute, but looking at the words only half the time. Therefore, by a simple calculation, we must conclude that the reader is recognizing the words at a rate that is twice as fast as he is speaking, or at a rate of 240 a minute. This must be the rate of recognition of words of a minister who reads a sermon but looks at the congregation half the time and at the words only half the time.

But silent reading rates go higher. Many high school students and most college students perhaps read at the rate of 300 words a minute, or 5 words per second. That is a pretty rapid rate of word recognition. Then we are assured that some individuals, through their own desire to cover ground or through special speeding up exercises, go up to rates of 600 words per minute or 10 words per second. At this point we need caution because it is entirely possible for the very rapid "reader" to begin to skip parts of lines and to get sense from seeing only parts. This problem is considered fully in Chapter X.

Enough has been presented, however, to indicate that word recognition can go on at various rates. Apparently the rate of any individual is controlled by several factors. *First,* one factor may be the individual's native verbal ability, since speed of dealing with symbols depends on that ability. Some persons may be naturally fast and some naturally slow at word recognition. *Second,* there is the element of drive which may at times make a person go faster, or the lack of drive which may keep him going more slowly. If a person finds it comfortable to recognize words at a certain rate, why should he go any faster? It is like our speed of walking. People have different speeds, not because all cannot go faster but because many of us just prefer to walk more slowly.

Third, there is the element of practice. Surely, one who seldom sees words cannot become very fast at recognizing them, and others who read thousands of words every day are much more likely to recognize those words rapidly. This factor of practice is seen with special kinds of reading matter. Every special line of work has its own vocabulary, and workers in that line become very fast at recognizing that special vocabulary, but not other vocabularies outside their work. The doctor can read medical material rapidly, but not mathematical material. The mathematician cannot read medical material rapidly unless he practices at reading it a great deal. Speed of recognition of general vocabulary is, of course, possible for anyone who reads much general reading matter.

The factor of speed, including devices for speeding up perception, is discussed further in Chapter X.

From Sound Language to Sight Recognition

LANGUAGE IS SOUND

An understanding basic to all study of reading is that language is sound. More generally, language is any system of signs by which individuals communicate, but in the human race, our standard system is a system of sounds. We do use other kinds of symbols or signs, such as movements, facial expressions, figures, and the like, but all of these are thought of as something outside of the usual meaning of the word "language."

We can see this fact best with young children. With them, we do use signs of various kinds, such as nodding the head, but we begin to make sounds to influence the child and he comes to know what those sounds mean. Soon by imitation he begins to make those sounds himself in order to convey meaning to us. We communicate with young children almost entirely with sounds. With older persons, we can at times communicate by representing those sounds by written or printed words.

PRINTED WORDS REPRESENT SOUNDS

Children very early learn that printed words "say" something. They ask us, "What does that say?" There is no doubt in their mind that language is sound, and that printed words represent sounds.

We must then recall that the *meaning is connected with the sound,* because sound words have been connected with the experience that gave the meaning. *The sound word has the meaning.* How does the printed word get meaning? To the young child, the printed word suggests the sound word, and the sound word suggests the meaning. The process in reading is

Sight . . . to . . . *sound* . . . to . . . *meaning.*

Adults tend to forget this fact because to them the word they see seems to suggest meaning directly. With adults the process of "sight-sound-meaning" operates so fast that they are not conscious of the middle step. This is a case of mental "short circuiting" in which middle steps in a process seem to disappear. For instance, the ten or more operations used in tying a shoestring have dropped completely out of consciousness because we run through them so rapidly and smoothly. They are still there, however. When the express train goes through a local stop, the local stop is still there; only it is not noticed. But any doubt or hesitation which slows up the reading will at once bring the middle step into consciousness again. In slow, cautious reading, the reader finds himself thinking the sounds.

It is true that some persons have taught the deaf to read without sound, since the deaf do not and cannot know sound. But in that case, the process of learning is "sight . . . memory image . . . meaning."

If there were no memory image, there would be no meaning, for the meaning comes from the experience remembered. Some persons have also tried to teach normal children reading without sound, but they have deceived themselves. Conferences with the children will show that they *think* the sound even though they do not say it. So they still get "sight-sound-meaning," even though they are forbidden to say the sound out loud.

How Is Sight Vocabulary Learned?

We have said that when the child who is learning to read sees a sight word, the sound word to which the meaning from experience it attached flashes into his mind. How is this sight recognition learned? We are very much interested in this question because we wish all children to acquire quickly a great store of these "sight-sound-meaning" associations so that they may read.

The See, Hear, and Remember Method

The simplest way to teach a sight word is called, from the teacher's viewpoint, the "telling method." She points to the word, or in some other way has the child look at the word, while she or another pupil says the word. This can be called the telling method, but from the pupil's standpoint, the proper description would be the *"see, hear and remember"* method.

Most teaching of reading begins with this "telling" method, and *"see, hear and remember"* remains perhaps the chief way in which the average person builds a sight vocabulary. In the primary grades, oral reading is much used, and the child who does not know the words watches as someone else reads. He hears another child or the teacher say a word that up to now he has not known. Now he knows what the word "says," and he need only remember it to add that word to his sight vocabulary.[1]

Some teaching plans have the teacher put the new words on the board first and tell what they say or have some child who already knows them tell what they say. The other children *see, hear and remember*. Some systems claim to begin with silent reading, but they always have oral reading later at which time the children who did not know the words can *see, hear and remember* them. Some plans for teaching seat the children so that one child can tell the child next to him. Some plans provide for the teacher to assign silent reading and then go about the room telling words to those who raise their hands.

In practically all the content subjects, the telling method is used by the teacher and therefore the *see, hear and remember* method is used by the children.

----

[1] Sometimes a child, when told a word, notices especially the last letter. Then when he sees a word of similar form, but *beginning* with with that letter, he thinks he is seeing the original word. This mistake is called a *reversal* (see p. 348 in Teaching Primary Reading).

Sometimes in arithmetic or science or history or geography, the teacher puts words on the board and tells what they say. Sometimes she has the children hunt through the text to find words they do not know. Sometimes she tells the words in answer to questions. In many cases no word attack is used by the bulk of the children and therefore there is only asking and telling, and then seeing, hearing and remembering. Even in high school this is the current method in most content subjects. In the study of literature, there is often reading of masterpieces aloud, and the child who does not know words listens and watches his book and thus learns what the new words say. Of course, in audience reading there is no learning of sight vocabulary.

The telling method has one thing to recommend it; it is the quickest and easiest for the teacher and pupil alike. There need be little stopping, and no struggle. As the reader hesitates, the teacher says the new word, the child repeats and goes on. The story is not disturbed. Attention is not distracted.[1]

Telling is an efficient method for teaching sight words in the beginning grades and it is almost universally used there. For one thing, in the primary grades the text repeats every word often, so that there may be many tellings and thus better remem-

---

[1] The Tracing method advocated by Fernald is a variation of the telling method, the child tracing the new word he is told so that he will "see" it better and so remember it.

bering. Then there is much rereading for various purposes, and again the child who does not know may, through the oral reading of others, be told words many times without embarrassment. In the texts in the usual school subjects, telling may also be an efficient method. The new words are often new in meaning as well as in appearance, and the teacher tells the new words as she explains the meaning, thus getting strong attention to the word. The words are likely to be used a number of times in any lesson, or in succeeding lessons, and thus there is repeated seeing and hearing, and enough vividness for remembering. In fact, the special words of the content subjects, such as *addition, subtraction,* etc., are usually well learned as sight words and almost entirely by the seeing, hearing, and remembering method.

The place where the telling method cannot help is in the outside reading at any level, or wherever the pupil has to read to himself. Then many different unknown words will appear, and there is no one to tell. We can see how this problem develops if we ask what proportion of the child's reading is done in class and what proportion outside. In the first grade all is done in class, or practically all. Gradually the class reading ceases to be the major kind of reading. By eighth grade the class reading is usually a small part of the whole, with silent reading to oneself and reference reading to oneself being the major part. Thus the telling method which seems to be satisfactory in first grade actually becomes less and less so grade by grade.

The Spelling Method

Another method of learning sight vocabulary which is still common in some parts of the country is the spelling method. It was at one time the universal method, but intelligent persons discovered how inadequate and cumbersome it was and began to use other methods instead.

By this spelling method of recognition, the pupil looks at the word, says the *letters* to himself, and the sound of the total word comes to mind. Some persons, the author included, can remember hearing children in school reading by this method. Here is a sample. "T-h-e the m-a-n man w-a-s was t-double-o too t-i-r-e-d tired t-o to g-o go." It is hard to imagine that this was at one time the prevailing method of reading but it was. Old books will tell of a person "spelling his way" through a paper. That was just what he did.

The spelling method was based on what appeared at that time to be invincible logic. A word was made up of letters, was it not? Therefore get the letters and you get the word. The slip in logic was in confusing the spelling word, which was made up of letter *names,* with the sound word that is made up of letter *sounds.* Our modern psychology understands that *language is sound,* and we also understand that the printed word is a symbol which should *suggest that sound* immediately. Using the letter names puts the letters between the reader and the word. We know now that we can go directly from the whole sight word to the whole sound word. That is why the telling method (or the see-hear-and-remember method) has replaced the spelling method.

We must admit, however, that the spelling method in reading is still with us in several ways. First, parents often teach children to spell the words about them. They do this because they themselves know a word two ways, by sight and by spelling, and they do not realize that these two ways were learned separately. So they ask a child to spell words and then tell him what the words say. Thus they give the child the connection of "letters-word-sound-meaning" instead of "whole word-sound-meaning."

Then, two things may happen. First, for the child to recognize words learned this way, he may have to repeat the learned process; that is, he may have to spell the word, which is a very slow, disturbing method of reading. Second, the child may get the *habit of attacking a new word by letters* rather than as a whole. Instead of looking at a whole word, he looks at the first letter. Instead of giving a word "one look," he gives it as many looks as there are letters in the word. "Man" is a three-look word instead of a one-look word. "Little" is a six-look word. And so the habit operates to slow down all word learning and to put letter names in between the child and reading.

To prevent this, we often try to explain to parents how we recognize words by wholes by showing them how they recognize a friend at one look, and not by examining his hair, his eyes, his nose, his mouth, and his chin. If parents cannot understand why spelling is wrong in reading, we have to ask them not to try to teach reading but just to listen to the child read, and we send home only books he has already read. Thus since he does not need to ask about words, he will not be told to spell them out.

The other problem with spelling and reading is the spelling program of the school. This program affects reading in two ways. *In the first place,* the regular spelling program begins in grade II or III. The commonest words are listed first. Those are the words that were supposed to have been learned as one-look words the previous year. Usually the reading words of one year are the spelling words of the next, or approximately that. But many children do not learn the words in reading at the time they are supposed to. So they meet the words in spelling before those words have been learned as reading words. Children often point to a word in reading and say, "I learned that in spelling last week." If they did, they learned it by the beginners spelling method, which is usually reciting the names of the letters. Thus with many children, the words in the reading lesson are learned through the spelling lesson and thus learned by the spelling method.

Second, spelling also comes up in the school through the writing done in language work. Even in the first grade, the children are writing letters and compositions of various kinds, and they ask how to spell the words they need. The teacher tries to give them the total word picture by printing the word asked for on the board or on a slip of paper, but the child will write it in his letter by painfully saying one letter at a time as he copies it. This is a spelling situation that cannot be avoided. There is only one way to keep this spelling from interfering with reading. After all, the child writes only a very few words a day in his composition work. He should read a very great many words a day in order to counteract the effect of his writing. We learn to do as a habit *what we do most.* If the spelling is only occasional, and the reading is constant, the reading habit of whole word recognition will prevail.

Sounding to Build Sight Vocabulary

Two points only need to be made here about sounding and sight vocabulary, since the whole subject of sounding will be discussed completely in Chapter VII. The first of these two points is that *sounding is absolutely necessary if sight vocabulary is to be built up after the school stops using the telling technique.* In the primary grades and later, new words are told to the pupil as a matter of course or if he asks. But during the middle grades, and

more and more throughout school, work is supposed
to be done by the pupil alone and unassisted. He is
to read to himself. If he meets a new word, no one
tells him what it is. If he cannot sound it, he must
skip it or guess. Neither method works very well to
teach sight vocabulary. So the pupil's sight vocabulary stands still, no matter how long he stays in
school.

We find all through the later school grades so
many children whose reading is at third grade level
just because up to grade III they were told words
and they accordingly learned by the see, hear and
remember method. But that method was stopped in
Fourth grade and the child's reading ability never
improved because he had no means of adding to
his sight vocabulary. But by using sounding, anyone
can teach himself sight vocabulary. He sounds a
new word once or twice and then when he meets it
again he does not need to sound it. As he looks at
the word, the right sound word leaps into his mind,
and he goes right on reading. This is the way the
experts have built up their sight vocabularies of
many thousands of words. Nobody told them all
those words. They sounded them out for themselves.

The second most important point about sounding
is that *it is unwise for most children to use the
sounding method at the very beginning of reading.*
We know, of course, that sounding is the method by
which many children teach themselves how to read.
These children discover the rule, "Look alike, sound

alike,'' and they use this rule on all the words they see. Soon they have a sight vocabulary, and keep on building up that sight vocabulary by the same method. But that method is too full of danger to be used with most children in the public school.

The trouble with beginning with sounding is very like the difficulty with the old spelling method. The method teaches the child to look at a letter at a time. Instead of seeing ''man'' as a unit, in one look, the sounding child says ''m-m-m a-a-a n-n-n,'' looking at each letter. Sounding is necessarily an attack by letters or groups of letters. But we want small children to look at words as wholes just as they look at faces as wholes, or chairs as wholes, or flowers as wholes. Experience shows that sounding at the start does teach many children a very bad habit of slow, letter-by-letter attack. The more capable child gets over this difficulty. He goes from the part to the whole. But far too many children do not. They continue a partial word attack all their lives and are slow, hesitant, laborious readers all through school. It is for this reason most schools defer sounding until the habit of *whole word attack* has been established. Then for a few minutes only, now and then, there can be *attack by parts*. ''You get the habit of doing *what you do most*.''

GUESSING TO LEARN SIGHT VOCABULARY

It is very common for teachers and for teachers' manuals to advise children to ''guess'' when they do not know a word. This is good advice if the purpose is to get along with the story. In that case, one can usually guess close enough to the intended meaning to get enough of the story to go on. But guessing just does not work if we are thinking of learning sight vocabulary, for it is seldom possible to guess the right word. And if the child guesses the wrong word he is matching a sound with a word to which it does not belong. Only *correct* matching of sight and sound teaches sight vocabulary.

The best way for the reader to convince himself that he cannot guess the right word is for him to try an experiment. Let him guess the words omitted in the following paragraph: (Put the words on a sheet of paper. Do not write in the book.)

"The *method* .... of guessing from context has been tried with many teachers and college students. They were *confronted* .... with a page, reprinted from an upper grade reading book, that contained ten sentences. In each sentence, one word had been .... The blanks were of the same length so as not to give a *clue* .... to the word. The subjects were told to read the *sentence* .... and to guess the right word. This *experiment* .... with several dozen different groups gave always the same result. Some of these *excellent* .... readers could not guess even one of the words correctly. A few .... with as many as six. But most got a .... three or four right out of the ten. Are you now ....*convinced*.... that guessing the right word from context is easy?''

This experiment indicates one thing rather clearly, that guessing from context is a test of intelligence. In fact, it is a standard method used in intelligence tests. When you have a word before you, you are sure you could guess it easily if called upon to do so, but when the word is not there, it is an entirely different matter. The teacher looking at a word in a book thinks the child is stupid not to guess it. But how well did you do on the test on the preceding page? Perhaps you made a good score at guessing *meanings,* but we are thinking of getting *the right word* so as to add it to your sight vocabulary. How many of the following words did you get right when you tried to guess from context?

1. experiment. 2. presented. 3. omitted. 4. clue. 5. context. 6. try-out. 7. skilled. 8. succeeded. 9. mere. 10. convinced. If you are not satisfied with your own experience, try this out on your friends.

CONTEXT AND ''READING AHEAD''

An interesting use of context that we all make is in the process of ''reading ahead'' that is a part of all reading. As already noted, in reading we are at any moment (1) perceiving the immediate field of vision, (2) remembering what we have read before, and (3) imagining what is coming. We realize that we are ''imagining what is coming'' when we are reading something poorly written and we expect a sentence to wind up in one fashion and are shocked to find it wind up in another. Good writers never lead the reader to expect what he is not given. Sometimes, of course, the good writer may mislead the reader on purpose and thus give a shock that is characteristic of humor. This shock caused by an unexpected turn of the sentence shows that we did expect something different.

The reader can make an interesting trial of his "imagining what is coming" if he will take a book, read the last sentence on a page, which is continued on the next, and then before turning, try to say what the rest of the sentence is going to be, or at least what the next word will be. Are you not bound to think of what is coming as you are turning the page?

THREE FACTORS IN WORD RECOGNITION

We need here to emphasize that, as we read, context is one of three different factors in word recognition. (1) The mere "looks" of the word makes some suggestion to the mind; (2) the context tends to suggest possibilities; and (3) the sound of the first letter or some part may also be suggesting some avenue of association. We hardly ever know which of these three are present or which is stronger than the others. Surely all three are usually involved. Their interaction seems to explain a great deal of miscalling of words. With some children, general appearance will dominate and they will say "learning" for "leaving." With some children, context seems to be dominant and they will say "good" for "well" or otherwise use a word of similar meaning instead of the exact word. With some, the beginning will dominate and they will say "low" for "lone." We cannot be sure just what the balance between these three mental operations should be. We can only watch miscalling, try to discover which process is not doing its part, and then emphasize that process so that the child can call upon all three for help when needed.

How Fast Can Children Learn Sight Vocabulary?

The school makes definite plans to teach sight vocabulary. It chooses a basic reader for that purpose. The basic reader contains words that the child is supposed to learn by sight. How many words should there be?

One thing can be clearly said at the outset. No one really knows how fast children can learn sight vocabulary, but the experience of the schools has been that we have expected them to learn faster than many are able to. For this reason, the publishers have been steadily cutting down the number of words used in school readers. Twenty years ago, it was common for a series of readers to present 2500 words in the primary books. Now series are coming out with 1300 words or less for the first three years.

VOCABULARY CONTROL

Time was when the author of readers for children just wrote what he thought appropriate in the best way he knew how. As a result, a typical case was a reader series in wide use in 1925 which had 2500 different words in the primary books and 1100 of these were used a single time only. Nowadays, the author writes what he thinks the children should read, and then a battery of editors goes to work on the manuscript. Stories are rewritten and rewritten. Pages are worked on as page units. Sentences are shaped and reshaped. Words are left out or inserted. Finally the result conforms to certain rules. Some typical rules are:

1. Word burden control. No more than 2 new words to the page for preprimer or primer, 3 per page for first reader, 4 per page for second reader, 5 per page for third reader.

2. Repetition control.
Every word repeated on same page or next page.
Every word repeated at least 5 times in the book.
Every word repeated in every other succeeding primary book.

As a result of this severe control of word appearance and word repetition, each publisher can show for his primary books a table something like the following:

TABLE II
Vocabulary Control for Reading Series X

	New Words	Total different words
First preprimer	26	26
Second preprimer	32	58
Primer	127	185
First Reader	180	365
Second Reader	377	742
Third Reader	498	1240

It will be seen that every book adds some new sight words and repeats all the ones previously used. In the case of this set of readers, a closer look at the figures is interesting. It will be seen that the new words in the primer are double the number of preprimer words. The new words in the First reader about equal all the words in the primer. The new words in the Second reader equal all the words in the First reader.

Some persons denounce vocabulary control as a mistake. They say children can learn many more words than are thus doled out to them. But such persons are not thinking of the average school in the United States. They are thinking of the favored schools or favored children. It is true that such children can learn two or three or four times as many words as are given out in a basic series. But experience of the publishers all over the United States tells them that entirely too many children cannot learn large numbers of sight words per year. It is for those children that a basic series is made.

The basic series *is a minimum, not a maximum.*
Let the capable children read the basic and go on
to read a dozen other books. They can do it and
they should. But the basic is *required* of every child,
no matter how slow. This requirement must be low,
or the child is doomed to failure. So the publishers
are justified in putting out easier and easier books,
and the schools are justified in using them. The basic
gives just a minimum sight vocabulary and never
has restricted any child from reading other books
in order to learn as many more words as he wishes.

Adjusting the Load of Sight Words

After such a favorable view of the basic reader,
we still have to question the number of words presented. Several studies have indicated rather clearly
that all we can expect of the average child is to
have learned 200 words the first year, or about one
per day for a 40 week year. If this is true, the
series described in the table above has too many.
It has, in fact, 365 words in the first year books.
It does no good to say that many words are learned
temporarily. Since each word appears in the next
book of the series, *permanent learning* is expected.

This discrepancy between what the average child
really learns of sight vocabulary, (as tested at the
end of the year, and not from week to week) and
the number of words presented in the readers has
led to several plans on the part of schools to remedy
the situation.

The first of these plans to adjust the books to the school situation is to delay use of the First reader until the beginning of the second year. This plan reduces the sight vocabulary load for the first year down to about 200 words. It is found that if the child learns these 200 words *solidly* he is much more able to go on with speed and confidence than if he tries to learn a larger number poorly. By this plan, if the first year load is 200, the second year load can be 400, and the third year load 700, making a total of 1300 for the primary years. Certainly the second year child can learn twice as many words as the first year child, instead of only the same number, as shown by the table above. And the third year child can learn much more rapidly than the second year child. This plan would make a sensible *progression of vocabulary load.* The usual present plan, by which the first year child is supposed to learn as many words as the second year child, is contrary to the nature of language development.

The second plan used to meet the possible overload of sight words in a series of readers is to review each fall the books of the previous year. According to this plan, at the beginning of the second year the children reread the book they finished the preceding June in order to refresh the sight vocabulary that book was supposed to have taught and also to teach again the words not previously learned. At the beginning of the third year, the class would reread the book they finished in June, also in order to clinch the sight vocabulary that book included.

This review is the more needed in that studies have shown that over the first two summers children forget a great portion of what they have learned. This is especially true of reading because the typical child of that age plays all summer and never looks at books. In fact, he has not enough reading ability to practice it on newspapers or magazines anyway. So in the fall, the teacher often finds that most of the sight vocabulary that is supposed to be known seems not to be there. In practice, she has to reteach the words as they come up in the new book. So why not review them in the old book?

Many teachers object to this plan because they say it is boring to the children. First, we must ask whether it may not be boring to the teacher, and that therefore she assumes it bores the children? Second, we may say it is a question as to *how* the review is conducted. A successful plan is to have the children look over the whole book and find which stories they would like to reread. Different children will pick on different ones, and a sort of popularity contest can be staged, with arguments on all sides. Old stories can be read as audience reading, with a contest to see who can read the most dramatically. Or old stories can be reread as dramatizations. Stories can be compared as to interest, reality, truth to life, or what you will. Children can search for favorite characters or events. There are many things

to do with a book except march through it page
by page. If these methods are followed in a review
after a summer vacation, there will be interest, the
sight vocabulary will be reviewed, and good basis
made for a successful attack on the new book.

Which Sight Words?

We have mentioned the huge number of sight
words that the expert possesses to use in his reading
and we have discussed the first steps in learning
sight words. Does it matter which words are learned
as sight words or which ones are learned before
others? Should the school have any plan about
the teaching of sight words, or should it be a mere
matter of chance with each book read?

Meaning Before Sight

One principle is followed in the primary grades,
"The child should have a word in his meaning vocabulary (that is, hearing vocabulary) before it is
taught him as a sight word." That is, "meaning
before sight."

This principle is naturally followed in the making
of reading charts. The children talk about what
they are familiar with, and the teacher puts down
the words chosen for the sentences of the chart.
Those words are of familiar meaning. If reading
were always based on experience, this principle
would always be followed, since language in terms
of the child's experience would come first and then

reading matter would be built on that language. There is a movement to plan the teaching of reading in this fashion. If a school has its own print shop, why cannot it make its own reading materials? Some schools have done so.

We see this principle also followed in the beginning reading books where they are careful to use only words which are familiar to the child for meaning. The beginning readers deal with child experiences, with the home, with the neighborhood, and the like, all the time teaching a sight vocabulary but taking care that the meaning is already known. Of course, this principle cannot always be followed in a nationally distributed book, since there are great differences in climate, for instance, from one coast to the other. Perhaps the more surprising thing is that so many school readers can actually be used from coast to coast with the children who read having some understanding of what the children in the story are doing.

In the middle grades, however, the readers begin to go far afield into other times and other countries. We find history and geography stories, dealing with many things about which the children know little if anything. Here there is often definite violation of the principle of "meaning before sight." Theoretically the teacher explains every new word. Actually she may feel she does not have time to do so, or she may think she has explained when she has not gone far enough, or she is unaware that the children are ignorant of word meaning. This will be further discussed in Chapter IX.

A practical aspect of insisting on "meaning before sight" is that experiments tend to show that children do not remember as sight words those which do not mean much to them. From psychological facts, one would expect this. After all, the basis of memory is association. The more meaningful a word is, the more associations it has. Therefore, when a child looks at a meaningful word, many connections are made. The word "takes deep root," as it were. When he looks at a relatively meaningless word, there is little association to fix it. Perhaps this fact explains why we have so much difficulty teaching sight vocabulary to the mentally subnormal. They look at the word and say the word, but do not retain it. This may be due to lack of deep associations.

An implication from this common situation may be that the way to have children remember a sight word is not merely to repeat the sight-sound association, as for instance, by flashing it again and again, but to use the word in many ways or to have the children get more and more meaningful associations with it. For instance, if the children are to learn "cupboard" as a sight word, it will help a great deal if their attention is called to the parts "cup" and "board" and they are told that originally a shelf or board was made for the cups, and that became finally our "cupboard." Greater meaning makes for better retention at all times, and especially for retention of sight vocabulary.

Disagreement Among Series of Readers

A common practice is for teachers to have children read a large number of preprimers first, then a large number of primers, then a number of first readers, and so on. That is, they have the children "read on one step of difficulty" before they go to the next.

Teachers find, however, that the vocabularies of preprimers do not agree with one another. If one preprimer has 50 words, the preprimer from another series may have 30 new words, the preprimer from still another series 30 more new words, and so on. Why, they ask, if the preprimers have the *most common* words, do they not have the *same* words?

The answer to this failure of beginning books to have the same words is that there are just too many "common words" in the language. There are at least 1,000 words that are all about equally common, meaning that they are used constantly by everyone. Out of this pool of common words, reading series take 50 or 60 for the preprimer. It is easily seen how the preprimer words of many series can be largely different. It would be convenient if the beginning books overlapped more in vocabulary, but they do not. The best solution to the problem of "reading across series" at any primary level is to go from one preprimer to the primer of the same series and then back to preprimers of other series, or from one primer to the first reader of the same series and then back to other primers. In this way, going to a lower level, one will find much more overlapping of vocabulary.

Publishers of reading books are aware of this problem of "reading across series," as it is called. To help, they are trying to get out more books at each level. In the last decade, the practice has begun of issuing two books for each year during the primary years, and schools are beginning to buy the books for this purpose. Some publishers have "parallel series," which use largely the vocabulary of their basic series. All of this is to cut down the sight vocabulary burden which appears when competing books are read and also to get repetition of the sight vocabulary of the basic series.

Sight Words Common to All Series

We have just pointed out that basic series of different publishers do have common elements. Which are those elements? If we knew them, we could be sure that children learned them and therefore that they could read more books with greater ease.

First of all, we can be sure that *nouns cannot be common to all reading matter.* Stories about a farm use the nouns *farmer, barn, cow, pig, fence,* and so on. Those words cannot be used in any other kind of a story. Stories about an automobile use *engine, wheel, hood, windshield, horn,* and the like, but those words do not fit a story about anything else but an automobile. Similarly, through the whole realm of experience, nouns are tied to a particular content. When the content changes, the nouns change.

This fact, so obvious but so little recognized, is the more important just because children tend to learn the nouns first and most thoroughly. The nouns are represented by the pictures in the story, and the children point to the things in the picture and can tell which words stand for them. Labels around the room are nouns. When scrap books are made, the pictures cut out are pictures of things that are represented by nouns. The workbooks have exercises featuring the things or nouns. Naturally, things are of interest to children, and thus nouns are more easily learned. But when a new story is taken up, a new set of nouns appears, and the old set disappears. A sight vocabulary of nouns can never be widely used.

Second, therefore, we must realize that the vitally important words are actually the "connective words" or the "service words." These are prepositions and conjunctions, verbs, adverbs and adjectives, and pronouns. No matter what the story, it uses "to," "from," "with," and so on. Every story uses "was," "have," "said," and other common verbs. Nearly every story, no matter what the content, uses "little," "many," "very," "some," and other modifiers. And no matter what the names of the people, the story has to use "he," "our," "they," "what," and other pronouns of all kinds. *The really important words in learning a sight vocabulary are the service words.*

Unfortunately, children are not much interested in the service words. There are no pictures for verbs or adjectives or prepositions. They do not bring up vivid memory images. They are just "service words," and are slid over as such. But those are the words we want the child to be sure to add to his sight vocabulary. We know from research which ones they are,[1] and we know how useful they are. In fact, the 220 most common of the service words are a major part of all the books the child will read in school or out. The following table shows what a large percentage they are of the total running words of school books:

TABLE III

Percentage That the Basic Sight Vocabulary of 220 Words is of Running Words in School Textbooks in Four Subjects

Subject of Textbooks	No. of Books	Grade I	Grade II	Grade III	Grade IV	Grade V	Grade VI
Reading	4	70	66	65	61	59	59
Arithmetic	2	....	....	62	63	57	57
Geography	2	....	....	....	60	59	54
History	2	....	....	....	57	53	52

Since these service words are so important in reading, the teacher should see that they are learned. The best way is to emphasize them as they

[1] See Appendix A, also Chapter IX, Problems in Reading, Garrard Press, Champaign, Ill.

come up in the reading books. In every new story are some of the important service words. The teacher should give extra practice on them with her flash cards or she should write them in a list on the board or put them on a special chart. Those are the words everyone must be sure of, no matter whether other words are missed or not. The words can be taught by special individual cards and also by games in which the children delight.[1] At any rate, those important service words are the ones every child must know by instant recognition if he is to be a skilled reader. All of them appear during the first two years, and an average second grade child knows half of them and an average third grade child knows all of them. And "knowing" these words means no spelling, no sounding, no puzzling, but *instant, flash recognition.*

Summary

Each person reads with his stock of sight words. The expert has a reading vocabulary of many thousands of sight words. We can tell when we are reading with sight vocabulary by the fact that we do not hesitate in reading. Speed in recognition varies, depending on the individual's native verbal ability, the amount of his drive, and the amount of practice he has had.

---

[1] See Appendix for Basic Sight Vocabulary list. Also write Garrard Press, Champaign, Ill., for catalogue of games teaching the Basic Sight Words.

Language is sound, and printed words represent sounds. The child must know what the printed word "says."

Most teaching of sight vocabulary is by the telling method, and, from the child's point of view, this is the "see, hear, and remember method." This method is used continually all through the grades and high school. But in outside reading or silent reading by the children, this method fails, since no one can tell them what the new words "say."

Originally the spelling method was used to teach sight vocabulary. But this plan put the names of the letters first, and so put the spelling between the child and the recognition of the word. Many parents still teach children to spell words in reading, and our spelling program causes some children to learn to spell a word before they learn to recognize it as a whole. Language work may also teach the spelling of reading words.

Sounding will be discussed in Chapter VIII, but here we must emphasize that sounding is the only way for a child to build up his own sight vocabulary through the years. However, sounding is not wise at the start since it, like spelling, causes the child to look at each letter rather than at the word as a whole.

Guessing is often used in reading, but it does not teach sight vocabulary because, though the correct or approximate meaning can be guessed, the exact word usually cannot be.

In the past, the schools have tried to teach sight vocabulary too rapidly, and consequently too many children have been left behind. Publishers have recently been lightening the vocabulary load of primary reading books, so that the words that all are required to learn may not be so many. The quick learners can of course learn from other books as many words as they wish.

The load of sight words may be adjusted in several ways. One plan is to delay use of the First Reader until the second year of school. Another plan is to review each fall the books read the preceding year so as to reteach the sight words which will be used again in the new books.

Since some sight words must be chosen, which should they be? First, they should be words of already known meaning. "Meaning before sight" is an essential for interest and for retention. Different series have different sight words just because there are at least a thousand common words and the beginning books use different ones from this thousand. Since most schools use several series of readers, this disagreement must be dealt with somehow. The simplest method is to emphasize those words which are most necessary for reading, and they are the 220 service words which research has shown to make up two-thirds of the running words in primary books and over half the running words in other school books.

CHAPTER VII.

Independent Word Attack

It is true that many persons grow up to adulthood and live out their lives without ever developing independent word attack. They know those words that they have been told, and no others. If they see a strange sign, they ask someone, "What is that?" They are told, they remember, and thereafter they can read that sign. In school they were told the common words, and they can read most of the newspaper or the ordinary magazine by using that sight word knowledge. In such reading, there are often words they do not recognize, but they just skip them and go on. These adult readers feel that such unknown words are not important anyway, since obviously one can get along without them. For ordinary reading, "they get enough without knowing every word." Sometimes they may be puzzled about a sentence, but they just go on to the rest of the story.

We have no way of knowing just how large a proportion of our adult population is represented by the description we have just given, but we know it must be a considerable one. We are sure of this because we know that a large part of the high school population is in this condition, and they will grow older and take their places in the world without any independent word attack. If they have failed to learn or to discover for themselves methods of word attack by the time they reach high school, there is usually little chance that anyone in high school will teach them. Word attack is supposed to be grade school subject matter.

Attack by Guessing From Context

In Chapter VI we have discussed guessing from context as a method of increasing sight vocabulary. An experiment given there, and figures resulting from research, clearly indicate that there is little chance for a reader to guess *the right word* from context, if he has the context alone to go by. If the word is a complete blank, either the reader can think of no word to fill the blank, or he can think of several and he does not know which the right word is. Our language is such a rich one that we have many words of nearly the same meaning but with varying shades of meaning or emphasis. For instance, if one said that "an active person does not want to spend his life in ....," there might be two words to go into the blank, "loafing" or "idling." The reader cannot tell which shade of meaning the writer may have intended.

However, in reading, one does not meet blanks but meets unknown words. Even if the word is not recognized, the letters which make it up can be. Therefore, in the case just given, one could look and see if the unknown word began with "l" or "i," and thus tell which word is intended. Either the name of the letter or the sound of the letter may be used, depending on whether the reader thinks of the spelling of the word or the sound of the word. Actually, this looking to see how the word begins is the greatest help in guessing from context.

In the research study referred to in Chapter VI, the teachers who made the experiment could guess only about 30% correctly when given blanks alone in the test reading selection, but when they were also given the first letter of the missing word, they were able to guess 60% or 70% correctly. This means that when one sees a word he does not recognize, he is usually able to think of some word that might fit in. He then looks at the way the word begins and thus tells at once if his guess might be correct. If the word he thinks of begins with the wrong letter or wrong sound, he tries to think of some other word that begins with the right letter or sound. Thus the first letter of the word both narrows the guessing from context, and checks the guessing from context.

We should certainly urge children to guess from context if they have no other method of word attack, but they should also check their guesses at least by the beginning of the unknown word. Naturally, the checking can go beyond the first letter. For instance, we may guess "limp" and spell or sound out "l-i-m-b-e-r" and thus discover that "limp" cannot be the word. We should encourage children to do this checking by sounding if they can. We have discouraged the spelling method in learning to read, but spelling can be used along with sounding as a check on guessing from context.

As also suggested in the previous chapter, the chief use of guessing from context is to find a word that might fit in for meaning and thus make the sentence or story complete. When we guess only for meaning, we usually do not bother to check the correctness of the word. If the meaning fits, we accept it and go on. But wrong guesses certainly do not help in building sight vocabulary.

Attack by Use of Sight Syllables

WE DO USE SIGHT SYLLABLES IN READING

The reader who has learned to recognize long words tends, for several reasons, to see those words in parts or syllables. First, his eyes tend to move across a long word with several stops. Long words may be up to fifteen letters in length, and at a single fixation the student cannot take in that many letters Many students' eyes habitually move along the line a distance of only four or five letters at a time. Therefore their habitual fixation in reading is bound to take in less than the total word length. Hence they are bound to see long words in parts.

A further reason for our seeing syllables is that a part of one word will often appear in another word. The words "telephone" and "microphone" have identical parts. The boy who pronounced "Persephone" as "Per-se-phone" was using familiar parts that he had learned in other words. Children even of average ability get used to seeing word parts that appear in a number of common words. The prefixes "un" and "sub" and the like are seen separately after they are seen as parts of a number of words. The suffixes "tion," "able," "ment," and others are soon seen as familiar parts.

These familiar parts become "sight syllables" and operate just as sight words do. As soon as the eye lights on them, the corresponding sound comes to mind. Some words seem to be made up entirely of sight syllables, such as "con-tent-ment," but generally only part of a new word is recognized in this way.

When part of a word is recognized by sight, it has the same effect as when the first letter is known by sight. The sight syllable suggests the word that ought to fit into the context, or it corrects a wrong guess because the word thought of does not have that familiar part. Thus familiar parts, or sight syllables, are valuable in the process of reading by aiding guessing both of meaning and of the right word. These sight syllables are of course more useful than single letters since they are more suggestive and because they check a wrong guess more quickly.

SHOULD WE TEACH SIGHT SYLLABLES?

There has been speculation as to whether we should not try to teach a large number of sight syllables just as we teach a large number of sight words. There has been discussion as to which were the commonest syllables, with the idea that if we had a list of such syllables, we would know which ones to teach and thus aid in reading. This subject is dealt with at length in Chapter VII of Problems in Reading (Garrard Press, Champaign, Ill., 1948). The author sampled the polysyllable words in upper grade elementary textbooks. He then divided the words found into syllables according to the standard dictionary. He found over 1200 different syllables. He then tried to see which were the hundred commonest. He found that the list of the 100 commonest covered only 35% of the total syllables used. In other words, no syllables were common in the way that some sight words are common. The common service words must be used in all communication but there are no syllables that appear in all communication. The only syllables which the investigation showed to be at all common were the endings -ing, -ed, and -er, and these accounted for only 6% of the total. No others accounted for more than 1%. Compare this to the list of 220 sight words that account for more than 50% of all reading matter.

In practice, of course, we are constantly teaching sight syllables (1) when we call attention to the parts in which a word is sounded, whether in reading or spelling, (2) when we have children look up words in the dictionary, where they see the word divided into syllables, and (3) when we teach rules for syllabication. That is, whenever the child sees the syllables of a word and at the same time thinks the separate sounds of those syllables, he is learning those syllables as sight units just as he learns separate words as sight units.[1]

PREFIXES AND SUFFIXES

The most common sight syllables are of course prefixes and suffixes. These are important because of the way they help tell us word meanings. It is urged that they be taught as meaning elements rather than chiefly as sight elements. For instance, from the words "unknown," "unseen," "uneasy," "unable," and the like the class may discover that the prefix "un-" means "not." When thereafter the children meet a new word that begins with "un-," they will think that meaning "not" at the same time that they separate the syllable "un-" for the sake of pronouncing the new word.

The danger in teaching prefixes and suffixes is that we will try to teach too many. There are a vast number of these units, but by actual count not many of them are very common. In addition, there is the danger that a child who is told that *de-*, for instance, is a prefix which should be taken off, will take *de-* off of every word in which it appears whether it is

---

[1] If children do not "get the idea" that long words are to be divided and can be divided, there is a game they can play which presents words in parts. It is called Sight Syllable Solitaire and can be played by the pupil alone or with others. It uses and teaches the common syllables, but its chief purpose is to teach that words *can* be and *are* divided into parts. (Garrard Press, Champaign, Ill.)

a prefix or not as in "debit," "deputy," "definite," and so on. In practice, one should tell children, "If you see a familiar prefix or suffix, pronounce it as a separate syllable," but usually the rules for syllabication (given later) will take care of the pronunciation of prefixes or suffixes.

LITTLE WORDS IN BIG WORDS

It is very common for teachers to advise children to "find little words in big words," thus seeking to help them to sound out the big words. It is true that teachers can point out little words in big words that will help the children to recognize words. But is it wise to give children the general rule to look for little words in big words?

A count of the "little words in big words" in school readers showed that the little words would hinder more times than they would help. Teachers should be aware of this. For instance, one teacher, in trying to teach the word "then," said, "What little word do you see in it?" Surely the word "then" is not made up of "t-hen." In a published phonics work book, the directions are, "Find the little word in "nodding." We can imagine what the author intended, but if you look at "nodding," you will find two little words in it, "no" and "in." Do we pronounce the word as "no-dd-in-g"? The "little word in a big word" should mean a *basic word in an inflected form* as "go" in "going" or "wish" in "wished." There is a place for such teaching. But all in all, it is better not to teach children at all times to "find little words in big words."

Word Attack by Sounding

No situation is entirely new; otherwise we would not be able even to be aware of it. Every new situation is familiar in part. And it is the function of intelligence to seize upon the familiar part and to master the situation thereby. We have already discussed two illustrations of the general principle that in reading, as in all our activities, we tend to perceive or see familiar elements in new situations. The two cases we have mentioned are (1) *seeing familiar letters* to check a word that is guessed from context, and (2) *seeing familiar parts* or syllables in new words. We now come (3) to *sounding,* which is a direct application of the same principle, in that every new word is after all made up of English speech sounds that we know already.

In discussing sounding, we shall first deal with how the child uses sounding in reading and how he learns to sound. In the next chapter we shall deal directly with the teacher's problems in teaching sounding.

Language Is Sound, and Words Are
Symbols for Sound

We now repeat the basic fact, already stated on page 154, that Language is sound. We communicate by making noises. Different races or nations make different sets of noises to communicate with one another. Many years ago, men began to make signs or symbols to represent these noises. Our own set of symbols began with the ancient Egyptians, and came up through the Phoenicians and the Romans. The Chinese symbols are, as we know, very different, but the great difference is in the way the symbols were planned. The Chinese symbols represent ideas and do not represent the spoken words. But our symbols represent spoken words. The men who first wrote what we now call English were trying to suggest the spoken word.

This fact, that symbols represent sounds, can be seen in the way the teaching of foreign languages is often begun. The books usually give a key to show just which sounds each letter of the foreign language represents. An attempt to do this most scientifically is seen in the International Phonetic Alphabet. A group of experts in many languages decided just what are the sounds in those languages and decided on symbols to represent those sounds. They used all of our 26 letters and then devised others. The most commonly known new character is the *schwa,* which looks like an inverted e, and that stands for the obscure sound that begins ''about'' and that is so common in the way we speak ordinary English.

Another illustration of the way symbols represent the sounds of words is in the writing of dialect. Authors try to tell us how words are spoken by the letters they use. In the study of dialect in different parts of this country and in different levels of society many writers have tried to show by the way they spell words the differences in sounds used. This further illustrates the fundamental fact that word symbols are supposed to represent sounds, since language is fundamentally sound.

Is Sounding a "Logical" Method of Teaching Reading?

Because, as we have just pointed out, printed words are symbols for sound words, it might seem logical to teach reading entirely by the method of "unlocking" the printed word to see which sound word is meant. This is logical in one sense, but it is not true to the "logic" of human nature. Experience tells us that a total printed word can stand for a total sound word without need for analysis into parts. Experience tells us also that for most children, this "whole sight word for whole sound word" association is the most practical at the start at least.

Sounding a Very Laborious Method

In practice, the sounding method as the sole approach to reading fails at two distinct points. The first of these is that sounding is a laborious method. When children are presented with words at six years or age or thereabouts, they must have quick success. If they do not learn to read something rapidly and easily they will "quit" on us. They will then be "set against" reading. Therefore, children must be able to recognize a few words right away and to be able to read a few sentences and to get a story out of it. They must have a "quick success" method. Such is the sight method of teaching, called the "look-and-say" or the "see-hear-and-remember" method. We can teach the children a dozen words just as we can teach them the names of a dozen objects or animals. Then they can do some reading and will want to go on and do some more.

In contrast the sounding method is painfully slow. Before the child can do any real reading, he has to learn the "elements." And in reading, the elements seem to come all at once. The first dozen words a child looks at may contain most of the sounds of the language. One "method" has tried to solve this problem by beginning with only a few elements and making words out of them. For instance, it teaches the sound of "a." Then it teaches the sounds of "s," "r," "m," and "n." After these five separate "teachings," the child can read for himself the sentence, "Sam ran." Another method follows the same line but it includes in the reading "teacher's words," that is, words the child is not supposed to read but which are told him by the teacher. More interesting stories can be read; the pupil sounds part of the time and the teacher tells part of the time. This plan violates its own logic, however, because it really expects the children to learn the "teacher's words" by sight after a few repetitions. Any completely logical sounding method sticks to sounding, and it finds that it must begin with laborious drill.

DRILL SOUNDING METHODS HAVE NOT BEEN SHOWN TO SUCCEED WITH ALL CHILDREN

There are now being used several of these laborious drill-sounding methods in phonics. The claims of the users is that the children are not harmed by the hard work, and that the method makes good readers out of them. Users of these methods never tell us about the children who *fail* by this method. They tell us only of those children who succeed. We want to know also about those children who, after being taught sounding from the start, hate reading, and also about those who have perhaps for life the bad habit of puzzling out words. No method can be approved because it succeeds with part of the children. We must know about results for *every* child, since we value the success and happiness of every child.

Some persons will insist, of course, that, (in their experience) a certain group of children, or a certain child, did not find sounding a laborious method. This may be entirely true, but in every such case that has been reported, we find two conditions that do not prevail in the general school population. The *first* of these is that the children had an eagerness to work at reading. Certain children have this eagerness. Children from certain kinds of environments or who are stimulated to imitate parents or older children or companions, have this eagerness. With eagerness, the laboriousness is accepted without resentment. The *second* of these conditions usually found in the reported cases is a higher mental age than the average. That condition is discussed in the next section.

SOUNDING REQUIRES A HIGHER MENTAL AGE

The second obstacle to the use of sounding as a beginning method in reading is that success with it requires a higher mental age than the sight or see-hear-and-remember method. It is true, the first grades of some schools use sounding with good success, but when one finds out the mental ages of the group, they are in fact seven years or better. Many individual children in first grade do learn to use sounding, but on investigation we find that the mental age of those children is seven years also. Parents tell us of how they learned to read by sounding, but if we investigate those parents we find them of superior I. Q., and we know that when they began to read, they were seven years or more in mental age.

That sounding requires a higher mental age than the sight method is shown by a careful experiment that covered two years study in the schools. The children of the primary grades of a school had all been given some phonetic teaching in every one of the three grades. They were tested for their ability to use phonics and also for mental age. The study was repeated the next year for verification. The results showed without a single exception that no child could use phonics if he was below seven years mental age. Some children in all three grades used phonics and all these children were seven years mental age or over. The article, therefore, gives seven years mental age as the age of "phonic readiness." [2]

We must emphasize that the "phonic readiness" of seven years mental age is built up by experiences with sounds during the first school year and before. Work with singing in the kindergarten is training the sound discrimination of the children. Their listening to the talk of others and to the stories read to them by the teacher develops their attention to sounds and their ability to tell sound words apart. Attention to their own correct saying of new words is fine exercise in sound discrimination. Finally, the first grade teacher conducts all sorts of exercises in comparing the sounds of words. All this practice is essential with most children to their final ability to *use sounding* when they reach seven years mental age or thereabouts.

Sounding Attack on Short Words

The need for a higher mental age to learn by sounding brings us naturally to the mental process required by sounding attack. What goes on when we

---

[2] See Phonic Readiness, in Problems in Reading, Garrard Press, Champaign, Ill.

"sound out a word"? For clarity, let us consider at the moment only one syllable words.

LETTER PHONICS

First, as we look at a word to sound it we have to concentrate on part of it, since we cannot "sound all the word at once." Here there are several possibilities. The most usual thing is to look at the letters, one at a time. This conforms to our habit in spelling of dealing with words letter by letter. After all, there are only 26 letters, even though in English there are about 40 sounds. *This method of sounding a letter at a time can be called "letter phonics."* It is the method most widely taught. In work with all kinds of children at all levels, it seems they naturally look at letters when they begin an analysis of a word.

Some persons object to letter phonics, however, and point out that letters can be sounded together. The most simple case is in the blending of consonants, as "bl" or "sp" or "tr" or the like. Those who teach blends should, however, remember that consonants do not *always* appear in blends. They also appear *alone*. So this plan of teaching blends would also have to teach the consonants separately. Instead of teaching only 21 consonant items, it would teach these 21 and also 20 or more blends. Does this doubling of the task help the child or hamper him? After all, a blend can be sounded from the parts.

Phonograms

Another plan tries to teach combinations of vowels and consonants as units, or "phonograms." *This is sometimes called "phonogram phonics"* to distinguish it from "letter phonics" (though technically a phonogram is a symbol for a sound, and therefore, a single letter is a phonogram). These combinations or phonograms are of two kinds, beginning phonograms, such as "ca," "le" and so on, or ending phonograms such as "at," "an" and the like.

One problem about the *beginning phonograms* (or beginning consonant-vowel combinations) must be considered. This plan of dividing would take "cat," "can," "cap," etc. and derive the phonogram "ca" from them, take the words "sun," "such," "supper," etc. and derive "su" from them, take "hop," "hot," etc. and derive "ho," and so on. Note that all these vowels would be short. The only trouble is that if one sees these combinations as syllables he naturally calls the vowel long, as in "cā-ble,' "sū-per," "hō-tel." This is because of the rule in English that *a vowel ending a syllable is long*. For this reason it seems inadvisable to use the beginning-phonogram system which teaches the child to see a consonant and a short vowel, because we would be teaching a habit of sounding that we would have to "un-teach" later.

The *final-phonograms* are widely used, largely no doubt because of the use of rhymes in ear train-

ing in the first grade. Children like to listen for
rhymes or to make rhymes, and finding rhymes may
be easy because, after a word is said, the final sound
seems to linger in the ear. There is a still further
argument for this use of the end of words in that
there are groups of familiar words which are non-
phonetic and which therefore can be taught by phonograms better than by letter phonics.

The most striking case of a "non-phonetic family" is the "-ight" family, of *light, might, right,
sight, fight,* etc. The combination *"ight"* cannot be
sounded out, but can easily be learned as a sight
unit. Similarly the *"-old"* family, of *gold, cold, told,
hold,* etc., does not fit letter phonics. Lists of words
with final phonograms have thus been successfully
used to teach non-phonetic words. Perhaps we
should call the method "sight word teaching of
words grouped by similarity." Usually, if we are
dealing with *phonetic* words, the final phonogram
which we might teach could just as well be sounded
out by letter phonics.

This fact, that most phonograms can also be
sounded from the letters, makes us ask whether the
added burden of learning the phonograms is worth
while. No matter how many phonograms are taught,
the sounds of single letters will still be needed to
add to the phonograms to make words. For instance,
the "-at" family of *bat, cat, fat, hat, mat, pat, rat,*
and *sat,* requires the teaching of eight single consonants to put before the "-at." Some reading sys-

tems have fifty or more phonograms to which have to be added the single letter sounds and any blends that are taught, thus giving the child over a hundred items to learn. Is this advisable? It is not too much for the child with sounding ability, but we must consider the average child who has trouble even with the single letter sounds.

To go back to our first problem, as we look at a word to sound it out, we must look at part of it, since we cannot sound it out all at once. At what part should a child look? Here we have another strong objection to use of the final phonograms. They must cause a child *to look at the end of a word first,* since the child must see what the ending is and then take the beginning from it. That is, if the ending is "-old" he sees that part first and then takes the initial "t" from it. He cannot take off the beginning until he knows what is the ending. This looking at the wrong end of words is not to be encouraged. The children do too much of it under the best of circumstances.

Using "Consonant Sounds"

If the word begins with consonants, as it usually does, the child is supposed to think "consonant sounds." Here we run into the difficulty that some consonants are easily sounded alone, and others are not. Three groups of consonants can be distinguished. *First,* some consonants can be sounded very easily. A group of these require a hum, such as *m* and *n*. One can make a humming sound for these. Some consonants are hisses, such as *f, s, v,* and *z*. It is possible to make a hiss for each. These two kinds of consonants can be sounded alone and used in word attack very easily.

Second, another set of consonants can be sounded by using the proper formation of the mouth, tongue and throat and making an obscure, vague sound that seems largely breath. Such consonants are *h, j, k, l, q* and *r*. The important point is that the sound which we make as we try to "sound" these consonants does not seem to disturb a child in his joining the consonant to the next vowel. For instance, if we put each of these before the sound of short a, and sound the consonant first and then the short a, there is no difficulty in blending the consonant and the a. These forms, as found in simple words, would be *h-a-t, j-a-p, l-a-d, q(u)-a-ck, r-a-n*.

Third, the greatest difficulty in sounding comes with the third set of consonants, those that are explosive in their effect. They represent different ways of attacking a vowel sound, and there should be no sound between the attack and the vowel. But it is impossible to sound an attack by itself. It must attack something. That is why these consonants are usually sounded *b-buh, d-duh, g-guh, p-puh, t-tuh, w-wuh, y-yuh*. They are attacks, and must be followed with *some* sound. The sound of *uh* is commonly used because it is the obscure sound which we use in reading when we do not accent a vowel.

But suppose we try to sound these consonants separately in sounding some short words. We would get something like *buh-a-g* (bag), *duh-a-n* (Dan), *guh-a-l* (gal), *puh-a-t* (pat), *tuh-a-p* (tap), *wuh-a-g* (wag) and *yuh-a-m* (yam). A child is very naturally confused by this added sound of *uh*. The difficulty caused by children's attempts to sound this group of "attack consonants" has confused the whole question of the sounding of consonants. As we have seen in preceding paragraphs, most of the consonants *can* be sounded separately with some success. The last seven mentioned, *b, d, g, p, t, w* and *z* do cause confusion. We can only try to overcome that confusion by having the children sound them by giving the "uh" sound just as lightly as possible.

Some of these seven "attack consonants" are used in common blends. The *b* is in *black, bridge; d* is found in *drink; g* is in *glass* and *grass; p* is in *place* and *price*. In these cases it will be seen that the attack consonant is used as *an attack on the sound of the following* consonants. For this reason, the two seem to blend into a new sound, and it is probable that we might well teach these particular blends as units. Blends of other consonants can be made up more easily of the separate parts. An interesting difficulty is *tw* in which two attack consonants come together as in *twice*. In the combination *wh* (as in *what*), the sounding is *hw* and the breath of the *h* blends into the *w* very easily.

THE WORD METHOD AND SOUNDING CONSONANTS

An attempt to overcome the problem of the consonants which are hard to sound alone has been called the "word method" of teaching phonics. By that method, consonants are supposed never to be sounded alone. We would not say the sound of "c," but always "*c* as in *cat*," never the sound of "b" but "*b* as in *boy*." Such a plan tries not to take the consonant away from a word but always to keep it in a word. The plan may be used as far as analysis of words is concerned, but when the child comes to use his sounding, he cannot "keep the sound in a word," as this plan proposes. If he meets a new word he cannot sound it by saying "*b* as in *boy*" with "*a* as in *apple*" and "*th* as in *thin*." He has to think "b-a-th." To *use* phonics, the separate letter sounds must be known.

THE THREE POSITIONS OF CONSONANTS

An unsolved problem is whether children need to be taught to use consonants in three different positions, at the beginning, the middle and the end of a word. Many systems teach each consonant in all three positions (if it can be so used) and the assumption seems to be that there is something different about sounding a consonant at one place than the other. However, it is hard to see how the sound of *n* in the word *Nan,* for instance, is any different in either position at beginning or end. Or are the sounds of the "t's" different in their different positions in the word *tot* or in *Tom* or *not*? If a letter suggests a certain sound, it can suggest it in any place in the word. We are not here dealing with speech difficulties in which children make the sound at one place and not at another. Such are special disability cases and need special training.

IRREGULAR CONSONANTS

The consonants "c" and "g" have what is called the "soft sound" before "e" or "i" and the "hard sound" at other times. That is, there are two sounds of "c" as seen in *circus*, the first like an "s" and the second like a "k." In fact, some authorities may say that "c" has no sound of its own but only the sounds of "k" and "s." The two sounds of "g" are seen in *go* and *giant*.

The letter "y" can be called irregular because when it comes at the end of a word it becomes a vowel with the sound of "i," as in *try* or *city*. This is sometimes true when "y" comes at the end of a syllable within a word, or sometimes within a syllable as in *sympathy*. When children discover the irregularities of these letters is time enough to give special attention to them.

USING VOWEL SOUNDS

After a child who is attacking a short word has sounded the beginning consonants, he comes to a vowel or several vowels. Here there are a number of possibilities that complicate the situation. In the first place, he must notice if there is one vowel or two.

If it is a single vowel in the middle of the word, the child is supposed to think the short sound of that vowel immediately, since *all single vowels are short unless there is a special reason for their being sounded otherwise.* But then the child has to check on two other possibilities. First, is there an *e* on the end of the short word? If so, *the last e is silent and the vowel in the middle of the word is long.* Second, if there is no final *e,* the child must still note if the single vowel is followed by *r.* That will give the special sound for *the vowel when followed by r.* So, if only one vowel is seen, the child must decide (1) whether the single vowel is short or (2) is long because of final e or (3) whether it has the sound with *r.*

Third, suppose the child notes immediately that there are *two vowels together instead of just one.* Now there are three possibilities (please note, we are speaking of how a reader uses sounding, *not* giving a method for *teaching* it). (1) The child may immediately recognize one of the familiar two-letter combinations called vowel digraphs, each of which has a definite sound. There are two groups of these combinations. In one group, the sound is the long sound of the first vowel. These are *ai-paid, ay-day, ee-speech, ea-peach, oa-boat.*[3] The other group of digraphs which do not have the sound of the first vowel but have some other single sound are *au, aw, eu, ew,* and *oo.*

(2) Another group of two-letter combinations are called *diphthongs,* which means "two sounds." That means that each of the two vowels in the combination is sounded, but they are "sounded together" in one syllable. The diphthongs are *oi, oy, ou,* and *ow.*

(3) But suppose the child sees two vowels and he notes that they do not make one of these two-letter combinations that he has learned? Then he knows that the two vowels are sounded separately. (Unless he has come across the *ie* or *ei* combination, which does not follow a rule.)

We have tried to show the process of analysis that the user of phonics must follow on small words. It is complicated, just because our language is complicated. One will see at once that this is not a job to be done by a typical six-year-old. One will also see that learning to use phonics takes time.

---

[3] It must be noted that we are not using the technical classification of the speech specialists. We know that the sound of *ai* and *ay* are correctly termed diphthongs. But in all reading instruction this combination is said to have the sound of long *a,* and we are following that tradition. We have also called the long vowel sounds "long vowels," though speech specialists call our attention to the fact that long *a,* long *i* and long *u* are actually diphthongs. To avoid confusion we are following the terminology universally used in the teaching of reading.

Combining the Sounds Into a Word

The process of "analysis" or sounding the pieces of the word, which we have just described, is not, however, the chief difficulty. In fact, many children can get so far but cannot do the next step; they cannot put the sounds of the pieces together into a word. That is, they can do the "analysis" but not the "synthesis." They sound the letters or combinations of letters but cannot think what word is intended.

Here we must insist upon a point that is not sufficiently realized. The sounds of the letters or of parts of a word, said one after the other, are not the word. They are only a suggestion of the word. They may come close to the word, but they are not the word. If we sound the parts of the word "same," we get "s-s-s ā-ā-ā m-m-m," but that is not the word "same." "Same" is a monosyllable. It is the sound of long *a*, attacked with the hissing sound of *s* and closing with the hum of *m*. It seems to be a single sound, and not three sounds. The sounds of the three letters come close to the sound of the word; they suggest the word; but they are not the word.

Consequently, there is always a gap between the sounding of letters and thinking of the word. This gap must be bridged by intelligence. The mind must catch the suggestion of the letters and then it must do a final act of finding the word itself. This final act is much helped, of course, by the suggestion of context. The words before and after give a mental set which makes it easier for the mind to jump from letter sounds to word sound.

Sometimes the teacher finds that when the child says the separate letter sounds he is too occupied with the effort of making them to concentrate on combining the sounds into a word. In that case, she can often help by herself saying the separate letter sounds and having him listen. Very often, with his attention entirely on the "synthesis" the child can accomplish it. If the teacher in this way has the pupil first try to combine the sounds himself, and then helps him to do so, he may develop his ability to change over from the analysis of a "seen" word to the synthesis of the letter sounds into the sound word. This situation, in no way unusual, emphasizes that there is this extra step from sounding the word parts to getting the sound of the word.

Of great importance is the fact that fear or anxiety on the part of the child does much to prevent this act of discovering the word from the sound of the parts. Many children who fail at this point do so only because sounding has not been the fun it should be, and they have no confidence that they can get results with it.

Sounding Attack on Long Words

Looking Over a Long Word

When any person meets a strange long word, the chances are very great that he will run his eye over the word. He knows he is going to have to attack the whole of it, and he estimates, as it were, the situation.

In this preliminary survey, the eye of the reader often catches known sight words and he knows he has met a "compound word." We urge children to look for known sight words in the long words they see so that they may easily recognize compound words. This is seeing little words as *making up* big words rather than seeing little words *in* big words, which we have discussed previously (page 192). Sometimes there is a known word followed by an unknown part, as "postchaise," or an unknown part followed by a known part, as "turcoman."

Very often compound words are taken up as a preliminary to syllabication of long words. It is logical to take them up at that time because they emphasize making a preliminary survey of the whole word. The preliminary survey of a long word is important, though it is to be supposed everyone makes this survey quite naturally. But compound words teach nothing else about syllabication, since the separate words which make up a compound are not syllables.

LETTER BY LETTER ATTACK

This glancing-over or preliminary survey of a long word may give no helpful suggestions, no sign of familiarity whatever. In that case, the reader may do one of two things. First, *he may make a letter-by-letter attack,* just as we have described in the case of short words. This letter-by-letter attack may yield a long string of separate letter sounds, and if it does, the chances are very small that the reader will ever get an idea of the long word. The sounds of too many single letters in succession give only confusion. Or after a few letters are attacked, they may come together into a known sound of a small word or a syllable. For instance, if one tried to sound letter by letter the word "connect" the chances are that after the first three letters he would hear the syllable "con" and would thus have a part of the word.

ATTEMPT TO BREAK INTO PARTS

This natural grouping of the letters as they are sounded one after another suggests a second kind of attack, which is to *try to see in the word some familiar syllable or part.* This "attempt to break into parts" is a habit every reader should have, no matter whether he has a system for breaking into parts or not. It is found that many children get to upper grades and high school without this idea that you can and must break a long word into parts. We find that when we do give such a child this idea, he will begin to try to break up long words, and he may have considerable success just by a sort of trial-and-error method.

RULES FOR SYLLABICATION

We have discussed (1) *the letter-by-letter attack* and (2) *the attempt to break into parts,* because those are the methods a child is likely to use first in an attack on long words. Letter-by-letter attack is the method which the phonics of short words would lead him to use if that is all the preparation in sounding he has had. Knowledge that there are compound words may lead him to break up all long words into parts. He is also bound to have learned some prefixes and suffixes or other sight syllables and thus have a basis for breaking up long words somehow. Many children succeed with these methods. Many children attack long words by their own private methods and succeed in recognizing them. But both these methods are hit or miss and quite inadequate. There is a definite way of attacking any and all long words, and that is by applying rules for syllabication.

Before applying the formal rules for syllabication to a word the reader may symplify his task by taking off any prefixes or suffixes he sees. He is likely to do this anyway during his preliminary survey of the word. Often the removal of these known parts will leave a word which is recognized at once. For instance one may see the word "uninhabitable." If one takes off prefixes and suffixes and therefore sees the parts as un-in-habit-able, he will also see that the central word is "habit," one which he may recognize at sight. But this step is not necessary.

Usually the rules for syllabication apply also to prefixes and suffixes.

1. The first rule for syllabication is, (1) *"There are as many syllables as vowels."* This assumes that the vowels are known and that the reader has learned from primary phonics which vowels go together to make vowel digraphs and dipthongs. The reader therefore glances through the word to see how many different vowels or vowel combinations there are. Each vowel or vowel combination is to be the basis of a syllable. If possible, the pupil should put a check mark over each vowel or vowel combination.

2. The second process is to divide the consonants that come between vowels. To tell which consonants go with the preceding vowel and which go with the following vowel, the rule is (2) *Divide between two consonants or in front of one.* One may make this division with the eye or with a pencil stroke or one may write the syllables separated by space or by a dash so as to see the syllables better. A subdivision of this rule is (3) *you never separate the r from the vowel before it,* since the r determines the sound of that vowel, and the two are pronounced together.

After the long word is thus divided by rule, how shall we sound by syllables? This is usually a simple matter because the syllables are seldom more than two or three letters long. Here letter phonics comes into use or any knowledge the reader has of blends or larger units. But there is a rule (4) that *the syllable ending in a vowel is long and the syllable ending in a consonant is short.* Otherwise stated, open syllables are long and closed syllables short. This is due to the simple physical fact that when you keep your mouth open, you tend to make the vowel long and when you shut it with a final consonant you tend to cut the vowel short.

This rule, that open syllables are long, assumes that *when you sound out a word, syllable by syllable, you are bound to emphasize each syllable as you do so.* That is the way you say a long word for spelling. As you write, you say each syllable, unconsciously giving it emphasis. It is to this slow, formal, emphatic pronunciation that our rule applies, "open syllables long, closed syllables short." By the rule, you would say the word as *pō-tā-tō*, or *au-tō-mō-bile*. This is in violation of the speech principle that *open syllables are long only when accented, and that otherwise they are obscure.* You usually say *puh-ta-tuh,* and *au-tuh-muh-bile.* The child attacking a strange-looking word cannot know where the accent is; so the rule "long when accented" can have no meaning for him as he tries to sound out the word. But a child, when sounding, *does* know when a syllable is open. So his only safe device is to make all open syllables long until he recognizes the word. Then he can know which syllables are long and which are obscure, for he already has the word in his speech or sound vocabulary.

Do the Rules for Syllabication Work?

Here we must state that the rules for syllabication just given "work" only with about 85% of the syllables in the language. English was not made according to rules. English just grew up, and it had many adventures on the way. First, an Anglo-Saxon dialect was affected by Danish. Then Norman French and Church Latin took top place and Anglo-Saxon was for a long time an unwritten language of the common people only. But all these elements interacted and then there began to be added Modern French and classical Latin. With the expansion of the British Empire, all the languages of the world were borrowed from. At the same time usage changed as generation followed generation, and some spellings changed too and others did not. Certain vowels took on a great number of different sounds under certain conditions. All of this is much too complicated for us to analyze here, but the upshot of the whole matter is that English is only partly phonetic. As said above, about 85% of syllables are phonetic. Long words tend to have at least one syllable that does not follow the rules.

In addition, *division for sounding is not the same as division for writing*. We divide in writing to help the reader. Therefore, we have a rule that you never divide the root part of a word. However, in saying a word, we divide it the customary way which is usually the easiest way to say it whether that is the writing way or not. The only way to be sure how to divide a word at the end of a line in writing is to look the word up in the dictionary.

SOUNDING FOR RECOGNITION ONLY

From all these considerations, we must see that the rules for syllabication have two distinct purposes. *First,* they are to give the reader *some* system of attack that will get him *near* the correct word. They are not intended to give the exact correct word sound for the three reasons given, (a) English words are full of exceptions to sounding rules, (b) no rule can tell where to accent the word, and (3) the syllables said one after another usually sound different from the word itself as ordinarily said or thought. When the reader gets near the word by using his rules for syllabication, he must use his intelligence and the context to tell him what the word is. *Sounding is for recognition only.* If you do not recognize which word is meant, or if you do not have the sound word already in your hearing vocabulary, you must look it up in the dictionary. *No rules can expect to tell you how to sound a word that is entirely strange.*

SOUNDING TO LEARN SIGHT SYLLABLES

The *second* purpose of sounding rules is to train the eye in seeing familiar parts in long words. If one uses rules for a time, he soon begins to see the parts of words without having to use rules to get them. The expert finds he does not have to use rules. He "sees the parts." But at some time he had to learn to see the parts. This is a fact that teachers especially have a hard time realizing. They look at any word and it seems to fall apart into syllables. They cannot understand the child to whom a long word is a lot of letters. But even the teacher had to learn to see the parts, though that was so long ago she has forgotten when it happened.

Unconscious Learning of Sounding

A strange phenomenon that must be considered is the way many children learn how to use sounding in reading without ever knowing that they are doing so. They attack new words by the sounding method but cannot tell you how they do it or when they learned to do it. They are somehow "unconsciously aware" of the parts of words and of the sounds of those parts. They somehow unconsciously separate a new word into parts, think the sound of the parts and then put those parts together. They do this very quickly, sometimes it seems almost instantly. The process appears mysterious, but must have a natural explanation. It is very like the unconscious process, already mentioned on page 131 by which children recognize sight words.

One natural explanation would be the one we have just given for the sounding ability which teachers have. Perhaps these children have in the past, when they were very young, consciously divided words into letters or familiar parts and thus learned to think letters as sounds and to see the sounding parts of words. They may have been using this method for such a long time that they have forgotten the steps they used. A child of seven who can sound any word may have been sounding since four years of age. He may well have forgotten his laborious early steps in sounding.

Another explanation is that the whole process may have been unconscious. The awareness that certain letters stand for certain sounds may have been borne in upon the child while he was thinking of the meaning of the words he looked at. The familiar sounding parts may have been registered with him unconsciously, just as so much of what we perceive registers unconsciously. Surely no one learning to drive a car can be conscious of all the things that are registering with him. He is thinking only of keeping the car in the center of the road, but the objects going past him and their relative distances from one another, and the angles of vision, and the varying distinctness of objects which tell him how far away they are and how fast they are going all register unconsciously.

The same situation is found in any complex learn-- ing in which we are reacting to a mixture of circumstances. Some of the circumstances do seem to be in consciousness, but all the others are also having their effect. It may be that while the child is struggling with the meaning of signs and with the stories in a book, the similarities of the appearance of words and the similarities of their sound are registering with him so that in reading he is guided by these similarities without knowing that he is. At least, this must be the explanation of the unconscious sounding we find in children. In adults, the fact may more often be that the learning steps have been forgotten.

As previously noted, this chapter has dealt with how the child learns to sound. The next chapter will discuss the school's teaching of sounding.

Summary

Many adults lack any kind of word attack because they never learned any in school. Guessing from context is widely used but enables one only to get some meaning that fits in, and not the exact word the author used. Attack on new words by recognizing in them certain sight syllables is common, but it is not practical to teach sight syllables the way we teach sight words. Prefixes and suffixes are the sight syllables that are most readily learned. It is not a good idea to teach children to "find little words in big words."

Language is sound, and words are symbols for sound. It is not truly logical, however, to teach sounding attack alone. Sounding is a very laborious method, and drill-sounding methods have not been shown to work with all children. Sounding requires a higher mental age than that of the average first grade child beginning school at six.

Sounding attack on short words has been taught in several ways. Letter phonics, or sounding each letter, is most frequently used. Beginning phonograms teach the combination of a consonant and a short vowel whereas in English a syllable ending in a vowel is long. Final phonograms are more widely used and are useful for the sight teaching of non-phonetic words, such as the "-ight" family. The real problem is whether it is advisable to teach phonograms when all the single letter sounds have to be taught anyway. Final phonograms might cause the habit of looking at the end of words instead of at the beginning.

Consonants are of three types, those with which we make a humming or hissing sound, those with which we make a breath sound, and those with which we should not make any sound except that of the vowel following them. These last are the "attack consonants" to which we incline to add the sound of "uh," and thus cause confusion. The "word method" of sounding which tries to keep the consonant always as part of a word will not work when it comes to using phonics, for on a new word the child must use the letter sounds separately.

There seems to be no great need for studying consonants in the different positions in a word.

Certain consonants may be called irregular, as "c" and "g" with their two sounds each, and "y" which is sometimes a vowel.

When, in a short word, a child meets a single vowel, he must either call it short because of the general rule, call it long because of a silent final e, or give it a different sound because of the r following it. When the child sees two vowels together, he must recognize a vowel digraph, or a diphthong, or he must sound them separately.

After the "analysis," which we have described, must come the "synthesis" of the sounds of the word. Here there is always an extra step between the best sounding and the complete word. Fear hinders that step.

Long words may, first, be merely compounds of short words. True polysyllables may be attacked a letter at a time or by a mere attempt to break them somehow into parts. But the systematic method of attack is by the rules for syllabication. These are: (1) There are as many syllables as vowels or vowel combinations, (2) Divide between two consonants or in front of one, (3) Never separate r from the vowel before it, and (4) a syllable ending in a vowel is long, one ending in a consonant is short. These rules imply that each syllable is being stressed as it is being sounded as we stress each syllable when we are spelling a word.

These rules for syllabication work in about 85% of the cases, and divide words for sounding only, not for writing.

Sounding rules are, first, for recognition of words already known by hearing, and second, for training the eye to see familiar parts in long words. Use of the rules makes use of the rules unnecessary later on.

We must consider the problem of the way many children seem to learn sounding without knowing how they do it. It may be that they have forgotten their first steps, and it may be that similarities of looks and sounds of parts of words register with them unconsciously as they read.

CHAPTER VIII.

The Teaching of Sounding

One reads with his sight vocabulary, and an enormous sight vocabulary is needed to handle the reading materials now available. Up to a certain point, that sight vocabulary can be built by the "see-hear and remember" method, someone telling the reader what a new word is. But as soon as anyone is expected to read by himself, there is no one to tell him, and he must skip the words he does not know unless he has some way of working them out, the chief way being sounding. Then, as he meets a word and sounds it out several times, it becomes unnecessary for him to sound it, and the word becomes a new sight word. It is in this way that most of our sight vocabulary has been built up. An average adult has a sight vocabulary of perhaps 20,000 to 50,000 words, most of which he learned by himself through sounding attack.

Such being the major importance of sounding attack in reading, we must give adequate attention in the schools to the teaching of sounding. At one time, the teaching of sounding was discontinued, but experience has shown the schools the necessity of including sounding training in the teaching of reading. At present the questions about sounding are, What to teach? When to teach it? and How to teach it? We shall try to answer these questions.

Underlying Principles

All efficient teaching must be based upon how children learn. As we have seen, the learning of sounding is not a simple process. We shall now try to derive some principles for the teaching of sounding that will enable us to guide efficiently the children's learning.

1. No Sounding of the Common Words

There are three reasons why the common words should not be sounded out but should be *recognized instantly* as sight words. The *first* of these reasons is that for the common words to be sounded either by letters or in parts would slow down the reading process and greatly discourage the beginner who must learn those common words before he can read. From the very first day of reading instruction, the beginner meets the common service words—verbs, adverbs, adjectives, pronouns, prepositions and conjunctions. He continues to meet them every day. He will not find reading easy and a pleasure unless he recognizes those often-met words instantly. Therefore we teach them as sight words from the start.

The *second* reason for the learning of common words as sight words is that we want the child to get the habit of *whole word perception*. We want him to look at words as wholes, and not as made up of pieces. We point to a whole word and tell him the whole word. We want him to get the habit of looking at words that way. So we begin with whole word perception and continue it most of the time. If we at any time do point out how a word begins, we do so for just a moment and then go back to whole word perception. This is one value of vocabulary control, that it keeps the reading matter almost altogether within the already known sight vocabulary. The child only occasionally comes to a word he does not know. The best ratio is not more than three unknown words per page. In the case of these unknown words, the child may look at letters, but he looks at all the other words as wholes.

A *third* and a very important reason for teaching the common words as sight words is that so many of them violate some rule for sounding. The common words have a long history of use by the English speaking people. During that long history, there has been much change of pronunciation and of spelling. Usually the original spelling of a word was phonetic, according to the usage of the time. But when the spoken usage changed, very often the spelling did not. Or the spelling changed for some incidental or arbitrary reason. At any rate, a large number of our most common words, such as *have, were, any, was,* and so on are not sounded as they are spelled. To try to sound such nonphonetic words confuses the child and lessens his confidence in sounding. For that reason, we delay sounding until most of these common words are known by sight.

2. Sounding Is for Recognition Only

Whenever we ask a child to sound a word, we should be sure that he already has the word in his hearing and meaning vocabulary. Otherwise, he will seldom get the correct word by sounding. We must keep clearly in mind three facts in this connection: First, under the best of circumstances, the child by sounding the parts merely *comes near* the word and never gets its exact sound. He must already have the exact sound in his mind and be able to get close enough to it to guess which word is meant. *Second,* English has many words that are largely exceptions to rules, and very many long words have a single syllable that does not follow the rules. So sounding by rules will not always give the right sounds. *Third,* correct pronouncing requires that we know where to place the accent, and there is no way of telling where to accent a word you have never heard. Of course, we teach children to discover from the dictionary how to accent new words but we are here discussing sounding in reading without dictionary help. If the pupil has a dictionary handy he does not need to sound: He merely opens his dictionary and compares the marks on the word with those on the key words at the bottom of the page. That is a good practice, but it is not sounding in reading.

3. Sounding Attack on Short Words Must Be Taught Separately From Attack on Long Words

There has been an attempt to teach sounding rules that would apply both to short words and to syllables in long words. For instance, we find at times the rule that "a vowel at the end of an accented syllable or of a monosyllable is long." That rule is intended to cover words like *me, by* and *no* and long syllables as in *dē-mand* or *lā-dy*. The rule does cover them, but we have to point out that from the child's point of view such words seem entirely different problems and are learned at entirely different times. The grammarian may consider together short words and syllables of long words, but we cannot do so in the elementary school without confusing the children.

In the primary grades the children are meeting the many everyday words of the language, most of which are short. The reason for this is that, for communication about everyday things, people have found it easier to use monosyllables. They even reduce long words to shorter ones for everyday use, as calling an *automobile* a *car,* and a *telephone* a *phone.* Among these common, short words, some are so common that we teach them by sight only. Others we try to get the children to work out for themselves.

Working out of monosyllables (aside from basic words known by sight) is a special concern of the primary children. We teach them to listen to a short word and to hear how it begins and how it ends, and what is the sound in the middle. That is, we first teach the process of sounding the beginnings and middles and endings of monosyllables and of putting the parts together to get the word. Thus it is seen that monosyllables are the special interest of the primary grades, and monosyllable phonics is naturally the chief kind of sounding that is used. The long words met in primary grades had better be taught as sight words, without any attempt to sound them out.

By the time the middle grades are reached, however, most of the monosyllables of the language have been met with and have become sight words. The new words are practically all long words. There is now little use for the method of attack we have taught for monosyllables. We have taught the children to listen to word beginning and to sound out word beginnings, but the beginning is only a small part of a long word. We have taught the sounding of letters and the putting of those letters together, but this method will not work if there are ten or more letters in a word. One cannot remember and synthesize so many sounds. Therefore, middle grade phonics is naturally polysyllable phonics, and it naturally begins with the process of breaking the long word into parts so that we may attack it more successfully. So the sounding of short words is taught at one time, and the sounding of long words at another, for very good reason.

4. SOUNDING HAS THREE STAGES: KNOWLEDGE, HABIT AND SKILL

Sounding or phonics may be thought of first as knowledge. The child may *know* certain things about sounding. He may be able to repeat them on an examination. He may be said to "know about" sounding. But if all the child has is mere knowledge, he will not be much benefited. Sounding is something to be used, and the child must be in the *habit* of attacking words with his knowledge. Sounding habits must be taught in addition to or along with the knowledge. From this point of view, we do not ask "Does he know sounding?" but "Does he use sounding?" It has far too often been assumed that knowledge is automatically used, that giving knowledge necessarily implies the use of it. This is far from the case, as we all find in everyday experience.

Finally, sounding knowledge has to be used and used until it is used with speed and precision, until it is used easily in all kinds of different situations, until any word can be attacked surely and skilfully. When sounding has reached that stage it has become a *skill*. With us adults it has reached that stage. We are so skilful that we use sounding almost unconsciously. This is the stage we want all children to reach but to reach it requires long practice under all kinds of circumstances. It takes years for this kind of sounding skill to develop. That is why we must see that sounding is used year after year, in all school subjects, even on through high school.

Nothing less than sounding skill, almost unconsciously used, will make an expert reader.

5. A Sounding Rule or Principle May Be Told to the Children

There are several ways in which sounding knowledge may be taught. *First,* teachers sometimes
begin by first calling attention to sounds. They may
make a sound like a hum, and then tell the children
that sound is represented by the letter *m.* That is
the method of "going from the sound to the letter."
A *second* method is for the teacher to "go from the
letter to the sound" by pointing to an *m* and telling the children that the sound of the letter is "*m-
m-m-m-m-m-m-.*" This statement is sometimes called
a phonic fact, but it is actually a rule or principle,
for the teacher is really saying, "Every letter *m,* in
any word, has the sound of *m-m-m-m-m-.* She is
making a generalization about all words that contain
m, and is not just speaking of one *m* in particular.

A *third* variation of this "telling method," is for
the teacher to give the children or get them to find a
key word by which they can remember that a certain
letter has a certain sound. Since attention should
first be given to beginning consonants, the key words
can be the names for very familiar things as *boy* for
b, cat for *c, dog* for *d,* and so on. Key words for the
vowels are usually *a* as in *apple, e* as in *elephant,
i* as in *Indian, o* as in *ostrich,* and *u* as in *umbrella.*
It is difficult to find more familiar words that begin

with the short sounds of the vowels. Sometimes, as is often done with these vowel key words, a key picture is also used, with the letter beside it. The letter should be a small one, not a capital. Then when the child looks at a letter and no sound comes to his mind, the picture is remembered, the name of the thing is thought of, and the sound of the beginning letter is thus found out. When it is desired to teach the sounding of capitals, names may be used as key words, as *T* in *Tom*, *M* in *Mary*, *B* in *Ben*, *R* in *Robert* and so on.

Fourth, there is another possibility, little used however, when a child looks at a letter and cannot think of the sound. He surely can think of the name of the letter and usually does. Then he may be told to say the name of the letter and listen for the sound of the letter in the name. This plan works with most of the consonants. Eight of the consonants have names that *begin* with the sound, namely, *b, d, j, k, p, t, v* and *z*. Seven of the consonants have names that *end* with the sound of the letter, namely, *f, l, m, n, r, s* and *x*. The two consonants *c* and *g* have names that begin with the less usual soft sound of the letters. Some of the consonants have names that do not contain their sounds at all, namely, *h, q, w* and *y*. This use of the names is an interesting possibility that should be experimented with. It may be that this fact that "the sound is in the name" helps some children who seem to get the sound of a word by spelling it.

6. A Sounding Principle May Be Best Taught as a Generalization From Individual Cases

The "telling method" which we have just described, with its four variations, is perhaps the one usually used in teaching sounding, but it is not the best. It is a general rule of learning that the best way to learn a generalization is to discover that generalization by oneself. This is called the "development" method. It can better be called the "finding out" method. It has two outstanding benefits. *First,* principles discovered by oneself have the maximum of meaning. Many children just do not see the value of phonics because they have been *told* all about it but they have not discovered any of the principles for themselves. *Second,* principles discovered are not easily forgotten. We are now having to teach phonics over and over again, year after year, in the grades and high school. Perhaps if the children discovered the principles or rules for themselves they would remember them.

Finding out (or generalization) can be done with sounds first or letters first. Sometimes the teacher asks whose name begins with the same sound as Mary's name. The children think of Mabel, and Mamie, and Mildred and so on. The children listen to the names and realize that they all begin with the same sound. Then the teacher asks, "What is the letter they begin with when we write them?" and the children notice that all these names begin with an M. So the generalization is made that a certain sound is represented by the letter M. Or the teacher may write on the board some sight words the children know, such as "man," "me," "my," "mother," and so on. She will ask what letter they begin with and the children will see that they all begin with the letter "m." Then she may ask, "What sound do they all begin with?" As the words are said aloud, and the beginning sound is held a little, the children become aware of the separate sound of "m." So the generalization is made that "m" stands for that sound. Whichever way the thing is done, the children arrived at the generalization that a certain sound is represented by the letter "m" and that an "m" always stands for that certain sound. A separate generalization is made for each letter. From all of these cases the child begins to make the "wider generalization," of "look alike, sound alike."

Even the rules for syllabication can easily be found out by the children themselves. A list of long words can be divided according to the dictionary and written in a column in separate syllable form. Then the teacher can ask to have the number of syllables in each word written to the left of the column. Then she can have the number of vowels in each word written at the right side of the column. The class will quickly see that they are about the same. But what about cases where they are not? The class will discover that the silent final e does not count as a syllable. Then the class will find that

there are vowel combinations, that is, two vowels
that count as one. With these corrections, it will
be found that the number of syllables and the number of vowels or vowel combinations agree. So the
rule is discovered, "There are as many syllables as
there are vowels or vowel combinations." The other
rules can be discovered in the same way.

Two cautions need to be made. *One* is that this
method of "finding out" takes time. But it is very
well worth the time. Sounding is to be used for life.
It must not be forgotten. If it is not learned this
year, it can be learned next year. It need not be
learned in a hurry. We are not rushing through it to
get to something else. The *other* caution is that
the teacher must not be fooled by the success of only
a part of the class. The leaders will rush through
any developmental process; this means that they
themselves have done it but it does not mean that the
others have. Special methods must be used to make
sure that each student finds things out for himself,
and does not just listen and watch as others find it
out. Only one's own discovery is his discovery.

7. SOUNDING HABITS MUST BE DEVELOPED

We have pointed out that the rules or principles
of sounding are items of knowledge that are best
derived by comparing sight words and sound words.
These rules and principles can be developed, can
be known, and can be repeated. But then certain
habits of using them must be developed. *The use of*

a sounding principle must become a habit before it is of much value in reading.

There are two ways in which the principles of sounding can be used. One is *in exercises* and the other is *in reading*. Concerning the value of exercises, we have very little scientific information. Whatever value they may have is to be measured by the amount of transfer to actual reading. When doing exercises, the child knows that he is to use a principle and he usually knows what that principle is. Then he is given material especially constructed to give a chance to use the principle. The stage is set, and the child performs according to plan. There are only two things we can be sure of about the use of exercises to teach use of principles: (1) the child learns to repeat the principle, and (2) he learns to use the principle when he knows he is expected to use it.

In reading, however, we find that there are certain differences from the doing of exercises. First, the child in reading may not think of using his principles of sounding. He may look at a new word and puzzle, and the teacher has to remind him, "How does the word begin?" The child will say, "With an r?" The teacher will remind him, "What is the sound of r?" and so on. So she has to try to develop *the habit of trying to sound*. Many children have considerable knowledge of sounding, but never use it. The have not developed the habit of trying to sound. Perhaps they find sounding is too much trouble or they find it easier to guess, or to use other clues. *Knowledge* of sounding is useless unless there is the *habit of trying to sound*.

Many different habits are included in sounding. First, there is the *habit of trying* that we have just discussed. Then there is the *habit of looking at the first letter* or the *habit of glancing through the word*. When a vowel appears, there is *the habit of noting whether it is followed by an r or by a final e*. In the case of c and g, there is the *habit of looking to see if it is followed by e or i*. In the case of long words, there are a whole series of habits involved in syllabication. The child may "know" phonics in the sense of being able to repeat the rules. He must have a series of habits if he is to use phonics. Nearly every step in the learning of sounding has a special habit required for its use in reading.

8. Habits in Sounding Are Built First by Selective Practice, and Then by Mixed Practice

We all know how, in arithmetic one process is practiced on exercises especially designed for it, and then mixed practice is introduced, that is, exercises that include the new process and also old processes. In the first kind of practice, which is "selective practice," the students know just what process to use. In the mixed practice, he must consider what process is needed in each exercise. Pupils may make a good showing in selective practice but not do so well in mixed practice, where they must understand the different requirements of the different kinds of exercises.

In sounding also, selective practice can be used, that is, *exercises* that practice one principle, such as the long vowel with silent final e, or the sound of c before i, and the like. Such practice is good as far as it goes. But we cannot tell whether students have sounding habits until they meet with mixed practice, that is, words in which different principles are to be used, according to the different situation. The pupil must show that he understands *what* to do, and not just *repeat a set pattern*.

In reading, it at first would seem that only mixed practice would be possible, since the words met with may call for use of any of the sounding principles. But there is a method of securing in reading selective practice on a single sounding principle, and such practice is better than selective practice in exercises, since it is in the real reading situation. There is always doubt whether what is learned in exercises will transfer to reading.

For practice in reading on a single sounding principle, the teacher must first have clearly in mind her program for teaching sounding. She knows just what the class has learned and she expects the children to use all the principles that have previously been worked on. Then she decides what is the next principle for them to learn. She may then plan to use either oral reading or silent reading. *If the reading is to be oral,* whenever the reading comes to a word that illustrates the new principle, the teacher stops and uses the new word as an illustration, perhaps adding it to a list on the board of words which illustrate the principle. There will be other new words which bring up principles that she does not want to take up as yet. She will tell those words instantly and have the reading go on. Thus she can keep all discussion of sounding during the reading entirely on the new principle to be learned.

If the teacher is using silent reading she will look ahead in the text and locate the words that illustrate the new principle. She will take them up ahead of the reading, listing them to show how they illustrate the new rule. The other new words, which bring up principles she does not want to attack, may be told beforehand by the teacher, or she can have the children find them and tell them to the class. Thus all attention to sounding may be restricted to the one principle. Of course in either oral or silent reading, the class may stop for attention to some or all of the previously learned principles if the teacher wishes.

In most reading, use of many sounding principles is required and therefore we have the conditions for mixed practice when we want it.

A fact that is hard for an adult to remember is that habits are learned in terms of years, and not of days or weeks. Our work on language habits has taught us this fact. Suppose we try to change from saying "ain't" to saying "isn't"? We *know* what the right word is. We know that we *should* get the new habit. We *want* to get the new habit. But how quickly does one change from the habit of saying one thing to the habit of saying the other? Months or years are required. Seemingly endless reminders are necessary. The old habit is strong and dominates us and can be broken only after a long struggle.

Similarly, the child who has the bad habit of puzzling over each new word or making guesses as to what it says will continue to puzzle or guess. He will do so without thinking of what he is doing. We need to remind him, "How does the word begin?" and we will need to remind him dozens and dozens of times. That is very natural. So let us cheerfully remind him and keep on reminding him, confident that the habit will develop in time.

9. Sounding Skill Is Developed by Different Children at Different Rates

After children *know* phonics, and after they try earnestly *to use* phonics, we find that some quickly learn to work out strange words and do so with the greatest ease. Others learn very slowly and seem to use sounding with difficulty. This is a question of the rate of developing a skill, and we must consider the special problems involved in learning skills.

Ability in learning and using phonics seems to be very much like ability in learning music or foreign language. Some children have a "good ear" for music and others do not. Some children grasp foreign language sounds very easily and others do not. There is something about the perception or remembering of fine distinctions of sound that varies in the individual. Our training develops the perceptual skill but does so at different rates. In sounding, this perceptual skill is called *skill in word analysis* and means ability to "hear" word parts clearly and easily. (This *sounding word analysis* is not to be confused with "visual word analysis" discussed by some authors.)

Sometimes we have the situation that the child seems to learn easily the sounds of the individual letters, but seems unable to go from the letter sounds to the word, the step we have called *word synthesis,* that must always be taken no matter how accurately we have recalled and combined the sounds of letters or word parts. It is hard to know what is the particular skill needed at this point. Perhaps it is skill in using a kind of imagination. In extreme cases, we sometimes have to give up the attempt to teach sounding to certain children who seem to be utterly unable to learn this skill in word synthesis. Usually, however, the great individual differences in speed of learning how to sound can be met by adjustment in our teaching.

10. To Develop Sounding Skill Requires Continual Reteaching

All these considerations show the folly of trying to demand that all children learn to use certain phonic principles at a certain time. This does not mean we cannot have a "curriculum in phonics." We can, if it is understood that the curriculum tells when we will *try* to get children to learn the principles, and if it is also understood that a large number of the children *will not* learn the principles at that time.

The curriculum in phonics should therefore specifically state for each year, "Introduce such and such new principles and *also reteach all preceding ones.*" Initial consonants are taught the first year and learned by some. They are taught again the second year and learned by some. They are to be taught again the third year and fourth year and so on until every last child has learned them. The same is true of every other principle. It is introduced and then taught and retaught until all the children have learned it. Teachers and administrators need to be prepared for this situation through an understanding of individual differences in children as explanied above in section 9. That is how it is and how it will be, and it is not the fault of the children. It is the nature of phonic skill.

School people are unprepared for this situation in phonics because they are accustomed to teaching

memory subjects. They can assign memorizing in
any certain grade and usually get it. But phonics is a
skill. You can assign an *attack* on a *skill* but *you
cannot schedule the learning* of a skill. It will be
learned when the child can learn it and no sooner.
We are fully accustomed to this fact with music, for
instance. We teach and reteach music and the children learn as they can according to their natural
abilities. We are accustomed to this situation in
physical education. We cannot schedule when a boy
will learn to hit a ball. We teach and reteach, and
he progresses as fast as he individually can. It is
the same with phonics. We schedule when we *try*
to teach. We cannot schedule when the children will
have learned. So we keep on teaching until finally
they do learn. And we do this calmly and not resent-
fully. It does no one any good to quarrel with
human nature.

11. Class Attack on New Words Permits Teaching at Many Levels

One of the advantages of class attack on any problem is that different children can be asked to do
different things, the task for each being adapted to
his abilities and needs. This is especially true of
sounding attack on new words by the entire class.

When short words are being attacked in the primary grades, the work can be distributed according
to individual needs. When the teacher asks how a
new word begins, she can ask the child who is still

at the initial consonant stage, and can even ask the child who needs practice on the particular consonant that appears. If there are two or more consonants together, she can ask the child who is learning how to blend. Then she can ask the vowel sound of the child who has progressed to the vowels. Finally, she can have the sounds blended into the right word by a child who is at that stage. The work can be shared, each doing what he can do, but all listening to the others. In this way, the children are teaching one another.

In the attack on long words, beginning with the third grade or later, this division of labor and mutual learning can be done with special success. The first question may be, "How many syllables are there in the word?" and a child who knows the vowels can be asked to go to the board and put a check over each vowel or vowel combination. This should be the job he knows how to do and that he needs to practice doing, not the job he cannot do. The others who watch learn from him. The next question may be, "How shall we divide the consonants between vowels?" Anyone who knows a consonant and who can remember "between two or in front of one" can do this, and therefore the job can be assigned to the one who needs practice in division of consonants. He can draw the dividing lines as all watch. Then the individual syllables need to be sounded, and this job can be given to the proper pupil or to several. Finally, "What is the word?"

Obviously, this is a question that requires knowing the sound word, and the teacher will call on a pupil who probably knows the sound word and not on one who does not.

This process of sharing the work and learning from each other is fundamental to the use of sounding attack in the class situation. The desired situation is "Everybody learning," but not necessarily everybody learning the same thing. Everybody will learn where he is, all will progress, and each will finally reach the goal of complete sounding knowledge, habit and skill.

12. Do Not Confuse Diacritical Marking With Sounding Attack

Knowledge of diacritical marking cannot help anyone with word attack in reading, just because no word in a reading book is ever marked. The word the child meets in reading is spelled in ordinary letters, without any marking to show whether there is the sound of a long or short vowel or what not. That is the word the child must attack, the word without any diacritical markings. If he has any knowledge of diacritical marks, he cannot possibly use it in reading.

Diacritical markings are used only when a child has the dictionary open before him. But when the child has opened his dictionary, he is not using word attack. He has given up trying to work out the word himself. He is not finding out the word for himself;

he is just finding out what the dictionary says. A person can use the dictionary without the slightest knowledge of word attack. The dictionary does the dividing and the dictionary tells just what sound to give each letter. The dictionary does it all. The pupil needs only to know how to use the dictionary.

Finding out what the dictionary tells about the sound of a word may make use of a knowledge of diacritical marking and it may not. The pupil may look at the diacritical markings on the dictionary respelling and from his knowledge of those markings, sound out the word. Or he may not know what a single one of the marks means and still get the word right. He has only to compare each marked letter with the similarly marked key word at the bottom of the page. The key that is now put at the bottom of each page makes it necessary to use diacritical marks only for comparison. The child who can compare each mark on a word with a similar mark on a key word can find out the correct sounding. But, as we have said, this is not word attack. Word attack means working out a word *that is not marked*. Therefore let no one think that teaching diacritical marks has anything whatever to do with the teaching of sounding attack.

A Program for Teaching Phonics

We have emphasized that each child learns sounding knowledge, habit, and skill at his own pace, depending on his native ability and upon his interest and the skill of the teacher. Learning sounding is actually an individual matter. But for school purposes, we need some kind of a tentative program to follow so that we do not just wander about in the field. We need a plan of attack on the whole subject, though we remember all the time that our plan is subject to change at any moment, and that we are not going to carry the whole group with us along our planned road at the rate we probably plan. Some will be ahead and some will be behind, but they will all be happily learning.

The plan we shall suggest is, therefore, strictly a tentative one. Since children learn in terms of needs, we have to estimate their needs beforehand, but we know that in actual teaching we must work with the needs of the moment. We also know beforehand that the needs of different children will be different. But we must make a plan, and then be guided by the development of the class and of each individual in it. We know it is folly to try to force a group to a plan that is not right for them. If it is the right plan, forcing is not needed.

When teachers read any plan that is put down in a book, they must realize that the writer of the book cannot possibly know the exact conditions of their own school and classroom. He is thinking of a sort of "average" that he has derived from his wide and varying experience. He knows perfectly well that each school and each class is different. He expects the teacher to be the "artist" who adapts the general principle and the average plan to the needs of her children at the moment. He would so adapt it if he were in her classroom. So let every teacher make the proper adjustments. She is the only one who can know what they are.

For instance, the home background of different groups is different. Where there is home encouragement and home advantages, children will advance much faster than ordinarily. But where homes are culturally poverty stricken and antagonistic toward the school one cannot expect the usual growth. Similarly, what any one class can do depends so much on what they have done in previous grades. After all, we built also upon what has been learned in school. Attitudes, habits, motivation, all these differ from school to school, and in the same school they differ from year to year. The teacher knows about these things and therefore will adapt a plan accordingly. Finally, philosophies differ in schools and with teachers. How much should we "push" sounding? Some people believe it is so important as a tool that much time should be given to it, and it should be hastened as much as possible. Other persons feel that sounding habit and skill will come in time and that one need not worry. Meantime, they say, let us tell the children the words and read. This difference in fundamental belief and attitude will make a very great difference in the sounding program.

Steps in Learning Sounding

Having fully pointed out that any plan for the teaching of sounding must be adapted by the teacher to her conditions and to her class, we now wish to present a plan that has three strong recommendations. *First,* it has succeeded with thousands of different teachers and with countless children of many kinds of abilities and backgrounds. The reason for this success lies perhaps in the other two recommendations. *Second,* then, this plan for teaching phonics is simple. It reduces the complicated subject to thirteen clearly defined steps which can be carried in mind by the teacher and also by the pupil.

For children to learn, they must see just where they are going and also see what progress they have made. With these thirteen steps, each child can know just what his progress is, and just what he has to learn next. Similarly, the teacher can see the definite needs and can detect definite progress. This simplicity and definiteness is intended, of course, for the learning of sounding in the elementary school. This simple plan is not intended for specialists or for mature students who can deal with the finer points of the sounding of the English language. It is, however, suited to the needs of the elementary school, for teacher and pupil alike.

The *third* recommendation for this plan of learning sounding is perhaps the most important, and is probably the one that contributes most to its success. That is, this plan fits, psychologically, the way most children actually find their way into knowledge, habit, and skill in using sounding. The plan was developed from actual teaching of sounding, and from observation of just how children learned.

We shall now take up the Thirteen Steps in Sounding, one at a time, and shall point out the psychological reason for the step's belonging where it does in the plan. We shall give recommendations and cautions that have been worked out from teaching very many children and observing their reactions and their success or failure. The plan is simple, but the teacher using it should understand just as fully as possible what is involved in each step.

The Thirteen Steps in Learning Sounding

Step One, Learning the Sounds of the Consonants

Knowing the sounds of the consonants is the most useful knowledge in sounding just because most words begin with a consonant. If one knows how the word begins, he can more accurately guess from context what the word must be since his guess must be a word that begins with that one consonant.

Ear training must usually precede the teaching of sounding, and the first ear training is to listen to how words begin. Later there must also be training in listening to the sound of other parts of words, but it is best not to confuse the child by asking him to listen to more than one part of a word at a time. It is hard enough to concentrate on one part. For this reason it is doubtful if the usual custom of having children listen to rhymes is a good one. Children like to do it and it is easy to do. But listening to the ends of words cannot help much in reading, where the first task is to find out how the word *begins*. We have no evidence that practice in listening to the end of words trains in listening to beginnings, though it may give "general ear training."

For the same reason it is doubtful whether there is value in "teaching a letter" in three positions, at the beginning, at the middle, and at the end of words as is often done. That is trying to teach three different habits of listening. It appears that the habit of listening to beginnings should come first and should be the only such habit for some time. If a child can easily and quickly think the correct sound of *beginning* consonants, he has a functional knowledge of consonant sounds and can go on to vowel sounds.

Blends of consonants may or may not receive separate attention. The best way to help children to make blends is not to teach blends as such but to thoroughly teach the single consonants. A child who can easily and accurately sound single consonants can easily make blends. If he has trouble with blends, the cure is usually to teach the single consonants more thoroughly.

With initial consonants, we have the three steps previously discussed: (1) knowledge, (2) habit, and (3) skill. After there is knowledge, there needs to be practice to develop habit and skill. One device is to have a child follow the lines of reading matter, not reading the words but sounding all beginning consonants. This is practice in something like a reading situation, and is better than using lists of words detached from reading.

Ear training and the sounding of initial conso- *nants are usually enough of phonics for Grade I.* Some children will go much farther and they should do so, but the average and the slow children will be disturbed if more sounding is attempted. The First grade is the time for instant sight recognition of the common sight words. It is not the time for puzzling and analyzing. The natural method of teaching words in First grade is telling, either alone or in oral reading. To develop much sounding in first grade is unnatural for most children and may produce lifelong bad habits of looking at letters instead of looking at words as wholes.[1]

STEP TWO. LEARNING THE SOUNDS OF THE CONSONANT DIGRAPHS

When a child is finding out how words begin, he will come across the combination *ch, sh, th,* and *wh.* At the end of words he will find the combination *ck.*

---

[1] The game, Consonant Lotto, is especially designed to teach initial consonants. Published by Garrard Press, Champaign, Ill.

If not told otherwise, he will try to sound each of
the consonants in these combinations whereas each
of the combinations has a sound of its own that must
be learned. These are called *digraphs* because they
are two letters with the sound of one.

The sounds of *ch, sh* and *th* are easily learned
from common words which begin with these digraphs — *chair, children, church; she, shoe, sheep;
this, that, they.* The digraph *wh* appears in the beginning of *when, what, why,* and so on, and it may
not be necessary or advisable to call children's attention to the fact that actually, instead of a new sound
for this combination, we pronounce the two letters
in reverse order, that is, as *hw.* Few people notice
this, and many persons actually do not pronounce
the *h* at all, but call these words *wen, wat, wy.* The
sound of the digraph *ck* does not bother children for
it is just two letters which have both the same sound,
the sound of *k.* In that sense, it is not properly a
digraph.

STEP THREE. LEARNING THE SHORT SOUNDS OF THE VOWELS

With children we often say that the vowels have
both names and sounds, that ā, ē, ī, ō, ū are the
names and ă, ĕ, ĭ, ŏ, ŭ are the sounds. We may tell
them to "Always use the *sound* of the vowels and
never their *names* unless there is a special reason."
Of course, the much more common practice is to say
that vowels have both long and short sounds, and

that the short sound is the most common and should be used unless there is a special reason not to.

The short sounds of the vowels are not in the names of the vowels, and hence some way must be found to help the child remember them. The usual way is to give a key word. Some key words often used for vowels in initial position are *apple, elephant, Indian, ostrich* and *umbrella*. These can be pictured and have the advantage of being unusual and therefore easier to remember. However, the more usual position of the vowels is not at the beginning of a word but in the center of small words of one syllable; hence the better key words are perhaps *bat, bet, bit, hot* and *but*. Or any group of convenient short words can be used. If pictured key words are desired, they might be *cat, tent, kitten, pot* and *rug*, or other common words easily pictured.

Step Four. Learning the Long Sounds of the Vowels

This step is put in just for completeness, for there is no trouble with learning the long sounds, since they are usually assumed to be the names of the letters. These names are learned very early. In fact, the problem in reading is to get the children *not* to use the names of the vowels, but to use their short sounds. One method is to say the vowels in English are *sounds,* and those *vowel sounds* are ă, ĕ, ĭ, ŏ, ŭ and *not* ā, ē, ī, ō, ū, which are just the *names* of the letters.

It must be noted that we are here following the practice common in all books on reading, of speaking of the long sounds of the five vowels. Speech specialists point out that this is not correct, but that what we call the long sounds of *a, i,* and *u* (and sometimes *o*) are really two sounds and therefore are properly diphthongs. But we are deliberately not teaching this fact to children because it would just confuse them. The one time we must watch out for this distinction is in words with long *u.* Some have the true long sound, such as *flute, rule* and so on, and others have the diphthong sound, such as in *mule.* Yet both types of words are often put together as long sounds of *u* and the children do not seem to have difficulty in shifting from the pure *u* sound to the diphthong *u* sound as needed.

Step 4 deals with what the long sounds of the vowels *are.* Steps 5 and 6, which follow, tell when the long sounds of the vowels are *used.* There is another case when a vowel is long, and that is when it ends a syllable, as stated in step 13, but it is best not to introduce this step 13 when short words are being attacked. It just confuses the children, since they are not concerned with open syllables at that time. Sometimes the rule is given that a vowel is long when on the end of a single syllable word or a syllable. This rule is intended to include the little words like *he, we, no, my, so,* and the like. But all these little words are early learned as sight words, and no one needs a rule for pronouncing them.

Step Five. Learning That the Silent Final e Shows That the Sound of the Preceding Vowel Is Long

Very few people have become conscious that the final e on a word is never pronounced (except in a few words from the French like *cafe*). Perhaps the reason is that among the early sight words there are a number with silent final e, like *same, time* and *hole*, and consequently in the very beginning one gets the habit of ignoring that final e. However, for sounding it is necessary to point out that the silent final e is usually a sign that the preceding vowel is long. When we are looking at words ending in silent e, we seem to use the long sound instantly without realizing that it is the final e we are noticing, as in the pairs, *fin-fine, hop-hope, rod-rode, mad-made,* and many others. This is an interesting case of unconscious awareness of a cue for pronouncing.

There is one very common exception to this rule which some children may notice but which otherwise need not be mentioned. In a large group of words such as *little, nettle, humble, bottle, saddle* and the like, there is a final e but a short vowel before it. The reason is that the *-le* acts as a separate syllable and there are two consonants before the *-le*. The word is divided between those two consonants. Therefore the syllable with the vowel ends in a consonant and is therefore short. Strangely enough, the final syllable in these words does not contain the sound of a vowel but is formed from the sound of the letter *l*.

Steps 3, 4 and 5 are usually taken up in Second grade. Some children do not master them at that time, however, and they have to be retaught in grade III. In grade II, many children go much farther than Step 5.

Step Six. Learning the Vowel Digraphs

Vowel digraphs are two vowels coming together that give us but a single sound. There are two groups of the vowel digraphs. In the first group, the sound of the digraph is the long sound of the first vowel. Teachers often say, "The first says its name and the second one is silent." This group consists of *ai* as in *paid*, *ay* as in *say*, *ee* as in *feed*, and *ea* as in *speak*, and *oa* as in *boat*. Since there are just five in this group of digraphs, it is more effective to teach each sound separately and not by the rule given above. That is, teach that *ai* says long *a*,[2] *ea* says long *e*,[3] *oa* says long *o*, and so on. If we tell children that when two vowels come together, the first says its name and the second is silent, they will apply this rule to all the vowel digraphs and also to all the diphthongs, with most incorrect results.

The other group of digraphs are also "two vowels together that give us a single sound," but that sound

---

[2] See Step Four concerning the sound of long a.

[3] Many words with *ea* have the short e sound, as *bread*, *head* and so on.

is not the sound of the first letter. This group consists of *au* as in *caught, aw* as in *saw, eu* as in *deuce, ew* as in *new, oo* (long) as in *food,* and *oo* (short) as in *good.* The combinations *aw* and *ew* each have one letter a consonant but they are listed here because they are held to stand for the sound of *au* and *eu,* which are properly vowel digraphs.[4]

STEP SEVEN. LEARNING THE DIPHTHONGS

The technical definition of diphthongs is that they are two vowels coming together *both of which are pronounced* ("A union of two vowels pronounced in one syllable") thus giving us a "diphthong" or a "two-sound," as the translation might be made. We may make this explanation to children, but if we do, we may be confusing them by asking them to break up or analyze sounds that they already make quite naturally. It is just as well to say that *diphthongs are two-vowel combinations with a "new sound."* For instance, the two letters that one sounds in "ou" seem to the child to be a new sound.

The common diphthongs are *oi* as in *oil, oy* as in *boy, ou* as in *out,* and *ow* as in *cow.* They may be developed from familiar words or taught by use of key words.

---

[4] The dictionary is inconsistent in calling *eu* and *ew* digraphs and then saying they are the equivalent of the diphthong sound of long *u* in *use, mule,* and the like. We have given for *eu* and *ew* key words that have the sound of *oo* (long) as in *food.* That is the sound more usually given these combinations.

As with so much of sounding, there is the problem of exceptions. The teacher should know that very many common words have the letters *"ow"* with the long sound, as *row, sow, flow, grow,* and so on. Sooner or later children notice this fact. Then we must say, "Try either of the sounds of *'ow'* to see which one will tell you what word is meant."

STEP EIGHT. LEARNING THAT VOWELS FOLLOWED BY R HAVE A SPECIAL SOUND

When *r* follows a vowel, the *r* is pronounced with the vowel and that vowel nearly always has a special sound, as heard in *car, her, sir, for, fur.* This gives a third sound of the single vowels, in addition to the short and long already explained. There are other sounds of the vowels, but none for which we can give any rules or need to. It must be remembered that we are not finding out just how to sound an entirely new word, but we are only using approximate sounds to "get near" the word so that we can recognize a word that we already know.[5]

---

[5] The attempt has been made to make other rules for cases of a vowel sound influenced by the letter after it. As an example there is the tendency to make *o* long when followed by *ld*, as in *gold, cold, told*, etc. Sometimes the rule is given that the vowel *a* has a special sound when followed by *ll*. This would cover many short words, as *ball, tall, call*, but it is not of value with longer words. When we divide words into syllables, as in the case of *"al-ler-gy,"* only one l is pronounced with the *a*, and the sound of *a* is short. In fact, it seems unwise to multiply phonetic rules which cover a limited number of cases. It is better to learn each such case separately. For instance, most of the small words ending in *-all*, are early learned as sight words, and never need to be sounded.

STEP NINE. LEARNING THAT C AND G FOLLOWED
BY E OR I HAVE THEIR SOFT SOUNDS

Most teaching of consonants begins by giving *c* its
"hard" sound which is the sound of *k* as in *"cat"*
and *g* its *hard* sound as in *"go."* At some time or
other, however, the children will discover words in
which *c* and *g* have different sounds, and they should
discover that in all such cases *c* and *g* are followed
by either *e* or *i* (sometimes *y* as in *gypsy*). In such
cases we can speak of the *soft* sound of *c* or of *g*. We
could say that *c* has the sound of *s*, and *g* has the
sound of *j*, but this seems only to confuse children.
It is better to say *c* has two sounds, hard and soft,
and *g* has two also. To bring in another letter is
an association that may explain, but it makes for
confusion. It is better to think directly of the two
sounds of *c* in *circus* and the two sounds of *g* in
gigantic.

This step is numbered nine just because there is
no distinct need for it in the progression from consonants to short vowels, to long vowels, to vowel
combinations. But these two sounds of *c* and *g* may
be learned whenever opportunity or need arises.

It is usually assumed that all steps through Step
9 will be taken up by Grade III. They will need to
be retaught, however.

Sounding Long Words

The Steps in Learning Sounding from 10 to 13
explain the breaking up of long words so that they

may be sounded in parts. Of course, in sounding the parts, all the previous rules are used, since the parts of long words contain consonants, blends, vowels, and vowel combinations. The teaching of steps 10 to 13 therefore assumes that the other steps have been learned. With older children, who need to know how to "unlock" long words, the beginning of sounding may be with step 10 and go on to 11, 12 and 13, for it will be found either that the students have unconsciously acquired knowledge of the letter sounds or they can be taught the letter sounds very easily because of their greater maturity and ability to apply themselves.

Sounding of long words may be begun in Grade III but is chiefly emphasized in Grade IV and later.

Step Ten. Learning to Take Off Common Beginnings and Endings

This step is listed as the first in the attack on long words because it is the most natural. The students have seen many long words and know a great many of them by sight. They are bound to have noticed common beginnings and endings. At least they have become conscious of *un*, in *unlike, unfair, unwilling,* and so on or of *sub* in *submarine, submachine* gun, and the like. They will be very conscious of the inflectional endings *-ed,* and *-ing,* of *-er* and *-est* which make the comparative and superlative of adjectives, and of the ending which make adjectives into adverbs as *-ly* in *richly, quickly,* etc.

Step 10 means to take off beginnings and endings which are familiar *to the student,* not ones which are familiar to the teacher. If the student does not see a beginning or ending, we should not go into a long session of teaching. The purpose is to recognize the word and not to teach prefixes and suffixes. Teaching prefixes and suffixes should not interfere with word attack. Sometimes, of course, the mere question, "Do you see a common beginning or ending?" will be enough to cause one to be recognized, but beyond that, we should not make too great a point of this step but go on to the others. Words can be divided into syllables without step 10.

The beginnings and endings which one can expect most children to have noticed by the middle grades are:

Beginnings	Endings
un-	-less
	-ness
re-	-able
	-tion
non-	-ly
	-ing
dis-	-ed
	-er
	-est
	-ful

It should be noted we have used the simple Anglo-Saxon terms *beginning* and *ending,* instead of the Latin terms, *prefix* and *suffix.* Sooner or later, the more learned terms can be used, but to younger children they form a block to thinking instead of an aid.

Children "see" the meaning in "ending" but have to "think of" the meaning of "suffix."

STEP ELEVEN. LEARNING THAT THERE ARE AS MANY SYLLABLES AS VOWELS

We are assuming the case of the children who do not see the syllables at once but who see instead just a long array of letters, without parting or division. Somehow, they must break this long string of letters into manageable groups. The way to do this is first to find the vowels and vowel combinations.

There is a kind of "readiness" for syllable division that should be developed orally. Children should be asked to listen to long words and tell how many syllables they hear. They should be told that each syllable is made by a push of the breath, and they themselves should say long words, feeling the push of breath at each syllable. In these and other ways they should realize that long words must be said in parts, and therefore they are read in parts. An excellent place for this preparation is in the spelling lesson. Long words should be sounded a syllable at a time as they are spelled, and if spelling is practiced in this way the meaning of "syllable" will be learned.

We here assume that the children are familiar with the common vowel combinations, that is, with the vowel digraphs and the diphthongs which have a "new sound" of their own. Children will assume that two vowels that come together are always a vowel combination, but they will find that sometimes two vowels come together but are sounded separately, because they are neither vowel digraphs nor diphthongs, as in the case of the two vowels in "dial."

In practice, if it is possible to have students put a mark or check over each vowel or vowel combination in a word they are attacking, they will get a *visual* idea of the number of syllables that is valuable.

STEP TWELVE. LEARNING HOW TO DIVIDE CONSONANTS THAT COME BETWEEN VOWELS (BETWEEN TWO CONSONANTS OR IN FRONT OF ONE)

The students must concentrate on "consonants that come between vowels," and disregard the ones that may be at the beginning or end of the word. They can separate the consonants according to the easily remembered rule, "between two consonants or in front of one," as in the words *sup ply, po ta to, num ber, la dy,* etc. This rule does not fit every case, but it follows the natural tendency in pronouncing to close one syllable with a consonant and begin the next syllable with another consonant. If there is but one consonant between vowels, the natural tendency is to end the first syllable with an open vowel, and then to attack the next vowel with a consonant. Consonants are used naturally to end vowel sounds or to begin vowel sounds.

At times there are three consonants between vowels. In that case the division can come after the first consonant or the second, depending on how the consonants can be sounded together. The purpose is not to tell exactly the right pronunciation but only to recognize a word that the child already knows by sound.

The fact that we have just mentioned needs continued emphasis, that this sounding of long words is *for recognition only*. The divisions made by these rules may not be the same as given in the dictionary, but they do not pretend to be. We are not finding out the "correct" division of the word, but only a rough division that will help us come close to the right sound. For the "correct" division, we must always consult the dictionary, since few persons know enough about the science of language to divide all words correctly. For instance, our pronouncing rules would give us the division *spel ling,* which tells us which word is meant. The dictionary gives us *spell-ing* because of the principle that an original monosyllable is not divided.

In the spelling period, and in the English classes in high school, the teacher may take time to explain about this principle, but in the reading class or when the child is working at reading by himself, he needs a quick general rule that will work somehow in most cases. The rule "between two consonants or in front of one" is such a rule and he can remember and use it for reading purposes. He should be told that when he is dividing a word *for writing* he must consult the dictionary.

In dividing into syllables, there is a sub-rule which should be mentioned, ''Never divide the r from the vowel in front of it.'' The student will infer this rule from step No. 8 which tells how the r influences the vowel sound and is in fact pronounced with it. This joining of the vowel and the r which follows is usually done automatically but students need to be told that step 12 does *not* mean they should separate the vowel from the r which indicates its sound.

Step Thirteen. Learning That Open Syllables Are Long; Closed Syllables Are Short

When we divide ''between two consonants or in front of one,'' some syllables will end in a consonant and some will end in a vowel. If the syllable ends in a vowel, it is called ''open,'' because the mouth is kept open as the long sound of the vowel is given. When the syllable ends in a consonant, it is called ''closed,'' and the vowel is usually short because the consonant sound usually closes the mouth and thus cuts off the vowel sound.

There are many exceptions to this rule, but it is of practical help in sounding. Very often in a long word one syllable will violate this rule, but usually most of the syllables will follow it. Therefore the syllables, when said one after the other, will come close to the right word, and it can be guessed. The reason for most of these exceptions is that there is a rule we have not mentioned, "never divide the root form of the word." We have not included it because it would be of no use to children. They have not studied Latin and Greek and therefore can have no way of knowing what these root forms are. But the teachers will understand the significance of this rule and why it gives us the soundings that it does.

It must be understood that this long or short vowel rule is a practical one only. Sometimes the student can get good results by trying the vowels both long and short and seeing which suggests a familiar word. In reading, it must be remembered that we are concerned with *sounding for recognition only* so that the child may gradually change his large hearing vocabulary into sight vocabulary for use in reading.

Summary

At present, the questions about sounding are: What to teach?, When to teach it?, and How to teach it? The answers to these questions must observe the following principles:

1. *No Sounding of Common Words.* To teach sounding of common words discourages the beginner, hinders his habit of whole word perception, and runs into the fact that many of the common words are nonphonetic.

2. *Sounding Is for Recognition Only.* By his attempt at sounding, the child gets close to the real

word, and he cannot guess what that real word is unless he already knows it by sound.

3. *Sounding Attack on Short Words Must Be Taught Separately From Attack on Long Words.* In the primary grades the child is attacking the short words of the language, and does so by sounding beginnings, middles and endings. By the middle grades, most of the short words are already known as sight words, and the problem is attack on long words, which must be divided before they can be worked out.

4. *Sounding Has Three Stages: Knowledge, Habit, and Skill. Knowledge* of phonics is taught first but is of no value until the child develops the *habit* of trying to sound out words. After many attempts to use phonics, *skill* at sounding develops.

5. *A Sounding Rule or Principle May Be Told to the Children.* The teacher may tell what letter goes with a certain sound, or she may tell what sound goes with a certain letter. She may give a key word that tells a sound, or she may have the children hear the letter sound in the letter name.

6. *A Sounding Principle May Best Be Taught as a Generalization From Individual Cases.* The development method for learning sounding is best because more understanding and more remembering result. But the method takes time and it is hard to have all the children develop principles for themselves.

7. *Sounding Habits Must Be Developed.* Sounding habits can be developed through exercises or in reading. First there is the habit of *trying to sound,* and then a long series of habits connected with the different sounding principles.

8. *Habits in Sounding Are Built First by Selective Practice and Then by Mixed Practice.* When exercises all require the use of the same principle, we have selective practice; when they require use of several or many principles, we have mixed practice. In reading the teacher can still get selective practice, but most reading requires mixed practice of sounding principles.

9. *Sounding Skill Is Developed by Different Children at Different Rates.* There seems to be a difference in native ability for learning sounding which results in great differences in learning.

10. *To Develop Sounding Skill Requires Continual Reteaching.* We may introduce certain principles at certain times, but because different children learn at different rates we must continually reteach.

11. *Class Attack on New Words Permits Teaching at Many Levels.* The process of dividing and sounding out a long word permits the teacher to assign parts of the work to different children who are at different levels of learning.

12. *Do Not Confuse Diacritical Marking With Sounding Attack.* Words are never marked in read-

ing, and thus knowledge of diacritical marks cannot help in reading, but only in use of the dictionary.

Any program for teaching phonics must be adapted to the particular school, since conditions of home background, previous teaching, and the like vary so greatly.

There are Thirteen Steps in Learning Sounding, which follow the natural learning of the children. These are:

1. *The sounds of the consonants.*
2. *The sounds of the consonant digraphs (ch, sh, th and wh).*
3. *The short sounds of the vowels.*
4. *The long sounds of the vowels.*
5. *Silent final e shows that the sound of the preceding vowel is long.*
6. *The vowel digraphs*
   Group 1. ai, ay, ee, ea, oa
   Group 2. au, aw, eu, ew, oo (long), oo (short).
7. *The diphthongs (oi, oy, ou, ow).*
8. *Vowels followed by r have a special sound.*
9. *C and G followed by e or i have their soft sounds.*
10. *Take off common beginnings and endings.*
11. *There are as many syllables as vowels.*
12. *Divide consonants that come between vowels, between two consonants or in front of one.*
13. *Open syllables are long, closed syllables are short.*

CHAPTER IX

Developing a Meaning Vocabulary

We have shown that the reader finds out what the words "say" in either of two ways. He may recognize the words as part of his sight vocabulary, or he may sound out the word to see what sound word is meant. It is apparent, therefore, that in his reading the child is finding sound words that he already knows through hearing. The reader is therefore using his hearing-meaning vocabulary in reading. The meaning of the sentences and of larger units is built out of this hearing-meaning vocabulary. All the ideas the reader can get from his reading are built out of his own hearing-meaning vocabulary.

Reading ordinarily implies a smooth progression of word recognition with the resulting thoughts and feeling. The process of sounding out a word interrupts the reading process; then just as soon as the meaning of the word is recognized, the reading process flows on again. But when the reader comes across a word that is really a blank—that means nothing—his thought process meets a blank also. The puzzling out of meaning from context that follows is very different from what we call reading. It is a very important process, however, and we shall consider it at length in the latter part of this chapter.

SIZE OF THE HEARING-MEANING VOCABULARY

A generation or so ago the hearing-meaning vocabulary of the average child was very small. The child heard only what his family and immediate friends said in their daily home life. The conversation that he heard was on a limited number of home topics. When adults gathered to discuss other things, the children were sent away or off to bed. When adult visitors came to meals, children were often fed in the kitchen beforehand, and were not present at the table. There were no telephones, no radios, no movies, and little traveling. In such a situation, the meaning vocabulary of many children could be counted in the hundreds of words rather than in the thousands.

Nowadays, things are very different. Children listen to their parents at all times and to other adults, both in and out of the home. Children listen to the radio or see television shows for an average of an hour a day, we are told, and many for longer periods. Children go to the movie an average of once a week, and there listen to spoken language, backed up with visual teaching of meaning, for from two to four hours. Children travel with their parents, because the automobile has made traveling easy and very common. On these travels, the children hear and see a very great deal of life under many conditions. Finally, children mingle on playgrounds and on the streets with many other children from many different walks of life, and the words

they bring home to their parents to explain often
baffle the elders. In short, the hearing-meaning vocabulary of the modern child entering first grade is
enormous, in comparison with what it used to be.
It is not as great as sometimes claimed,[1] but it may
average 2,000 words or more.

PRIMARY READING TRIES TO KEEP WITHIN THE HEARING-MEANING VOCABULARY

Just because we want the beginner to meet only
words he already has in his hearing-meaning vocabulary, the beginning reading books try very hard to
keep within the field of child experience. Objects are
used which all children will know, such as *ball,
wagon, doll,* and so on. The people are *mother* and
father, brother and *sister,* with whom all children
are supposed to be familiar. Even the situations are
those of the home and play yard which are assumed
to be common to all children's lives.

This keeping within child experience has, of
course, several purposes. *One* purpose is *interest.*
We want to present to children situations that will
have an appeal to them so that they will pay attention and so that the words they are told will be remembered because of pleasant association. There
seems to be conclusive evidence that words associ-

[1] See Implications of the Seashore report (Elementary English
Review, Nov. 1949) which demonstrates that the high figures claimed
by Seashore, which average ten new words per day during preschool
years, are humanly impossible.

ated with unpleasant experience are not easily remembered. *Second,* we wish to encourage *language participation* by all the children, and they would be able to talk only about things with which they are familiar. *Finally* we do not wish to hamper the teacher with the necessity of explaining things to the children when she should be conducting a pleasant story-reading experience.

The content of primary reading is supposed to begin with the home, extend from there to the playground and to visits with relatives, to include pets and toys and simple tools, and then gradually to go away from this center in ever-widening circles. As soon as we leave the home, of course, there is a question as to where to go and what to include. The purpose is always to keep within child experience and to stimulate language and thinking about that experience. But should we go on a visit to the farm? Does that mean staying within child experience or leaving it? Should we take up the policeman and fireman, or do all children live in towns with a policeman on the corner? What about going to the airport? How many towns have airports? This problem leads us to the next topic which we must consider.

Building Meaning Vocabulary Through Experience

IN THE PRIMARY GRADES

As just suggested, the attempt to keep the vocabulary of the primary reading books within the meaning vocabulary of the children runs into difficulties. We have explained how varied is the present day language experience of the modern child, how he listens to grown-ups, to the radio, to movies, how he sees television, how he travels with parents and sees and hears many things, thus building up a meaning vocabulary that is very great as compared to the meaning vocabulary of children a generation ago. But can we count on all children having this large initial meaning vocabulary?

Unfortunately, with the raising of the *average* of children's meaning vocabulary, there has not been an equal improvement in the situation of the children from unfavored homes and localities. There are still with us in large numbers children who are not allowed outside their own yards or immediate neighborhoods, and whose parents do not travel and take the children with them. We have many thousands of children from homes that do not have radios and who therefore do not have the steady flow of talk that the radio brings into the home. There are still many, many children who do not go regularly to the movies, and some who have never gone. And always there are children raised in homes where the language of the home is very limited because of parents' lack of education. So while the condition of most has improved, the conditions of many has remained very poor indeed. So the teacher of nearly every primary room has a few children who do not have the large hearing-meaning vocabulary typical of the others. And in some districts, a large number of the children are without the usual experience background of the average school child.

Methods of Giving Experience Background

Giving children experience background is done in three ways: first, by taking the children out to see the world, second, by bringing the world into the school in various ways, and third, by "experience activities" in school. We shall see how these apply in the primary grades.

1. TAKING THE CHILDREN OUT TO SEE THE WORLD

Trips are becoming more and more common as a means of developing word meaning for children. These trips are necessary when the reading book discusses a visit to the farm, and the children have never seen a farm; or when the characters in the book take some other trip such as to an airport, and the children in the room have never been there. Perhaps the authors of such readers assume that most children have been about a good deal; unfortunately, it is only the children of the favored homes who have taken trips to many places, though the children of itinerant workers necessarily see much of the world too. So the school tries by trips to make up for the lack of the assumed experience. Since the advent of school buses, these trips are becoming more and more easy and more and more common. The time will soon come no doubt when the school will systematically take children to all points of interest within many miles; at least within the possibility of going and returning in a day's time.

Visits to the local points of interest are also necessary in most schools. The school cannot count on all children having been even to the public park or to a filling station. Certainly it cannot be sure the children have seen a fire station or a dairy or the post office, or the city hall, or a court room. Because the educated parents tend to assume that all children have had the advantages of their own children, the public often doubts the advisability of these trips to "ordinary" places. Therefore, what we need in every town is statistics as to where the children have been and have not been, and then a plan to fill in the gaps that we find. Even if children have been to any one of these points of common interest, they may not have seen very much because of lack of guidance. A visit under guidance will do them all much good in the way of building vocabulary.

We must emphasize that this "going out to see the world" implies that *every experience is given a label, a word,* so that the child can use that label or word in his thinking and in his conversation. This necessity requires planning. The teacher may beforehand tell about what is to be seen, using the words for which she expects the children to get meaning. During the trip, the new things or situations or relationships may be pointed out by the guide or discovered by the children who have been looking for the new things they had heard about. And after a trip or visit, the words must be used again in discussion and in thinking so as to be sure that their meaning is clear and that the new meanings are tied in with other experiences. All new learnings must be "tied in" with other experiences if they are not to be promptly forgotten.

2. Bringing the World Into the School

The other method of giving real experiences that we have called *"bringing the world into the school"* may be carried out in many ways. One is to *bring objects* into the school. If a Teddy bear is talked about in grade I, some child can bring one from home so that children who have never been given a Teddy bear can see and hold one. Similarly all kinds of toys and small objects may be brought in by children or borrowed from other sources. Some cities have school museums that send exhibits about on request. The big advantage of objects themselves is that they can be handled. For instance, everyone is surprised the first time he picks up a Dutch wooden shoe to find how light it is. It looks heavy but it is made from light wood, and it is hollow. One would never get the idea of the lightness of wooden shoes if he did not hold one. Thus much meaning can be got from seeing and handling objects that cannot be got otherwise.

Pictures of things come next to the things themselves. In the primary grades, the chief dependence is upon pictures in books, especially the pictures in the basic reader or the illustrations in other books. After all, the illustration is to teach word meanings as well as to stimulate interest. Some day the makers of readers will send along with the books, portfolios of large wall pictures or pictures of other kinds. Right now, the teacher cuts pictures out of magazines and newspapers and files them for use in showing the children meanings of words. We must remember, of course, that *picture experiences must be accompanied with words* so that the experiences may later be used in talking and in reading.

Pictures in books have two drawbacks, however. *First,* they do not give an idea of size. Children never get an idea of how huge an elephant is from pictures; when they see an elephant in a circus they are always much astonished. Pictures of large things and of small things are likely to be all the same size. *Second,* pictures do not give adequate ideas of setting. A picture of a pig seldom gives any idea of the pen and the barnyard. A picture of a tractor does not give much idea of the tractor pulling a plow across an immense field. Large pictures help, and we should get away from the postage stamp kind of picture to pictures of generous size.

Movies and *slides* are intended to give greater reality than the printed small pictures, and they do have this effect. The larger the screen, the more realistic the slide or movie. Color also helps a great deal, since real life is in color. Movies are more realistic than still pictures, but when the object itself is still, such as a building or a landscape, the slide is better than the movie. The movie may show some leaves waving or other incidental motion, but the slide can be clearer and more vivid. Most important, however, the teacher can have a set of slides of her own from which she can pick desired pictures and use them just when she needs them. The movie fits into classroom procedure in a different way. Typically, we have to use movies when we can get them and we have to make the class work conform to the opportunity. That can be done but does not fit the needs of daily reading. Instead, the teacher should have a file of slides that illustrate the word meanings of her reading books, and she should draw on that supply at any minute that the reading requires her to do so. With cheap 2x2 slides and handy projectors, there is no reason why every room should not have "slides for the reading lessons," always ready. When the reader is changed, there would need to be an addition only of a few subjects, since most readers in the primary grades have about the same subject matter.

3. EXPERIENCE ACTIVITIES

The third way we can develop word meanings in children is through *experience activities*. When actions are described in the readers, we can often have the children do the same things themselves, preferably before the reading. If the children in the reader "build with blocks," our own children can build and discover the problem of balancing one block on another. If the children in the book give a show, let our children give a show, and thus get new word meanings. If the book describes a hobby, let our children participate in it. This "meaning through activity" has often been neglected in favor of "meaning through seeing," but it should not be. There is much *social* meaning and *muscular* meaning and *artistic* meaning that comes only through doing. For instance, if in the reader one child is "host" to his friends, how can one really learn what "host" means except by being a host? Similarly, one must learn the meaning of "guest" by being a guest. Teachers sometimes have one room invite another to a party just to learn the meaning of such terms. Some teachers have the children entertain their mothers at a party in order to understand about "entertain" and "planning" and "refreshments" and so on. Many of the concepts and word meanings of the primary grades are based upon activity and if the children have not taken part in such activity, now is the time to see that they do. We must note that in this case, the variations in experience in the class will be very great. Some children have done so much and others so little. We therefore have to plan so that the children who need the activity get it. For instance, we should put on the entertainment committee not our experienced entertainers only but also our inexperienced ones as well.

Going Beyond the Reading Books

As has already been evident, we have been thinking of a program of "giving meaning through experience" that goes far beyond the immediate demands of the vocabulary of the readers. That vocabulary is a good beginning, but we surely do not want to stop there. We are concerned primarily with child development and not merely with teaching reading or with reading a certain set of readers.

Good teachers have always felt this. If the book demanded that the children know what *barn* and *feed trough* meant, the teachers have taken the children to a farm and seen that they learned a hundred new words about farm animals and farm scenery and farm life. They learned about *milking* but they also learned about cream separators because the separator was there and the children wanted to know what it was. The children in the reader gave a little show and pretended their pets were tigers and lions. So the children in the room gave a show and went far beyond *lion* and *tiger* and the other things told about in the story. They learned about such things as *acts* and *juggling* and *clowns* and *freaks* and *sideshow* and *menagerie* and dozens of other things that come with shows. If child development is our aim, we use the needs of the reading just as a beginning. We go just as far in giving new experience and new meanings as the children will go gladly with us.

For this reason, many schools do not base their experience building program on the reading matter only. Many schools look about them to see what the children *can* learn and what the children *need* to learn, and then go about providing the experiences that will enable them to learn all that is possible. This means in fact an "experience curriculum," and our curriculum should always be basically an experience curriculum. Each school should study its own children, their needs and their deficiencies, and build its own program for them to *go out* to see the world, for them to have the world *brought to them*, and for them to *take part in* all the *activities* that make up full living for their age.

Three common dangers appear in this planning, however. *One* is that we will think only of the ideal child for our community and thus not think enough of the lacks of the actual child we have. Those lacks need to be made good first, after which we should branch out into building our ideal. *Second,* we tend to list experiences that are desirable and then go to books to read about them rather than actually to have those experiences. We should read about the topics in our experience curriculum, but books do not take the place of the experiences themselves.

Third, we tend to think of groups as experiencing, whereas all experience is individual. When we take the children to see the dairy, we must manage so that everyone in the whole group sees every part of the dairy. When we have the class entertain the mothers, we must see to it that every single child serves his mother or some mother, and not let a committee do the serving and the others just stand and watch. If the class is to give a play, each and every child must have a chance to say a line across the footlights, and not just a selected few. We may, of course, give a play for other purposes, but we mean here a play for the experience of being in a play. That means everyone must be in it. This can usually be managed by having the same play given by different casts.

Building Meaning Vocabulary in Middle and Upper Grades

We have discussed all phases of "Building Meaning Vocabulary From Experience" in connection with the primary grades because we wanted the discussion to be concrete and specific. Therefore all the illustrations and situations were taken from the primary period. We shall now apply to the Middle and Upper grades the same principles to building meaning vocabulary from experience.

THE NEED IS GREATER THAN IN PRIMARY GRADES

Naturally the need for building meaning vocabulary appears in the middle and upper grade period with even greater urgency. During grades IV through VIII, the reading material goes farther and farther from the original center, the Home, which guided first grade reading. The content of the reading goes away from this center geographically, taking in the state, the nation, and the world. It goes away from its original center in terms of age interests, going from child interests to adolescent interests and to adult interests.

Perhaps this progression goes much faster than it should; one may ask why it is necessary to put into the elementary school years all the adult concerns of government, commerce, vocation, and the like. The answer is of course a historical one. In the days when very few went beyond the eighth grade, the curriculum makers tried to make the first eight years a complete education. Now nearly everyone goes through high school, or at least goes to school ten years instead of eight. But somehow the old material that used to be felt necessary for the middle and upper grades is still there. So we must try to make it as meaningful as possible.

That the basic readers go into wider and farther fields is just one of the great problems of the middle and upper grades. A still greater problem is that in these grades we have the so-called ''content'' subjects, geography, history, science, health, and so on. These subjects all use books. In these books the children meet words they already have in their hearing-meaning vocabulary, and they meet an enormous number of words they have never heard of. This is especially true of the deprived group of children that we have discussed on page 276. In our middle and upper grades are great numbers of children who have not traveled at all, who have not listened to radio, who have not gone to movies. For these children the added "content," year by year, forms an almost impossible barrier to growth. The reading matter very soon leaves the area of their direct experience or the areas in which they have seen pictures and then it keeps on going farther and farther into the unknown.

For instance, in reading for the middle grades, the children in the books often take a transcontinental trip. This trip begins in a railroad station that a child may never have seen, and goes into a train on which he has never been. From the windows he is supposed to see things he has never seen or perhaps even heard of. For another instance, a science book takes the children on a trip in a woods. Many of the children have never seen anything but pavement or grass or a little barren park. In the undergrowth the characters in the story find mosses and ferns, and the burrows of little animals. All this is utterly strange to the child of the pavements. Instances could be multiplied without end of the almost impossible situation of children trying to understand in reading words that are infinitely far away from the hearing-meaning vocabulary that is based upon their own experience.

Principles and Methods to Be Used

Obviously, in the middle and upper grades also, the three methods of building experience must be used, *first,* taking the children out to see the world, *second,* bringing in the world to them, and *third,* giving them experience building activities.

1. TAKING THE CHILDREN OUT TO SEE THE WORLD

Trips and *visits* are not nearly as common in the middle and upper grades as one would expect. In fact, there is a tendency to take the little children places rather than to take the older ones. No doubt there is a feeling that the older children can go on their own account, but it should be perfectly obvious that they will not do so unless the school plans the trips and visits. The psychological principle that explains this is that "what you do not know does not attract you." It is only having *some* knowledge that makes you want to have *more.* Thus the older child is surrounded with unknown areas that he makes no effort to enter into just because these areas simply do not exist for him. Ignorance does not attract; it is only knowledge that causes a desire for more knowledge.

The second difficulty is that perhaps teachers feel the older children are too much trouble to take places. They tend to be uncontrollable just because they are older and are more used to doing things on their own. This fact only emphasizes, of course, the need for the social training which trips give. The difficulty of management should certainly not prevent us from taking children to see things they should see. One way of avoiding the difficulty of taking a whole room is to allow groups or committees to go and see things under the care and guidance of some cooperative parent. Many schools like this plan because by it the school is not responsible, it is not necessary to take unwilling students along, and there is some expanding of experience for many children. However, usually by this method the children who most need the trips fail to get trips. No such plan will release the school from its responsibility to see that *all* children have direct experience with as much of their environment as possible. In short, the school is woefully lacking in effort to expand the experience of middle and upper grade children through trips and visits.

As has already been emphasized, *all seeing of new things must include the naming of those new things* so that the children will have the words to tell about experiences and to think about them more effectively. Experience without accompanying language is bound to have little educational value because such experience is not likely to be used. No one can very well talk about an experience if he does not know what to call it or what words to use in describing it.

Words classify the new experience with old experience, since new things seen are called by old names. The name of the "cream separator" on a farm associates with its source the cream that has heretofore been seen only in a bottle, and it associates the idea of separating cream from the milk with all other kinds of separating known in the past.

Interestingly enough, new experience often gives meaning to old words which had little meaning before. The children may have heard that bulls "bellow," but they may hear such a bellow on a visit to a farm and now have some real meaning for the word. The children may have heard that nuts grow on trees, but when they first see a tree with nuts on it, they now have real meaning about the source of nuts.

It is also true that experiences often give the children labels for experience they have had but for which they had no names. Children may have seen farm machinery as they drove past along the road, but they did not know what to call it. On a visit to the farm they may get *plow, mower, binder, combine,* and other words to fit to the experiences they have had in the past.

2. BRINGING THE WORLD INTO THE SCHOOL

Pictures as a means of bringing the world into school should be especially pushed during the middle and upper grades just because there is such a need for them in all the expanding subject matter. The textbooks fail to supply this need because pictures take space in the textbook, and the author wants to put in words instead. Here is one of the chief troubles with teaching word meanings in the middle and upper grades. The authors and publishers do not seem to take seriously the need for experience of some kind to explain and give meaning to the vocabularies of the books.

Two steps should certainly be taken. First, the textbooks should control the burden of strangeness. One science reader for middle grades, for instance, had on one page the names of 22 small animals found in the woods. That is an impossible learning task for the child.[2] Vocabulary control is common in the primary grades. We also need concept control or vocabulary control in the middle and upper grades. We cannot believe that putting more before a child causes him to learn more. The chances are that he learns less. Therefore, we should know for each "content" book of the middle and upper grades, what its burden of uncommon words is, and what provision it makes for teaching each of those uncommon words. If this were insisted upon, very many of the books offered for the middle and upper grades would be seen to be obviously poor if not impossible teaching instruments. What is the burden of new word meaning, and how is it to be taught?

Second, we must insist upon more picturization in all the books for these grades. We need in the books *more* pictures, *larger* pictures, *better* pictures.

---

[2] See Fact Burden, Chapter XXII in Problems in Reading (Garrard Press, Champaign, Ill.), which tells of a tabulation of facts in textbooks and the discovery that a textbook may contain 10,000 facts or more.

This trend is seen in the science books now being issued for middle grades, but it has not appeared very much in the field of geography or history. *Third,* we should also have some kind of picture supplement to these content books, perhaps special teacher folios of pictures or boxes of slides, or even reels of movies. Each book needs the pictures that will teach the meanings in the book. Any publisher who will boldly attack this question will do an immense service to education.

Fourth, we must have special attention paid to the problems involved in learning words from words, a problem which is taken up in a later section. Children of the middle and upper grades have more maturity than those in the primary grades, and they can use with some success the method of learning words from words that are not appropriate with primary children. Yet it is a fallacy for makers of textbooks to think that they have solved the "strange word" situation by adding a glossary of terms to the back of the book, or by giving advice to "use the dictionary." This problem is discussed fully in pages 308 to 321.

Visual Education and Word Meanings

Advocates of visual education insist that visual education includes everything seen by the child on blackboard or bulletin board, in textbook, exhibit, museum, and what not, but visual education for most schools has come to mean moving pictures. The

schools have an investment in projectors and pro-
jection rooms, in film libraries, and in memberships
in film loan associations. All of this should pay dividends in hearing-meaning vocabulary.

Everyone is convinced of the value of visual education, but in most schools the film can have little
to do with the day by day learning of word meanings
in the textbook. It is just impossible for most
schools to make the tie-up needed for this purpose.
To do so, the school would have to have its own stock
of films and show them concurrently with the daily
lessons in the books. This is seldom possible. Instead, the school orders films that parallel the text
in a rough manner, and then gets and uses them
when it can.

By the present system the film is nearly always
ahead of the lesson in the textbook or behind it. If
ahead, the teacher can sometimes shift her assignment and make the film illustrate the technical vocabulary of the book. If it is behind, the teacher has
done her best already to teach meanings, and she
must go back and reconnect the word symbols of the
past lesson with the new experience of the film. All
this is the best we can do with the film situation.
We must return to our previous suggestion, therefore, that a school-owned file of slides or film strips
will serve the purpose much better if we are thinking of developing our meaning vocabulary along
with the text.

From another point of view, of course, the showing of films may be independent of any textbook learning. Each film is a unit in itself, carrying its own vocabulary, teaching its own word meanings, and being worth while on that score. This is perhaps the only practical way of looking at the use of films. Let us then not count on the film as a "backup" of the text but consider it on its own. In that situation, we need to know just what the technical vocabulary of each film is and just how we should use the film to teach that vocabulary. For instance, should we not have a list of the words illustrated by the film so that we can show the class that list beforehand and at least have them get used to the sound of the words? After the first showing of the film, should we not bring out this list and check to see if all the children saw the thing the words referred to? If they did not, let us look for those things on the second showing that should always be made if much learning from the film is expected. We are merely urging a systematic use of the film for the teaching of meaning vocabulary, and not an incidental use only. Films properly used are a tremendous educational force. We should use them to the maximum.

PICTURES MUST BE TAUGHT

The psychology of "seeing" is that something outside the individual connects through the eye with past experience within the individual. This fact explains why everyone, child or adult, sees in a picture

what he is already familiar with. In a picture of
some people standing before an old Southern plan-
tation house, a gardener will note the kind and condition of the plants and vines, the house painter will
notice the condition of the paint, the architect will
notice the proportion of the pillars, the seamstress
will notice how the dresses of the women are made,
the photographer will notice the angle of lighting,
the furniture dealer will notice the construction of
the chairs, the psychologist will notice the serenity
or worry on the faces of the people, and so on and
on to illustrate the basic fact that people see what
they know.

People who have taken children to a picture show
will have a positive experience with that fact. While
the adults are absorbed, the children will become
restless and want to go home, just because they are
seeing very little in the picture. Or ask children
after a picture show to tell about the picture, and
you will find that very little was seen, and the very
little that was seen had to do with the experiences
these particular children had already had. Similarly,
we often wonder why some people who have traveled very widely have so little to tell of what they
had seen. The fact is, they saw very little; they saw
mainly what they knew already.

The question must therefore be asked, if we "see
what we know," how can we see something new in
pictures? There are two ways, one is by *accident,*
and the other is by having something new *called to*

our attention. Accidental seeing often occurs, as when we notice for the first time some characteristic of a friend's face even though we have looked at that face a thousand times before, such, for instance, as the wide distance between his eyebrows. Our eyes happened at some moment to focus on the space between his eyebrows, and the space was called to our attention by this accident. We often hear people say, ''You know, I have never noticed before how so-and-so,'' indicating that chance has brought something to their attention.

The other and more practical way is to have the new brought to our attention by someone else. A traveler, for instance, should have a guide who points things out he would never otherwise notice. In a museum, the labels point things out; for instance, we read the label beside a mummy and it calls attention to the cloth in which the mummy is wrapped, and we look at the cloth which we had not noticed before. In a picture show, parents try to point things out to children, often to the great annoyance of their neighbors. In the picture books at home, parents point things out to children. In school, the teacher must do the pointing out, unless the author has put under the picture a legend which does it for her. But no matter what the author does, the teacher should still ''teach'' the picture. If it is a geography picture, she needs to point out how the people dress, how the houses are built, what kind of vegetation is growing, what signs of business there

are, whether there are telephone wires, how the
street is paved, what kind of carts or automobiles
appear, and so on and on.

If the teacher teaches pictures wisely, she will try
to get the children to build the *habit of finding things
for themselves* rather than to wait for her to point
them out. Of course some children will notice things
others do not, and thus the children will, as it were,
exchange help in seeing new things. But aside from
this exchange of experience, it is possible to find
things in a picture if the students get the habit of
"exploration of a picture." They can carefully look
over a picture, foreground, middleground, and background. They can examine each article in the picture separately. They can carefully look for the familiar and for the different.

This *habit of exploration* of a picture, looking it
over part by part, is one of the great needs for
building meaning vocabulary. Each apparently familiar thing in the picture, for which one has already
a word, will soon be seen to be a little different, thus
giving a new meaning to the word. But the teacher
or someone will also have to supply new names for
many things found in the picture by exploration. The
children will want to know the name for that special
kind of cart, for that kind of dress or ornament, for
that new kind of tree, and so on.

In the case of movies, a class can be given a very
enlightening exercise in seeing by showing them the
same film a number of times with directions as to

what to look at each time. (1) The first time a movie is shown, it will be found that all will look at the principal actors. (2) Let it be shown again with the understanding that everyone is to watch the minor or supporting characters. These will be found very interesting and worth while. (3) Then let the movie be shown again and have everyone study settings only. These settings are usually works of great care and even of art, and are well worth seeing. But no one looks at them while characters are moving or speaking.

(4) Finally, let the movie be shown once again and now have everyone watch the camera work. How are the sets lighted? What angles of shots? How are close or distance shots used? How are the shots alternated or changed and how fast and why? How does the camera work add to the feeling or the meaning of the scenes? There are many more aspects of a movie, but these four will show a class clearly that on one showing they see very little, and that really seeing something takes time and attention and thought.

In short, wherever we have said anything about use of pictures, it is assumed that those pictures will need to be taught if the children are to get much new out of them. Otherwise they see what they know already. This explains in large part why the great time and money spent on visual education has not yielded as great results as were expected. The adult and the educated person sees so much in the movies that the school shows; the children see so little. Similarly, it is assumed that wherever we have pointed out the desirability of trips and other ways of "seeing the world" it will also be assumed that there is a guide who points out the new. Otherwise, much time and money can be spent with little effect. Even in the presence of the Grand Canyon of the Colorado, children and others still see just what they know and that is very little compared with what they might see if someone would only point it out to them.

3. Experience Activities in the Middle and Upper Grades

A great advantage that the middle and upper grades have over the primary grades in vocabulary building is in the much wider range of experience activities the children can engage in.

Social activities bulk large in these grades. All children should have the experience of taking part in social meetings of all kinds. These may be handled as extra curricular, but they are an important part of the curriculum just the same. Then there is a wide range of *expression* activities. These may be oral before the class or before another group, or they may be written expression experiences of all kinds—story, poetry, factual, or what not. All children need to express themselves in many ways not only to expand their abilities but to expand their appreciation of the expression of others. Only he who has made a speech can appreciate a good speech by another. *Artistic* activities should be provided for all, in music and in the graphic and plastic arts. All children should do and make many kinds of things. Included are the *manual* activities that imply use of tools and materials in shops and laboratories. The print shop alone has been found to teach the meaning of about a hundred special terms. *Managing* activities are possible in the running of the school store, of school shows, papers, and the like. The word *budget* should be learned early and its powerful influence in both family and business life appreciated. *Homemaking* activities for both girls and boys carry an immense vocabulary of daily value. Even a boy should understand what a *recipe* implies. *Political* activities are possible partly through imitation, as when a national election is carried out in school, but also in school politics. Here the girls have a chance to discover the meaning of *politics,* something not taught in books. Finally, *athletic* activities naturally carry a vocabulary that all should know in order to understand the daily newspaper and the daily news broadcast.

Here, again, we should insist that *every activity have its vocabulary* specifically listed beforehand, and that the activities be watched to see that they yield the meanings desired. Otherwise, the activity may be very time consuming, and without the benefit that is supposed to follow. Likewise, the big problem of getting meaning for all is our greatest one.

Far too often, we let children choose the activities that they already know about and avoid those they do not know about, thus nullifying at the start the possible learning from the program. The program of activities is to learn to do what you *cannot* do, not merely to do more of what you can do already.

New Meanings From Imagined Experience

REAL VS. IMAGINED EXPERIENCE

Having described the development of new word meanings that may come from real first-hand experience, we must admit that our efforts in that direction will always come far short of our desires. We shall never be able to take children out to see the world as we would wish. Sometimes a single parent may take his child all over the country, have him visit every kind of farming and industry, have him engage in every sort of sport and activity, let him start and manage a little business of his own, and in these and other ways give him a rather complete range of first hand experiences. We see this happen. Then we ask, what is the possibility that we may secure this well rounded life of first-hand activities for every child in the school? Such a goal seems far off indeed, but that does not mean we should stop trying. Every year every school should add something to its program of first-hand living experiences and should see that more children engage in each activity.

This limitation to first-hand experience has at all times thrown the chief emphasis in school on *imagined* experiences through hearing and reading. By hearing we formerly meant the reading to the children that is so common in the primary grades and that goes on to some extent in all grades. Many teachers are good readers of literature and can hold a class enthralled with their rendition of some fine story. There is reason for such "reading to the class" in all grades, since such reading insures that everyone of the listeners experiences the thing that the author intended. Nowadays, however, the school can also provide hearing experiences through radio. Every school should give the children the benefit of the fine recorded programs of all kinds, as well as of the special school broadcasts available.

Usually, however, by imagined experiences through reading we mean reading by the children to themselves, either in school or at home as a result of stimulation by the school. This is the kind of reading that librarians are thinking of when they argue for more books and more reading done by all. Imagination is also needed in reference reading for factual courses, but the reading that is dear to the heart of all lovers of reading is the reading of works by literary artists, famous or not, who recreate life as seen and felt by them and who make the reader re-live that life as he runs his eyes over the pages.

The Great Range of Imagined Experience Through Reading

Having previously said that first-hand experience was more vivid and meaningful than imagined experience, we must now point out that imagined experience has an infinitely wider range than first hand experience. For instance, one cannot physically visit every one of the many countries of the world, but one can visit all of them repeatedly through imagination. There are, in fact, library book lists which are arranged geographically and, by reading books from those lists, one can live in almost any part of the world he wants to, from Madagascar to the North Pole. One can even take trips in imagination to the moon or the planets.

In the field of human activities, the same is true. One cannot physically take part in every kind of sport, from stratosphere flight to hunting tigers in Bengal, but one can easily do this in fiction. One cannot physically be a surgeon and a cowboy, a sculptor and a marine, but in the imagination one can be all these and all the other occupations one can think of. There are vivid books that will put one into the life and feelings and experiences of men and women of all occupations. This is a very important fact, since in our human relations we must understand and cooperate with men and women of all kinds and all interests. How can we do this unless we feel something of their hopes and joys and frustrations? And how can we feel those things in our own flesh? We can do so only in imagination. In our own bodies, we can live but one life; in the imagination, we can live many lives.

In history, the situation is even more important. It is a fact that physically we cannot live except in our own time. We cannot go ahead a thousand years or back even a generation. But in the imagination of fiction we can live in any period. The historical novel and not the ordinary history book is, in fact, the thing that gets people fascinated with the study of history. The meanings of history, the ways of life and of government, the housing and clothing, the fighting and the struggle, all come through the imagination, since they cannot come any other way. It is true we can see some historical objects in museums, but museums give us little indeed compared to the living in the imagination that the reading of a fine historical book or historical novel makes possible.

Movies and Reading

Here we may note an interesting relation between the real experience of seeing a historical movie and the reading of historical fiction. Experience has shown that after a fine movie has been made of a certain period or of a famous book, people in much greater numbers read that book or read about that period. The movie was "real" in the sense of being visual, and the reading is imagining. But the fact seems to be that the movie gives the public something on which to build their imagining, and then they delight in the imagining of reading. For instance, if a movie of mediaeval times shows living conditions and clothing and weapons of the time, then the reading public seems to find much more interest in books of that period, surely because they now can imagine the stories much more successfully.

How Imagination Gives Meanings

Now it is time to inquire further into this process of getting new meanings through imagination. Clearly, imagination must work with the material of memory and is limited by it. The most striking instance perhaps is that people who have never seen or felt snow or ice just cannot imagine what snow and ice are like. They use their ideas of white powder and of glassy appearance and construct something they think is snow and ice, but it is not clear enough to be of much use. So there must be a background of first-hand experience upon which and with which imagination works.

With this material from memory, the imagination can do three things. It can, *first,* alter memory by changing in size or degree. It can make a hill into a mountain, or it can make a person into a pygmy. It can make cold colder or hot hotter. It can make fear more fearful or joy more joyful. These are all remembered experience made more or less. The *second thing* imagination does with memories is to combine them. It can take a man and a horse and make a centaur. It can add fear to something to which it has never yet been attached. It can make a new person in imagination by combining the qualities of many persons the reader has known, of course, perhaps increasing or decreasing each.

A *third* element which is somehow added to this construction from past experience is a "feeling of reality." This is a vague but very real thing. It makes the difference between the work of literary art and the mere hack piece. This "sense of reality" is what makes a classic a classic. As we read a classic again and again, it seems each time more real until we are more sure that it happened than things that we know really did happen. For instance, the imagined Hamlet, Prince of Denmark, is more real to most persons than Henry III of England who actually lived, and Oliver Twist is more real to those who have read his story than any poor boy they read about in the daily papers.

Part of this reality of what is imagined is, of course, to be credited to the imaginative powers of the reader. Many persons can imagine with great reality the characters and events in a contemporary novel that may leave most other persons cold. We can never be sure how much of this reality of what is imagined is due to the reader and how much to the writer, but we know this reality to be a fact of experience. If anyone doubts it, let him recall how he has awakened from a dream shivering with fright; and the dream was only imagining.

Imagining Demands Easy Reading

Finally, we must emphasize a fact which all teachers have seen for themselves. Children do not imagine people and scenes and events if the reading material is too hard or too strange for them. *First,* too hard reading material repels the reader because reading it is too hard work. The labor is so great that the reward is not worth it. *Second,* the child must have the past experience out of which he may easily build the new experiences. If the novel is in a strange country, such as England, and in a strange time, such as the seventeenth century, we cannot expect the American child of the twentieth century to have experiences out of which to make the new ones. Here we must point out that novels for school should have much more illustration than novels for adults rather than less. The strange thing is that in classics for schools, just where illustrations are needed most, they are most completely omitted.

Third, a novel has to be easy to compete with other kinds of recreation. Time was when a child had nothing to do but sit down with a book. Now he seems to have everything else to do—radio, movies, television, clubs, hobbies, tools, pets, and what not.

There is at present a strong movement to bring the fine tales of the past and even of recent times into the possibility of imagined experience for all children. Several publishers have easy-reading editions of the classics. Some have sets of easy-reading biographies. We are getting easy-reading science.

The schools are at last realizing both the importance of imagined experience, and the absolute necessity for making this experience easily accessible and enjoyable.

New Word Meanings From Words Only

It is a very common practice, both in school and out, to explain a new word to a child by giving him old words, that is, words he already knows. As we say, we just "explain" the new word meaning. Adults at home "explain" new words to children when they ask. Teachers in school "explain" new words. The glossary in the back of the book explains new words by using old words. And the dictionary itself uses this means chiefly, though at times it does use pictures to explain some things which seem difficult to explain with words only.

The Fallacy of "Knowing Already"

We must recognize that adults and expert readers place too much dependence upon "explaining" or trying to give new word meanings by words only. We are always inclined to believe that we can give "new meanings from words only" because *we ourselves "know already"* the meanings we are trying to give.

The dictionary is very wise in this regard. If one will examine the dictionary, he will find that flowers and animals and machines are nearly always pictured. The dictionary discovered long ago that mere words cannot tell what a flower or plant is. Try to tell what a *geranium* is. Only one who "knows already" what a geranium is will get any real meaning from your words. The physical world about us is largely incapable of being imagined through words alone. So the dictionary does not rely on description of that world. It uses pictures, as indeed it should.

But the average adult tries again and again to tell children with words what things are, just because the adult "already knows." The child asks, "What is a snake?" The adult says, "An animal that crawls along the ground." The child imagines such an animal and asks, "But his legs will be in the way." The adult says, "Oh, he hasn't any legs." So the child takes off the legs and sees a legless body lying there. "But how does he crawl around without legs?" "He wiggles," says the adult. The child tries to make the legless body wiggle. "How does that get him to go forward?" The adult loses his temper. The peculiar way in which part of the snake pushes the other part cannot be described. It has to be seen. Let us go to the zoo.

Five Ways of Giving Word Meanings With Words Only

In trying to see how we can use words to give meaning to words, we can distinguish five different methods. These are not sharply separated from one

another but discussing the five separately will help
us in thinking about the problem.

I. The Synonym Method—Giving an Old Word for a New One

One of the most used ways of explaining to a child
what a new word means is to give him as a synonym,
an old word which he already knows. Cases taken at
random from a dictionary for schools are: a *cabin* is
a *hut; relinquish* means to *give up; lugubrious*
means *mournful;* to *singe* is *to burn; debris* means
rubbish; and so on indefinitely. An adult who is
helping a child with reading does this constantly.
Glossaries in the back of textbooks use the method
very often. And teachers in class are much inclined
in the hurry of daily work to give synonyms in this
way.

Of course the reader will at once object that the
cases we have cited do not constitute true synonyms.
Synonyms are words that mean almost the same. At
least the meanings of the two words should be so
much the same that they can be reversed, and either
one used for the other. For example, *somber* and
gloomy may usually be interchanged; *somber* means
gloomy and *gloomy* means *somber*. Now we have
not said that the cases we gave were synonyms, but
only that the dictionary gave them as if they were
synonyms. For the first word, the second word was
given. The child would assume that the new word
meant the same as the old word, since he was given

the old to take the place of the new. The child was really given "word substitutes," but he would consider them to be synonyms.

Of course synonyms or word substitutes are useful in reading. Instead of being stopped by unknown words, the reader substitutes known words. Instead of "The hound dashed across the avenue," the child substitutes known words and gets the meaning, "The dog ran across the street." If he had not been told these "synonyms," he could have no meaning at all. Now he can read the passage in terms of what he knew before. This method of "using old word meanings" is the "method of synonyms," that is, words that are presented as interchangeable. The pocket dictionaries that are sold in quantity at the ten cent store give an old word for a new word, and thus permit reading with old word meanings. They are of value for that purpose.

Synonyms Give No New Meaning. A moment's thought will show that when we or the dictionary gives a mere synonym or word substitute for an unknown word, *no new meaning results.* The child comes to the word "chow" and asks what it means. We say, "A chow is a dog." So the child puts the meaning for *"dog"* in the place of the word *"chow"* and goes on reading. He has no new meaning for the word *dog,* and to him *chow* just means *dog.* So he has two words for the meaning of *dog* where he had just one before. This is the case with all synonyms if given alone without explanation.

They give a new word for an old meaning. How can there be *new* meaning when we just say "This means the same as that." The meaning stays the same.

II. The Classification Method—Giving the Class or Group or Area in Which the New Word Meaning Belongs

As has already been noted, many words given as synonyms either by teacher or by dictionary, are instead *classifications* or *groups* to which the new word meaning belongs or *areas* in which it is found. We usually indicate this fact by saying that a hound is a *kind of dog,* that an avenue is a *kind of street,* that singeing is a *kind of burning,* and so on.

Unless we emphasize that we are giving a classification, and *not a real synonym,* the child will not only make the association the way we give it to him, such as "a hound is a dog," but he will tend to reverse the association and say, "a dog is a hound." This is natural, since we are always inclined to believe that if A equals B, then B equals A. It is true that "all hounds are dogs," but not that "all dogs are hounds." Similarly, *dashing* is a kind of *running,* but not all running is dashing. An *avenue* is a *street,* but not all streets are avenues.

The quick learning child is not so easily misled about the difference between synonyms and classification. He has discovered that as he meets new words, he keeps meeting divisions of the kinds of things he knows already. When he meets a new word for *house,* he suspects that this is a new kind of house, or a new name for a kind he already knows about. He is aware that *house* is the general word that covers many kinds. But for safety's sake, we had better emphasize with most children the words "kind of" when we are explaining. We might add "There are other kinds." For instance, when we say a *chow* is a "kind of dog," we might say, "There are other kinds such as a spitz, a cocker and so on." When we classify, let us make the fact clear to the child.

III. THE METHOD OF POINTING OUT DIFFERENCES— GIVING A "NEAR-SYNONYM" OR CLASSIFICATION AND POINTING OUT DIFFERENCES BETWEEN OLD AND NEW

As already mentioned, for practical purposes at times, and surely when we are in a hurry, we will use the previously described methods of giving a synonym or word substitute or of giving the group or class to which the new word meaning belongs. If we do so, we will realize that we are not being accurate and that we are not building new meaning as we should.

The really accurate way of teaching a new meaning with old words is to give an old word as a synonym or classification and then go on to *point out the difference* between the new meaning and the old. Typical cases found in a dictionary are: a *mustang* is a wild, prairie *horse;* a *cove* is a sheltered small *bay;* a *stool* is a *chair* with no back; to *bellow* is to *roar* like a bull; to *limp* is to *walk* lamely. In each case a synonym or classification is given and then differences are pointed out.

Space does not permit us to discuss all the ways in which an old meaning as represented by a synonym or classification may be modified to give new meaning, nor is such a discussion necessary for teachers. What we need to get over to children is that some words are *"wider" in meaning* than others; that is, include more meaning or a greater number of experiences or things. In the definitions given above, the wider words are *horse, bay, chair, roar,* and *walk.* The words defined are *narrower or more special in meaning* than the wider words. They are more narrow or special in definite ways. These ways are the *differences we want to point out.*

In our present discussion, we are of course dealing with the differences between *genus* and *species,* as the scientist would say. We are urging the pointing out of *differentia.* But such technical language would not help the children; hence our attempt to express the basic facts in terms children would understand.

IV. The Method of Pointing Out Similarities

We have emphasized that children early learn meanings for large groups of things, animals, actions, and the like. They get the general meanings of *toy, bird, talk, want,* and so on, since these wide, general terms are in common use in our familiar language. Then they gradually notice special kinds of toys, special kinds of birds, special kinds of talking, special ways of wanting. The new words for these special meanings are explained by giving them the general old word meaning and then showing the differences between the old and the new.

We now must add that, as children grow, they likewise learn *new general meanings* or classifications of familiar meanings. They know that sparrows are *birds* and they know what ducks and chickens are like, but they must learn that ducks and chickens are *birds* also. They know *whispering* but think it is different from *talking;* they learn later that whispering is considered just one kind of talking or both are kinds of communication. They know crying, ill-temper and fighting, and they are later told these are all kinds of the same thing called *aggression* or *resentment.* They know engines and washing machines and lawnmowers and so on, but have to learn that all these are called *machines* because they are all alike in a certain way.

In this method of giving new word meanings there may not be the telling of a new word, but only the combining of old experiences under an old word, thus giving that old word new meaning. Or there may be the teaching of a new word which is given meaning by gathering under it old meanings, since the new word is a "wide word" which includes the meanings of old words. In either case, the process is the pointing out of similarities or likenesses between old experiences.

V. The Method of Many Associations

The methods of giving meaning with words which we have discussed (1) Synonym or word substitute, (2) Classification, (3) Pointing out of Differences, and (4) Pointing out of similarities, have all been minimum methods. They have been the sort of methods used by a dictionary which wishes to do the job in the least possible space and with the least possible words. But such minimum methods should not be our limit or our ideal.

After all, the method of the school should be more the encyclopædic method. In using words to focus old experience on a new word meaning, we should use all facilities possible. *We should connect the new meaning with all the old experience with which it can possibly be connected.* The encyclopædia gives pages to word meanings to which the dictionary devotes five to ten lines. But the encyclopædia is not the ideal. It also is limited for space. Instead, one can write a book or a series of books on most worthwhile new meanings. Take the meaning, *government.* There are libraries on that word meaning.

The school is of course also somewhat limited for time. We cannot tell children everything about everything. We have libraries to aid us, and we do send the children to encyclopædias and books. But after all, the children have a whole life in which to learn, and they cannot learn everything at once. Thus we begin with our minimal methods cited above of classification, differentiation, and so on. But from this minimum we go on as far as we can with *the method of many associations*. Anything we can tell a child about a word, anything he can read about it, any association with it whatever, all add to its meaning. All through life the ''method of many associations'' adds to breadth and depth of our word meanings.

Do the Words Used in Defining Really Have Meaning?

It is assumed of course, in all this discussion of giving word meaning with words only, that the words we use really do have meaning for the child. This is a precaution not always taken by the givers of definitions and explanations. Very often we use unknown words to give meaning to known words. An attempt always to use words of already known meaning is all a dictionary can make, of course, because it cannot know the individual child who is reading the definitions. The teacher who is explaining can be much more certain that she is using known words to explain unknown words.

Merely Verbal Meanings

Is This New Meaning Real or Merely Verbal?

Here we must ask whether the new meaning secured from "adding up" old words is a real meaning or is just a word formula. We have seen how in reading with imagination the reader perceives combinations of familiar words and gets as a result of a creative process a real new mental image and a new meaning. Is this adding up of words in a definition a real creative process or is it a mere mechanical one, giving us just a verbal result?

To illustrate what we mean by merely verbal meanings versus imagined meanings, let us take a common case. Let us take the beginning of the Gettysburg Address, with which everyone is familiar.

"Four score and seven years ago our forefathers . . ." Here the word *forefathers* may be explained simply by a synonym as our *ancestors*. It might then have a merely verbal meaning. If, however, we use creative imagination, we will think of the men of the revolutionary day as actually being our very own great, great grandfathers. Their blood actually flows in our veins. We are here because they lived and worked, married, and had children whom they cared for and protected. They are actually our "fathers who went before," our fathers in blood and in tradition and in culture. We know how they lived in hard and strenuous times, without present day safety and comforts. They wore rough clothing, ate rough food, and lived in much discomfort and danger. But they are our forefathers, and we cherish their memory.

"brought forth on this continent"

Verbally speaking, that means just "made in this country." But "brought forth" is a figure of speech that means "gave birth to." Our forefathers actually thought up in their minds and spirits the idea of this country. They gave birth to this idea. And they did it "on this continent." "Continent" means all America. But creatively thought of, here "continent" means a land separate from Europe, far from home and friends, stretching from the icy Arctic to the tropics.

We might go on with the rest of the famous Gettysburg Address. If the meaning is conceived verbally only, it is not very impressive. If the meaning is by imagination conceived realistically, in terms of the lives and peoples referred to, the meaning is thrilling indeed.

Our conclusion must be that merely verbal meanings as far as they go, are very useful in reading. Without them, our reading would be stopped. But we can also say that if we stop at merely verbal meanings, we will not have much meaning. The man who wrote "The blood of peasants isn't red a thousand miles away" meant that we read in the paper of massacres and killings in other lands and go right on eating our breakfasts. Massacre has a merely verbal meaning to us. But if massacre really had

the meaning of butchery of the helpless, soldiers
sticking bayonets into women and children or smash-
ing skulls with their clubs or feet, we could not go
on eating our breakfasts so easily. Similarly, the
man who said "none would go hungry if we all ate
at one table" meant that we read easily about people dying of starvation just because we have merely
verbal meanings for starvation. If starvation has a
real meaning for us, we would be so upset that we
could not enjoy our own full tables.

Some persons believe that mere verbal meanings
have a special place in some fields, such, for instance,
as geometry. The student can have a perfectly good
verbal meaning for *parallel* without knowing very
many cases of parallel lines and without seeing
parallel lines all about him in the house, on the
street, and so on. The student can have a useful
verbal meaning of *line* without wondering about all
the lines he sees in the world about him, as at the
corner of the house or along a telephone wire, and
so on. Of course if he has real meaning for *line*, he
would know that none of the things he sees are lines.
They are all surfaces. By definition, a line has
length but no width, and everything he calls a line
has width or he would not see it. We might go on
to many more instances. Shall we conclude that verbal meanings in geometry are enough? Surely they
are useful, but not enough.

Perhaps our conclusion must be that in practice
many of the words we use or read have merely ver-

bal meaning. They have little or no concrete reality behind them. They have no emotional tone. A little consideration will show, however, that real experts in any field have far more than mere verbal meanings for their words. They do have concrete reality behind the words. They do have feelings of importance or attraction or repulsion about those words. It is only the beginner or the novice who has the superficial verbal meaning only.

So the goal in any field is to go beyond mere verbal meaning. If we do not do so, it is the fault of our teaching or of our learning. We should have some meaning from concrete reality, experienced or imagined, for every term we use or see. Then the world we read about would be a real world. The people of our present century that we read or hear about would be real people to us, living, breathing, working, struggling, enjoying. Even the people of history, the long cavalcade of the past, as it has been called, would be real, breathing persons, and we would look back at their lives with wonder or with satisfaction, as the case might be. With this kind of real meaning for the words we read, *reading would be living*—as it should be.

Summary

Meaning of the words read is obviously a prerequisite for any meaningful reading of sentences or larger units.

Children now come to school with an enormous hearing-meaning vocabulary. Primary reading materials keep within that hearing-meaning vocabulary as far as possible, but try to make up for lack of it when such lack exists by giving experience background in three different ways. First, the school takes children out to see the world by trips to places of interest and importance. Every experience met with in such trips is given a label, that is, a word, so that the children can talk and think about the experience more effectively. Second, the school "brings the world in" by means of objects, pictures, slides and movies. Third, the school conducts experience activities that are social, muscular, artistic, etc.

Though experience background is given to aid in the reading of basic books, the experience program goes far beyond the needs of such books and tries to fulfill the needs of child-living as far as possible.

In the middle grades, the need for experience background is greater than in the primary grades because the middle grade subjects go far beyond the familiar environment of the school child. The middle grades try to give experience background in the same ways described for the primary grades. Trips are used to take the children out to see the world. Pictures are especially important in bringing the world into the school. Here the greater burden of new words in the middle grade books demands much more attention to illustration of texts, supplementary pictures, films, etc. Special attention must be given to teaching the pictures since little new is seen in pictures without guidance. Experience activities in middle and upper grades are especially important since the children's maturity permits all sorts of activities, social, expression, artistic, manual, managing, homemaking, political and athletic.

Granting this need for first-hand experience, the school must give much more emphasis to imagined experience as a basis for new word meanings. Imagined experience can cover the whole of the world, all of human occupations, and the whole of history. Imagination changes past experience, it combines past experience, and it gives a sense of reality to its creations.

New word meanings may be given by the use of words alone. Much use of words alone is ineffective because the teacher is deceived into thinking an explanation is adequate since she is subject to the fallacy of "knowing already" what she is trying to explain.

At least five ways of giving word meanings with words can be distinguished. They are:

    I. The Synonym method—giving an old word for a new one.

    II. The Classification method—giving the class or group or area in which the new word meaning belongs.

III. The Method of Pointing Out Differences—
Giving near-synonyms or classification and
pointing out differences between old and new.
IV. The Method of Pointing Out Similarities.
V. The Method of Many Associations.

The word meanings formed in these ways may be
merely verbal or may be given more real meaning
by use of the imagination. It should be our aim at
all times to go beyond the merely verbal so that
reading may become living as it should be.

CHAPTER X

Fluency at Some Useful Level

Fluency in reading involves something more than just sight vocabulary and word attack. Those two steps in reading development are necessary for fluency but fluency goes beyond them. The word *fluency* means "flowing." It means such immediate *recognition of words in patterns* that the thought of the reading matter is followed smoothly and without hesitation or distraction.

FLUENCY AT DIFFERENT LEVELS

Obviously, readers may possess fluency at different difficulty levels. Children may be fluent at second grade level of reading matter or fluent with sixth grade reading matter, and so on up to difficult adult material. This fact is referred to by Betts in his concept of Basic Reading Level. He points out that the difficulty level at which a child can read without hesitation or stumbling and with almost complete understanding can safely be called his *basic reading level*. It is the level at which he has fluency. At higher reading levels, he can be said to read with greater or less success and with greater or less difficulty but at those higher levels he does not have fluency in reading.

FLUENCY IN DIFFERENT FIELDS

In speaking of difficulty at different levels, we have been referring to "general" reading matter, usually fiction or factual material about things with which all persons are acquainted. There are also, however, many separate fields of interest in which a person may or may not be fluent. One may be fluent, for instance, in reading sports but not in reading science, or the other way around.

Having fluency in different fields involves two different things. *First,* there must be rapid recognition of the vocabulary of the special field. The doctor, for instance, immediately recognizes a large vocabulary that the rest of us would have to stumble over. The historian recognizes instantly a large vocabulary that is rather uncertain to the average person. So in every field, fluency requires first of all that the special vocabulary be immediately recognized.

Second, every field has more or less of a thought pattern of its own. This may be an *actual idiom,* as in the case of baseball with its "drew up at first," "inside corner," "grounded out to second," and so on. Many fields of activity have these special ways of putting words together. In addition, each special field has its *habitual associations of ideas* with which one may become acquainted. For instance, in history we have the phrases, "according to the constitution of the United States," and "by and with the consent of the Senate," and so on. In geography we have "coastal regions," "prevailing winds," "seasonal rainfall," and thousands of other customary

associations of ideas. Acquaintance with these habitual patterns of ideas enables a reader to be more
fluent in the particular field.

In content subjects, and especially in high school,
we wish the children to attain fluency in reading in
certain fields of knowledge. When some children become so interested that they begin to do independent
reading in a field, they actually achieve fluency in
the special subject. When they do, we can assume
there is a good chance that they will continue reading in that field after leaving school. Usually, however, all we can hope to secure for most children is
fluency in general reading matter, since only with
general reading matter do they get enough practice
to attain anything we might call fluency.

FLUENCY AT A USEFUL LEVEL

It is important that we realize that it is not enough
for children to attain fluency at some *school* reading
level. For instance, fluency at third grade level will
do a sixteen-year-old little good when he leaves
school. Practically no job that he could get would
have reading requirements as low as third grade
level. For school purposes, we may encourage and
build fluency at any level. For life purposes, we
need to ask ourselves what level actually needs to
be reached to be of some use in daily life.

The lowest reading level of use outside of school
is about sixth grade. At this level an individual can
read a good deal of the newspaper, especially the
advertisements and the news stories that are on the

front page. Sixth grade level will take care of the reading needs of most unskilled or semiskilled jobs. Therefore, in all our school work we should remember that we must aim at the sixth grade fluency if the boys and girls on leaving school will be able to take some useful place in society. And we must aim at *fluency* at sixth grade level, not just puzzling out at that level. If the individual has fluency, he will read; if he can only puzzle, the chances are that reading will be too hard, and he will not read. In consequence, he may lose much of the reading knowledge he has.

Since sixth grade fluency is a useful level, we should not be too unhappy if many of the children do not get beyond this. If they get no further, that is to be deplored, but the situation is not too bad. We have actually given them a useful level of reading skill. However, we should realize that if we do *not* get our children up to sixth grade fluency, we have badly failed them. We have taken years of their school life in trying to make them readers, and we have not made them readers for practical life use. So we should study all our children who are approaching leaving age and ask ourselves if they have *fluency* at sixth grade reading level. If not, we should do something about it quickly and decidedly before it is too late.

Is sixth grade level of fluency useful for success in high school? It may very well be just because the child who can read fluently at sixth grade level can usually puzzle out reading matter several grades higher up. In addition, it is possible to so advise high school students as to cause them to avoid courses which demand much reading or which demand reading at too high a level. Even though the courses taken still require some difficult reading, the work can be done if there is sufficient willingness and time and native intelligence.

For high school, eighth grade fluency is much more useful, and is about all that the great majority of high school students have. The difference between eighth grade and sixth grade fluency is in instant recognition of a much more literary vocabulary and the acquaintance with language patterns common to more literary material. The material of the seventh and eighth grade is full of such literary vocabulary and "long ago" patterns. If the student becomes at ease with such material, there is little that will hinder him in the quantity reading of high school.

What about college? Here we must know what course a student elects, and what the required reading courses are. If there will be much English literature, a fluency beyond the eighth grade is usually required for success, but students with a basic reading level of eighth grade sometimes get by. For required history and science, there must be a fluency in those fields built up through high school history and science. Just general reading ability is usually not enough to master a quantity of assigned reading in a special field.

We have not tried to give final answers to the problem of what are actually useful levels of fluency, but only to suggest what is involved. We need to know more about all these things as a result of research. Unfortunately, most of our present data is in terms of scores on tests. Getting answers on tests involves many skills aside from fluency in reading. A grade level on a standard test is not a fluency level because standard tests are usually done slowly and carefully. Therefore, we need more facts before we can decide what are ultimately useful levels of fluency in reading.

Speed of Reading

A great deal of what has been written on speed of reading is of little value because it does not specify the difficulty of the matter being read, and it does not tell us what thinking processes the reader was going through. Since reading, properly conceived, is thinking, then speed of reading means speed of thinking, and we must know what kind of thinking we are dealing with.

We do, however, have some figures on speed of reading which are meaningful. A number of investigators have conducted experiments (which any teacher can also duplicate) in speed of reading under conditions that are definite and clear. They have given children reading matter that they could easily read, that is, read without puzzling over words or ideas. That meant they were giving these readers material at their basic reading level (see page 325). They then told the individuals just to read, and that there would be no check on comprehension and no questions to answer. In addition, the material was story material of one kind or another, but definitely material in which the interest was in what was happening or going to happen. Therefore these investigators were measuring *speed of reading (1) easy story material (2) without any check on comprehension*. It was properly assumed that if the story had interest and if the reader had normal intelligence, comprehension of the usual story type would be inevitable.

We have put together figures from all these investigators and present below the results in round figures. These represent a curve of growth in speed of reading (1) of easy story material, (2) without check on comprehension.

TABLE IV

Speed of Reading: (1) Easy Story Material, (2) Without Check on Comprehension. Averages from Several Investigations, with Figures Rounded

Grade	Words per Minute
I	60
II	90
III	120
IV	150
V	180
VI	200
VII	220
VIII	240

This table indicates that, in this type of reading, the first reader starts at about one word per second. By the third grade he has progressed to two words per second. By the fifth grade the speed is three words per second, and by the eighth grade four words per second. But we must be sure to remember that these figures represent averages. In reading, the range of performance at any one grade level is very great and the average is more truly thought of as the point about midway between the extremes than as representing the whole group.

"Saving Up" in Reading

Since the usual speed of speaking of most persons is about two words per second, or 120 words per minute, it would be seen that we speak at about third grade reading speed. So at the third grade level, the speed of reading and the speed of speaking would be about the same. At higher grades, the speed of reading should be faster than the speed of speaking. But in first and second grade, the speed of reading is less than the speed of speaking. Because of this, a performance called "saving up" is carried on by good readers of the first two grades.

"Saving up" means reading the words at the slow rate of the beginning grades, but not saying them just as they are read. The child is told he should say the words he reads just as he would say them if he were talking. But he talks at 120 words a minute and reads at 60 words per minute. Therefore, the child pauses, says a few words, pauses, says a few more, and so on. During the pauses, he is "saving up" the words he reads and when he speaks he says them in phrases or other thought units. If he did not "save up," he would be saying words slowly, one at a time, and producing an unpleasant effect often called "word reading." By "saving up" and by the device of pausing between phrases, he sounds as if he were reading twice as fast as he really is.

Adults do a comparable thing. A skilled speaker may read a speech without many in the audience being aware that he is doing so. He glances down at the manuscript, sees a part of his material, looks up at the audience and slowly says it with emphasis, glances down and gets another section, looks up and continues his slow speaking progress. He is reading at a speed of perhaps four or five words a second, and speaking at two words a second. He reads, saves up, and speaks.

A technical term referring to this process is *eye-voice span;* that is, the space between where the eye is in reading and where the voice is in speaking. We see an illustration of the eye-voice span when someone reading aloud turns a page before he has said all of the last line. Sometimes we try to check the eye-voice span by quickly covering the page someone is reading and noting how much farther he can say the words after the point at which we covered the page. We would rather use the term "saving up," however, instead of eye-voice span because we are interested in the *process that goes on* between the use of the eye and the use of the voice.

How does the reader "keep" the words he has seen until he has a chance to say them? Let anyone try to process himself and try to tell how he does it. Certainly he does not say them to himself and then say them aloud, as has sometimes been suggested. To do that he would have to be doing both processes at once, since he goes on speaking without interruption. Rather, the eye takes in the words, and then as one looks up at the audience the words just seem to come to him. Obviously, meaning has a great deal to do with it, since one can have a wide eye-voice span on familiar material and not on strange material. In the case of a speaker reading his own paper, memory must function, since he wrote the material at some previous time and has read it over before. In any case, this problem is worth study as casting light on the reading process.

A device for increasing speed of reading is to try to read aloud to an audience and also to look at them as much as possible. In doing this one makes the effort to look down as little as possible so that he may hold the audience with his eye most of the time. Suppose one is speaking at 120 words a minute and wishes to look at the audience at least half the time. To do so, he would have to read the words twice as fast as he spoke them, or at 240 words a minute. Trying to do this has a strong effect on speed of reading.

Fluency and Eye Movements

Naturally, there is a very great connection between eye movements and fluency in reading. In terms of eye movements, reading is a steady, continuous forward jumping of the eyes, regular and rhythmical, without hesitation or backward movement. Fluent reading requires such eye movements. Anyone doing what he usually calls reading is using such eye movements. He is not struggling or puzzling out. He is "just reading."

Regular, rhythmical eye movements in fluent reading mean that comprehension is not a problem. The reader is confident. He is satisfied with what he is getting. He is not worrying about answering any questions. Words are being recognized instantly, ideas are being smoothly put together, thoughts are following one another without hitch. Please note that we are not saying just what per cent of comprehension of the material is going on. Whatever the degree of comprehension, it is satisfying the reader to the extent that he is not hesitating or questioning. He "reads right on."

Sometimes poor readers give a strange imitation of this fluent reading. They read ahead with rhythmical eye movements. They do not hesitate. They get to the end of a paragraph or section, say, "Well, that's all Greek to me," and go right on. These children have learned to put on a show or imitation of good reading. They go through the motions. But since comprehension is not there, the process cannot be called reading.

THE NATURE OF EYE MOVEMENTS

We have said that the eyes in reading "jump ahead." This is literally true and can be verified by anyone. Just ask a friend to read a book held up in front of him, and look over the top of the book at his eyes. You will easily be able to see the steady succession of jumps as the eyes move forward across the line. You may even be able to count them. The swing back to the beginning of the next line will show when a new line begins.

A moment's thought will show why the eyes have to jump ahead in reading and not move steadily. The eye is very much like a camera with the shutter removed. The light goes into the eye, through the lens which is in the front of it, and at the back of the eye hits the retina or nerve which you use in seeing. Since this light is reflected from objects, the picture of the object is "made," as it were, on the retina, just as it is printed on the film at the back of the camera. But suppose you move the camera while the shutter is open. All you get is a blur. With the eye, there is no shutter; the front is always open. So if you move your eye, there is also a blurred impression on the retina and you do not see anything. That is why the eye is made so that it jumps and stands still, jumps and stands still. You can see the necessity for this if you will look straight ahead of you and then suddenly shift your head to one side. You will find that you did not see anything clearly until the head was still again.

It is possible, of course, to follow a moving object with the eyes, but we do so by using the neck. We fixate the moving object and keep it fixed as we turn the head on the neck as a pivot. When looking at landscapes, we therefore use a combination of jumping the eyes and turning the head. But it is clear that we have to keep the eyes fixed steadily on anything for a fraction of a second at least if we are to "see" it.

WE READ WITH POINT VISION

In looking at a picture or a landscape, one can look from point to point and object to object, or one can see the picture or landscape as a whole. A photographer learns the trick of "field vision" as it may be called, which means seeing all that is in front of you or some large part of it, rather than looking from point to point. If you have never realized this difference, look across the room now and notice you can use either point vision or field vision. You can see the whole other half of the room as you keep the eyes focused on the center of it. What you are seeing is what a camera would get if pointed at the other half of the room. Or you can shift your gaze from object to object, seeing each more clearly. In driving a car, for instance, one may use either field or point vision. The driver may just look ahead and see the whole view more or less clearly. Or if he is passing a car, he may fix the eyes on the center line or on the fender of the approaching car. One way to avoid eye fatigue is to drive by field vision and not by point vision, but one must be prepared to shift from the one to the other.

Reading cannot be done, however, by this process we have called field vision. To test the matter out, pick up a book and start looking at the middle of the lines only. Keep the eyes firmly fixed on the middle of a line and try to find out what is on either side. You will discover that you can see where the line begins and ends but you cannot tell what the words are. If a proper name occurs often in the story, you can tell it when it is off to one side but you do so by its general shape and by the capital. It is hard to do this experiment at first because the eyes want to flit to right or left but you can soon learn to hold them in the middle. This inability to read to right or left even though you can see something is there, shows that to read we must fixate definite spots in the line and we can read just what is near that spot.

EACH EYE MOVEMENT IS A "LEAP INTO THE DARK"

Research has shown by actually photographing the eye movements of good readers that the good reader makes regular movements to the right as he reads. For instance if he makes five fixations to the line, these fixations are equally spaced across the line. That is, the line is actually divided into five almost equal parts, with a fixation point in the middle of each. If then we have a line with 45 letters or spaces in it, as is common with many books, this reader would be seeing nine letters or spaces at each fixation. He sees the first nine, the second nine, the third nine and so on. He would literally be seeing "parts of the line."

It is clear, therefore, that the good reader is not fixating words or phrases or parts of sentences. He is actually and literally fixating parts of the line. What do those parts include? We have seen that if there are five fixations and 45 letters or spaces to the line, each glimpse of the line might include nine letters. In some cases, those nine letters might be one word. In other cases they might be the last half of one word and the first half of the next. In other cases, they might be two or three little words or parts of little words. The reader is not fixating words or phrases. He is just fixating parts of lines. He sees whatever is in that part of the line and nothing else.

The way w|e have di|vided thi|s line il|lustrates.

Obviously, a good reader's regular movements to the right as he reads are all "jumps into the dark." He does not know what is coming for he has not seen it yet. He cannot see it until he moves his eyes, and after he has moved them, he takes in whatever he hits.

Do We Read by Words or Phrases or What?

The question whether we read by words or phrases or how, depends upon what we mean by "read." If we are thinking only of the eyes, certainly we do not read by words or phrases, just because the eyes cannot see what is coming and therefore have to take in whatever they hit. Each fixation usually includes one word and parts of others or just parts of several words. No such meaning of "read" makes much sense. So we certainly cannot identify eye movements directly with reading. If, however, we mean reading as thinking, then we surely read by words, phrases, and other thought units. That is, we *think* these units as we read, regardless of what the eyes are doing. We see parts of the line, but we think thought units. We do this because of the wonderful power of the mind to weld together scattered impressions and perceptions and to make logic and sense out of them. That is why good reading is so synonymous with mature intelligence. The process of putting together parts of the line certainly is an intelligent process.

Eye Movement Photographs

An eye movement photograph is just a piece of film on which is recorded by dark lines in stair step form the movements of the eyes across the page of reading matter. The diagram below gives a typical example of the stair step pattern of a good reader.

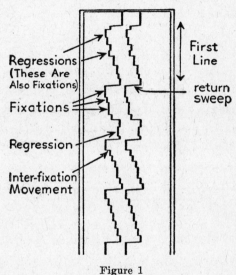

Figure 1

Diagram typical of the photographs of the eye movements of a good reader.

Diagram shows stairsteps formed by photographing the eyes while reading four lines. The "return sweep" is the return to the beginning of the next line. Vertical lines were made as the eyes stood still at a fixation point and the film moved up. Short horizontal lines were made when the eyes moved from one fixation to the next.

The dark lines represent the tracks made by two dots of light reflected from the eyeballs of the reader. As the eyeballs moved in reading, the spots of light were photographed to show the movement. The camera which is used has no shutter and therefore the film is continually exposed. As the film moved steadily upward in the camera, each eye, when it was still, made a vertical line on the film. When the eyes shifted to the next fixation, they made a short horizontal line. When the eyes returned to the beginning of the next line, they made a long horizontal line. So there are a series of stair steps, one for each line. The number of steps shows the number of fixations, the height of the steps shows the length of the fixation. All these dimensions have been carefully measured and the resulting figures published.[1]

Eye Movements and Speed of Reading

A better understanding of eye movements may be had if we correlate what we know about them with what we know about speed of reading. This is easily done from the figures already given. For instance, it has been pointed out that a first grader may read at the rate of 60 words per minute, or one word per second. How many eye movements does he have? Some studies suggest that he probably averages three fixations for each word. If he reads a word a second, this would mean a third of a second per fixation. But we must remember these are averages. A

---

[1] For a complete discussion of eye movements, see Buswell, How Adults Read, University of Chicago Press.

study of the actual photographs of a first grade child reading shows that for some words he needs only one fixation and with others he needs five or six. He may hold some fixations for a full second and hold others for a fifth of a second or less. In this highly variable performance, made so by the child's uncertainty about words and his general uncertainty about reading, we must beware of averages. They do not tell what the child does *all* the time; rather they are a mid-point between all his very different performances at different times.

The third grader may average a speed of 120 words a minute, or two words per second. He may get this speed by making one fixation per word, with half a second time for fixation, or he may have more fixations and stop less than a half second for each. But here again his real performance as seen on eye movement records is highly variable. Sometimes he spaces his fixations more widely, and sometimes he bunches them very close. As a result, he sometimes may take in two small words and at other times the distance between fixation points may be only a few letters. We must remember that when the fixation points are close, this does not necessarily mean that the child sees a less number of characters. He may see about the same number of characters each time, but he sees some parts of the words several times. That is, the fixation fields overlap.

As we get up to the better readers, those who read at about 300 words per minute, or five words per

second, we find much more regularity in eye movement performance. Such a reader may average two
words per fixation and two-fifths of a second per fixation. These round numbers would give a reading
speed of 300 words per minute. Again they are averages, but they are more truly representative than
the averages for poorer readers.

Regressions, or backward movements, have not
been emphasized, but they are important in comparing speed of reading and eye movement data. Poorer
readers make many regressions, and these do much
to slow down speed of reading, since they not only
put the eyes back in their progress across the line
but take time too. The chances are that the backward
looks may be necessary for comprehension. The better the reader, the less likely he is to make backward
movements. The very good reader makes them only
occasionally.

Do We Have Eye Movement Habits?

The phrase "eye movement habits" is often used,
just as though we had a habit of striding across the
page with our eyes in the way we do have of striding
down the street with our feet. This comparison between eye movements and walking is a good one and
can be used to make many things clear.

With regard to walking habits, we can say that,
other things being equal, we do have a habit of taking steps of a certain length as we walk. If we are

alone, if we are not in a hurry, if we are not tired, if we are not thinking about how we are walking, each one of us would probably take a certain number of steps to go a block of 300 feet. This means walking along the paved sidewalk. In that sense, we do have a habit of walking.

In the same sense, we probably have a habit of eye movements. Again we must say, "other things being equal." We must not be trying to hurry, we must not be disturbed, we must not be confused, we must not be thinking of our eye movements or our speed of reading. And we must be reading some easy interesting material, just as "smooth" in its way as the paved sidewalk upon which we would be walking.

Now we must ask, are "other things equal," in most of our reading? Are they equal, for instance, in the taking of reading tests? Most reading tests say "read as fast as you can but be sure not to make mistakes." If you give such a reading test to a large number of persons and ask them afterwards, "Were you going faster than usual or slower than usual or just the same as usual?" very few will say they were going just the same as usual. About half will say, "I hurried to make a good score." The other half will say, "I went more slowly to make a good score." Note that the directions told them both to go fast and to go slow. One advice "registered" with some persons taking the test, and the other advice "registered" with the others. But very few went "just the same as usual."

Do eye movement photographs give a record of "eye movement habits"? We can have no real answer to this until we have exhaustive studies of individual cases. We need figures for the reading done by these cases *without photographing,* under many conditions, and with many kinds of materials. For instance, we need to time their free fiction reading to get speed of easy story reading without check on comprehension. This is the kind of reading they usually do. What is the speed and therefore the probable fixations and time of fixation? Does this check with photographs while reading similar material taken over a long period of time so that the individual would get used to the photographing procedure?

Why Do Eye Movements Vary?

Why do speed of reading and kind of eye movements vary? Obviously, there are two sets of factors in speed of reading or speed of eye movements, one inside the reader and the other in the material read.

Differences in the emotional state of the reader are very important in producing variation in speed and in eye movements. The good reader is confident. He goes right ahead without hesitation or timidity. He jumps his eyes ahead, sure that he will recognize the words he will see and that he will make sense out of them. He is therefore likely to do his best, and gradually to stretch that best into something better. This confidence is of enormous importance in taking the "jumps into the dark," which eye movements really are.

The timid reader, on the contrary, expects trouble. He just "knows" he is going to hit words he will not recognize. He is afraid that even if he knows what the words *say*, he will not understand what they *mean*. He progresses like one of us feeling our way in the dark in a strange room, fearing any second to hit some furniture. Perhaps this timidity, this fearfulness, is the strongest element in hampering children in progressing in reading. It shows itself when we find a child with a high mental ability, with a good recognition vocabulary, but with very slow reading. The reason usually is that he really could move his eyes further and faster but that he is timid and fearful from some early unhappy experiences. Teachers who pounce upon mistakes and make children self-conscious about them are certainly producing this type of timid reader. We have to tell such children that mistakes don't matter. They should plunge right ahead and make mistakes and then correct them. If the mistakes are ridiculous, we will laugh with them and not at them. But we don't want timid reading.

Differences in purpose cause many of the other variations in speed of eye movements and of reading. (1) In the free type of fiction reading we have discussed under fluency, with no check on comprehension, the reader's purpose is to get the story and not the details. He keeps going steadily ahead and gets all he wants in doing so. If he does not get all the details, he does not care. But there are two other possible purposes. (2) One purpose is to get only certain information and to ignore everything else. (3) Another purpose is to get everything that is read, that is, to understand everything and to remember everything. Both of these special purposes cause special types of eye movements. They will be discussed further in Chapter XI where our concern is with comprehension.

Differences in reading material are very great, and produce very great differences in eye movements. To return to our comparison with walking, it is obvious that we cannot walk in the same way over all kinds of ground. Our strides change when we meet sand or soft ground; they must change if we wade through underbrush, and we cannot keep our stride when we have to climb fences. The difficulties with reading matter are comparable. There are all degrees of hard words, hard ideas, and hard sentences. Attacking some words may well be compared to climbing a fence. We shall have more to say about this problem in Chapter XI when we deal with the difficulties in reading material.

Should We Push Eye Movements?

There has been much interest in pushing eye movements of readers with the purpose of "improving reading." Pushing has been done by use of films, by flash exposures, by lowering a cover over the material, and just by having the reader hurry as much as he can. There is a wide literature on these devices and their results.

Let us repeat our definition of reading. "Reading is imagining, thinking, and feeling about ideas and thoughts made from past experiences suggested by perception of reading matter." That is to say, reading is done in the mind. The eyes are tools of the mind. If we push the eyes, what happens in the mind that is reading?

Unfortunately, none of the experiments on the pushing of eye movements tell us much that is helpful about the reading process that went on during the experiment. The most that we know about the reading is that the subject could repeat a certain portion of what was read or could answer certain questions on what was read. In every case, the amount repeated was a small percentage of all the ideas or thoughts that should have been suggested. Variations in this small percentage cannot be taken very seriously because they do not tell anything about the much larger percentage of "imagining, thinking, and feeling" that should have gone on during the reading. When questions are asked, in every case, the questions suggested ideas for the subject to recall. Recall made with the aid of such questions is little measure of the total process that went on during the reading. In fact, if we omit the questions, we get hardly any recall at all. Such *suggested recall of a small percentage of the material* tells us little of the total process that should have developed in the reader's mind. In short, the experiments tell us much about eye movements and little about reading.

A further difficulty is that all the values from pushing must be values through transfer of training. Any change must transfer from the pushing situation to the normal reading situation. Does it so transfer? Likewise, it must transfer from the pushing materials to the other materials used by the individuals. Does it? It is claimed that the pushing situation is very "similar" to the normal situation. The problem in the pushing situation has always been to be able to repeat something of what was read. School does have some such "lesson getting" situations. But modern education is trying to get away from this repeating of the book and instead to get fuller understanding, criticism, thinking, and application to life. Should we go back to repeating the book, even though we may develop such repeating to a high efficiency?

There is a sense of course in which pushing is a good thing. If we use a *natural* kind of pushing, we can hope for results that will be genuine and widespread. The only natural kind of pushing is self-pushing in normal reading situations. Then there is no problem of transfer, since we are pushing right

where we want the pushing to take effect. We shall
see in the next section how much pushing can take
place.

What Can the School Do to Improve
Eye Movements?

As we have seen, good eye movements and speed
of reading depend ultimately on instant recognition
of the words that appear in the reading matter.
Therefore, anything the school can do to improve
instant recognition will immediately improve speed
of eye movements. There are a number of possibilities:

1. The common service words can be speeded up
by all sorts of means which have been explained in
the chapter on sight vocabulary. As the service
words comprise more than half of all reading matter, speed on the service words will transfer to that
reading matter. We have told how games can increase speed. Another device [2] is to use a sheet called
the Basic Sight Word Test which contains on one
page 110 of the common service words in random order. It has been found that a student can time himself in reading this set of common words and then
practice reading them as rapidly as he can until he
can read the sheet much faster. A record of increased speed can be kept and is the incentive for
the practice. Then the other side of the sheet, which
has the other 110 common service words, can also be

---

[2] The Basic Sight Word Test, Garrard Press, Champaign, Ill.

tested and then practiced on. This speeding of the common words is a simple "stunt" that children can understand and in which they can see progress.

2. Phrase recognition can also be practiced by use of a game.[3] Phrases made up from the common nouns and the basic sight words are printed on small cards. The combinations are adjective-noun, noun-verb, auxiliary-verb, verb-adverb, preposition-object, and conjunction-pronoun-verb. These word combinations were first made in complete meaningful sentences, and the sentences were then broken up into the parts or "phrases" that are naturally used in reading for thought. Naturally, the term "phrase" here means word combination rather than the mere grammatical meaning of phrase. These 140 "phrase cards" can be played with in many ways, especially to form sentences of many kinds. It is found that as the phrases are in this way used as units, the child who is frequently looking at them gradually tends to perceive them as units rather than as combinations of separate words. He is thus not only perceiving more than a word at a glance; he is also becoming used to perceiving language patterns that he will constantly meet with in reading. In this way, his smooth eye movements are facilitated.

Transfer from use of the sight phrase cards is possible in several ways. If the perception of the separate words is speeded up, that faster perception

---

[3] The Sight Phrase Cards, Garrard Press, Champaign, Ill.

will transfer because these words appear in all reading matter. If the perception of these particular phrases is speeded up, the speeding will also transfer through meeting with the very same phrases in reading. Finally, the greatest transfer may be through the confidence built up through handling the phrases as units and from the skill in phrase combinations learned by using them in sentence building. Reading thought units is closely related to combining thought units in sentence making. In any or all of these three ways, practice with phrase units that are both made of common words and are also common themselves will increase speed in reading and make for better eye movements.

3. *Much, easy, interesting reading,* is also a formula for the improvement of speed of reading and of eye movements. We must have *interesting reading* or the child will not read. Interest also causes him to push himself little by little to try to finish the story and find out what happens. Action stories, especially detective and mystery stories, are valuable for keeping the child on his toes and for keeping him naturally pushing his speed of reading. Without this pushing, there may be no improvement in speed or eye movements. After all, one may walk a thousand miles without becoming a faster walker. One becomes a faster walker only when he is anxious to get where he is going.

The reading must be easy or the child cannot speed up on it and maintain regular, rhythmic eye movements. Every unknown word stops the reading process and the eye movements, at least momentarily. The hard reading we give children in school is definitely calculated to make them slow readers. It stops them with hard words, it stumps them with strange terms. In fact, the reading speed of many high school students goes down from the freshman to the senior year, due to the continual hard reading we require of them.

Since children are at such a variety of different reading levels in every grade of the school, we must provide for each grade some materials that will be easy for all the children. Tests show that every room has children reading at from one to three grades below the one in which they are sitting. Those children cannot do *easy rapid reading* unless we have in the room books as much as three grades lower in reading difficulty than the average of the room. Publishers are just beginning to accept the challenge of this situation and are putting out books at mature levels of interest but at low levels of reading difficulty. The teacher should write to the publishers and ask for their latest offerings of this kind. But without material at his basic reading level, no child can possibly improve his speed or his eye movements.

There must be *much* easy reading or there will be little change in the child. Here we have a clear case of conflicting habits. Easy reading says "go fast." Hard reading says "go slow." Which is to prevail?

Obviously, *the thing the child does most is the thing he will learn to do*. If slow reading is required most of the time, he will be a slow reader. If he does fast reading most of the time, he will become faster. We often forget that the good reader in school is reading outside school more than he is in school. And the outside reading is easy for him; he picks it that way. So he is in fact doing more easy reading than hard reading. But what about the poor reader? He does not read outside school. In school, everything may be hard. Naturally he remains a slower reader instead of becoming a faster one. Whatever a child does most, he learns to do.

The Rapid Reading Period

The only solution for the slow reading problem in school seems to be a rapid reading period every day in which we apply the principle of "Everyone reading on his own interest at his own level." Tests show that every room has in it five grades or more of reading ability. This means a wide range of books for the rapid reading period. The *range must be in interest as well as difficulty* because we must remember that we need the drive of interest to do the pushing in speed. And this rapid reading period must be scheduled every day.

Some schools try to secure rapid reading with a "library period" once a week. Does anyone ever acquire a skill by practicing once a week? "Once a week" will not make a golfer, a bowler, a bridge player, a singer, a piano player, or a reader. Of course it might be assumed that the library period once a week starts the child off on home reading the rest of the week. This is true for the child who likes to read. But the child who objects to reading is the one we are concerned with. The period once a week does not get him to read every day outside of school the rest of the week. So for the child who needs it, the once-a-week library period is a failure unless it helps him to get books to be read the rest of the week in the *rapid reading period in his own room.*

Pushing Machines

Does the school have a place for "pushing machines"? Experience shows that children like to play with these machines. Some of them like the challenge of keeping ahead of the machine. Anybody using the machine even once or twice gets a new idea of speed of reading. In fact, some people find that they have been "loafing" too much in reading and that they can brace up and go somewhat faster with just as much profit and pleasure. This results, of course, from their giving greater attention and concentration. Some children are willing to give this attention and some are not.

If a school can easily afford the cost of a machine, without taking the money out of the book supply funds, a pushing machine is useful in the hands of a good teacher of reading. She will not try to force everybody to work with it. She will not expect the same interest in the machine from all. She will expose the children to it, as it were, and take advantage of any values the children find in it. All persons do not react the same to any idea or device. The pushing machine may help some cases a great deal. But the benefit from trying out a pushing machine is not in the actual short period of practice with the machine. No short period of practice can do much for any skill. Rather, a short period of practice will give the child ideas about speed and develop in him interest and drives that may lead him to do the natural speeding up that will be beneficial. *Only natural speeding up will continue for a long enough time in a real reading situation to give much permanent benefit.* And speeding up the slow reader is a necessary requirement for "fluency at some useful level."

Summary

Fluency means the recognition of "words in patterns" with such ease that rapid getting of the thought is possible.

Children may be fluent readers at different levels and with different kinds of subject matter. But the lowest level of fluency that will benefit a child in out-of-school work is fluency at about the sixth grade level. High school work may sometimes be done with about sixth grade fluency, but not the work of college.

Speeds of reading of easy story material without check on comprehension range from one word per second at first grade to four words per second in eighth grade. The smooth oral rendering of material by a slow reader requires the process called "saving up," as does also the oral rendering by a speaker who is really reading from a paper before him while he appears to be looking most of the time at his audience.

Normally, smooth reading means smooth eye movements. Good eye movements are regular, rhythmical jumps ahead by the eyes. In reading we use point vision or the focusing on points along the line. The good reader takes regular "leaps into the dark," as it were, since he never knows what words lie ahead until he has focused on them. For this reason, we cannot be said to see phrases, since we are bound to see parts of the line which may include any combination of words or parts of words. Eye-movement photographs show this fact. The first grader may fixate an average of three times on each word and the good reader only five times per line. The more fluent the reading, the fewer the fixations and the shorter the fixations, as well as fewer backward movements.

Eye movement habits are like walking habits. If there are no disturbing factors, we may have a habitual length of step and speed of taking steps, but usually there are disturbing factors. Similarly with eye movements, we may have habitual fixating movements, but they are subject to change. Eye movement photographs probably do not represent those habitual movements because of the unnatural photographing situation.

Eye movements and speed of reading vary with the emotional state of the reader and with his purpose. They vary with differences in reading materials.

We know little about the results or the value of pushing eye movements chiefly because the experiments tell us little of what kind of reading process was going on during the pushing. Pushing may benefit the reader only if the results transfer to normal reading, and the pushing situation is hardly that of normal reading done in school.

The school can improve eye movements (1) by speeding up recognition of common words, (2) by speeding up recognition of phrases, and (3) by providing much easy interesting reading. A rapid reading period when each reads *on his interest at his own level* is a necessity for this speeding up.

CHAPTER XI

Reading and Study

We are all familiar with the distinction between "just reading" and other special kinds of reading. "Just reading" is what we ordinarily do when we read. The other kinds of reading are the concern of this chapter.

What We Get From "Ordinary Reading"

Up to this point we have been thinking of "ordinary reading," or what is sometimes called recreatory or recreational reading. It is the reading done for any pleasure or benefit resulting from the reading, without any special urge to get any particular information or any particular amount of information. In "ordinary reading" the eyes jump rhythmically across the page, stopping at regular intervals, taking in whatever part of the line is seen and getting enough comprehension to satisfy or please the reader. In other terms, it is reading at the "basic reading level" of the individual, that difficulty level at which there are no problems of word recognition and very little problem of meaning or comprehension.

This "ordinary reading" is the type most people will do most of the time, and some people will do all of the time. It is the kind of reading that educates

most individuals after school days are over. Even
if the individual goes to college, "school days"
mean a total of only sixteen years. But normal life
expectancy has risen to over sixty years. Therefore,
if one leaves college at the age of 22, he has a "reading expectancy" of perhaps 40 years, or more
than twice the school period. During all of that
time, "ordinary reading" will be the dominant if
not nearly the only type of reading done. It is for
this reason that developing skill in "ordinary reading" is so important, along with a permanent interest in doing this kind of "reading for fun." The
school may educate for a limited time, "ordinary
reading" will educate for the rest of life. The tragedy is that so many individuals leave the school
period without having any interest whatever in doing any more reading, or without fluency at any useful level so that they might do this type of "ordinary reading" if they wished to.

WHAT IS STUDY?

The many kinds of study have one thing in common. They are methods of using reading matter
that we use when we are not satisfied with just ordinary reading. For instance, teachers are not satisfied that children should "just read" their textbooks. They do not want the children to "just read"
the encyclopædia. The teachers would say that the
children do not get enough or get what they should
from "just reading." They should study, instead.

We shall now discuss the various types of study, thinking of them as ways of "getting more from reading."

"Speeding Up" or Getting More Per Hour

By "getting more from reading" we may mean getting more for the time put in, that is, *getting more per hour*. We may have only half an hour to devote to a book. In that half hour we want to get all we can from the book. How can we use that half hour to best advantage? The same applies to getting lessons in school. If a student has an hour and a half to get five lessons, his time is limited. He has so much to "cover"? How can he get the most in this strictly limited time?

Before we go further into methods, let us point out that this situation of having only a limited time to "cover" a great deal of material is often not a genuine or sincere one. The student who really wants to get his lessons can usually find more time to devote to them. Instead what a student often does, unfortunately, is to do everything else but study and then declare that he has just a half hour or an hour left to study. Similarly, if we say we have only a half hour to devote to a book, we really mean that we intend to spend only a half hour on the book. If we wanted to spend more we would find a way of doing so. So we must realize that much of the alleged pressure to cover a lot of reading in little time is not truly genuine, even though we do know that such pressure exists at times. For instance, we do know that reviewing before an examination is a pressure situation. In adult life, the work of an attorney in preparing for a trial may be a high pressure reading situation. Editors often find themselves in high-pressure reading situations. For those situations, we should certainly have a technique to "get more per hour." We shall describe three such techniques.

1. SKIMMING FOR GENERAL IMPRESSION

We have defined "ordinary reading" as jumping the eyes smoothly across the line and getting enough to satisfy the reader. Now the reader who wants to "get more in less time" is reading under different conditions. In the first place, he is going to be satisfied with less per page if he can get more per hour. The reason is that he does not need all the ideas he gets during ordinary reading. He wants only a survey, an overview, a general impression.

In the second place, for this "getting more in less time," or more rapid reading, we must assume that the material is not too strange to the reader. If it were strange, he could not go faster or he would get no ideas at all. But if it is familiar, he already has so many ideas in his head on the particular subject that they quickly respond to the reading matter. We must assume familiarity of ideas if there is to be much speeding up.

These two conditions, familiar ideas and willingness to take less than complete understanding, permit a kind of "reading" that is rather well termed "skimming for general impression." Remember our definition, that "reading is imagining, thinking and feeling about ideas and thoughts made from past experience suggested by perception of reading matter." How is "skimming" different? Two things may happen, or both of them, that make definite differences. First, the time of eye fixations may shorten until they are very rapid: therefore, what is perceived may make very slight suggestions to the mind. We know from laboratory experiments in speed of flashing words and phrases that very short glances often give vague or incorrect ideas. If the skimmer is giving extremely short glances to the parts of the line, vague and perhaps incorrect ideas may be suggested to the mind.

Second, when a person is skimming, the eyes may take such long jumps that parts of the line are missed and therefore are never seen by the eyes at all. Anyone who takes but two or three looks at an ordinary line of type cannot possibly get all of it onto the active receiving section of the retina. He sees parts and misses parts. Sometimes a skimmer will let his eyes drift across and down the page at the same time. As a result, the successive fixations may be on different lines. But the skimmer gets "some idea" of what he has covered. He is reminded of some things he knew. He has perhaps "a general impression."

Granting that the skimmer does get a "general impression" of what he has covered, *how can that impression be defined?* From experience we find it may be explained in at least three ways. *First,* the skimmer comes away with some impression of *what the material "is about."* From the total of ideas passed over, some did register with him. He therefore knows in what field those ideas were, and he may have an idea of how well that field was covered. Here we see an implication of our earlier statement that skimming could only be done with material that was somewhat familiar. *Second,* the skimmer may come away with a judgment as to *how valuable or important the material.* As we have said, some of the ideas registered with him, and he was giving an evaluation of those ideas. He therefore arrives at some evaluation of the whole. This is of course only a tentative evaluation, but it is a useful one if the skimmer has to decide whether he is to take the time to read the material entire.

Third, the skimmer may come away with some conception of the *organization of the whole.* As said above, some ideas did register, and the skimmer was getting a sense of the sequence of those ideas. He was taking, as it were, a sampling of the article or chapter. He estimates the organization of the sampling and thus decides that the sampling of the whole must be largely the same, as it really is. *Fi-*

nally, of course, some skimming is to refresh the memory of an earlier reading. In that case, the few ideas seen help to recall those not seen, and thus refresh the memory of the whole.

It should be pointed out that we have no real evidence of what people get from skimming. Various experiments have been made with reading that is speeded up to the point where it is skimming, but these experiments do not give us any idea of what comprehension goes on. *First,* all such experiments give questions for the reader to answer, usually the multiple choice type in which the right answer is in full view and merely has to be distinguished from wrong answers. It would be an entirely different story if we just said, ''You have 'read' this material at this fast rate. Now tell us what you have read.'' Trials of this kind have yielded very vague, very sketchy and often incorrect ideas as a result of skimming. *Second,* no experiments on skimming have given us the *per cent of comprehension* that results. It is perfectly possible to count the ideas in a reading selection. It is perfectly possible to have a reader tell what he got and so to count the ideas he reproduces. A measure of the efficiency of the reading would be the per cent of reproduction.

2. Skimming With a Clue in Mind

In skimming for a general impression, more or less attention is being paid to every part of the material covered. The mind is alert to perceive everything that can be perceived as the eyes go across the page or down it. But there is a quite different kind of skimming that may well be called *skimming with a clue in mind.* In this kind of skimming, the mind is ignoring everything except certain ideas that it is holding up before it. It is not alert to everything. It is alert only to certain very special material.

The commonest kind of skimming with a clue in mind is skimming *to find the answer to a question.* The question is held in mind all the time. The eyes rapidly cross the page or slide down it, waiting, as it were, until they light upon something related to that question. Usually the clue that will catch the attention will be a word or certain related words. For instance, if the question is, "What did the early hunters or trappers eat when in the woods?" the reader will rapidly skim over descriptions of the early hunters and trappers, looking for the words "eat" or "meals" or the like. When one of these words is met with, it will seem to "pop" into consciousness, and the skimmer will stop and begin to read.

A very interesting variation is when one skims for *anything related to a certain subject.* This is a very vague clue, but with the expert skimmer it serves the purpose. In the case of the early trappers and their meals, the eye might catch anything related to *food* or *cooking utensils* or *fires* or *hunger* or anything even remotely related to meals and eating.

This skill is widely used by research workers who must gather material on a topic from many sources.

One thing we do not know is whether all children can actually learn this skill in "skimming with a clue in mind." We may tell them how to do it, and say, for example, "Just run your eyes down this page and when you find the word 'taxes,' read what it says." They run their eyes down the page and cannot find the word "taxes." We glance at the page and point right to the word. How do we find it? Why don't they find it? Perhaps there might be a process of training. First, students may find it easy to locate dates on a page. Perhaps then they could find proper names. Perhaps later they could find words familiar to them. Finally, they might come to the high point in the skill when the skimmer is thinking of certain words related to his question or topic and his eye catches entirely different words but ones with related meaning. This skill in "skimming with a clue in mind" is so valuable as a time-saver that it should be given more study.

3. READING ONLY THE IMPORTANT PARTS

Granting that "skimming for general impression" has its uses, and that "skimming with a clue in mind" is most valuable when the reader knows what he is looking for, there is still another skill that is of paramount value in "getting more in less time." That is the skill in *"reading only the impor-*

tant parts" of a book or chapter or article. This skill has sometimes been called a kind of skimming, but that word does not seem appropriate to it. Skimming suggests rapid and hurried reading; but reading only the important parts is deliberate and planned. It is straightforward, thoughtful reading, but not a reading of everything.

Anyone who has himself done much writing knows that not all the sentences he writes are of equal importance. Not all his paragraphs are equally important. The writer has usually a basic or central point that he wants to explain or "put over." To explain or support that central point, he has a series of important thoughts or ideas. Then to support each one of that series of important thoughts or ideas, he writes maybe dozens of other sentences, explaining, enlarging, illustrating, restating, and so on and on.

The uninitiated reader may see an article as twelve pages of printed matter, all parts of it looking alike. He may believe that all he can do with the article is to read it from beginning to end. Very many children and even students in college have this idea. If you say to such a student, "I wish you would look at this article," he says, "Oh, I haven't time to read it." And you say, "I didn't ask you to read it. I said just to look at it." And he has no idea what you mean. Similarly so many people say they haven't time to read books; so they never look at a book. They still think that all one can do with

a book is start with the first word and continue until the last word.

Every writer knows that the *beginning or ending*
is the most prominent part of any article or chapter.
Therefore, he puts his main ideas either at the beginning or the end of the section of writing. Consequently, the skilled reader knows that if his time is
limited, it is wisest to read the first page and the
last page, rather than to try to skim through the
whole section. This is the first device of the one who
wants to "get more in less time."

In the case of a book, the preface is the first thing
to read, as the writer may have put his main idea
there. The table of contents should be studied to
discover the scope of the book. The number of pages
shown for various chapters will tell what the book
emphasizes. Then it is wise to look over the first
chapter and the last chapter. Book reviewers are
perhaps the group who are compelled more than any
others to get the main ideas from books in very short
time. They know the value of reading the preface
and the table of contents and of looking at the first
and the last chapters.

To get the train of thought of any writer, the
skilled reader knows all he needs to read is the *paragraph beginnings*. With some writers, this may
mean reading only the first sentence of each paragraph; with other writers, it may be necessary to
read the first two sentences, since the first sentence
is often used for transition from the preceding para-

graph. Most readers will be astonished the first time they try this method of "getting more in less time." They should take any chapter or article and go through it, reading only the first two sentences of each paragraph. They will be astonished that they usually have a smooth and connected sequence of the important ideas.

The better an article is written, the better this plan or method of reading works. Some poor writers "wander into" each topic and therefore the main point of the paragraph is somewhere around the middle. Then, if a subject is controversial, a writer may adopt the policy of leading up to his point. In that case, the point of the paragraph may be at the end. The reader who is looking only for the important parts to read will have to become skilled enough to size up both the writer and the subject and so determine how to get the gist of the paragraphs. But it is obvious that if one sentence somewhere tells what the whole paragraph is about, the fastest possible method is just to read that sentence.

Summaries and transitions are also important in "getting more in less time." With practice, one becomes skilled at locating places in a chapter or article, usually near the beginning or end, when the author summarizes what he is trying to say. One also learns to spot the usually short transition paragraphs where the author tells what he has tried to say up to that point and what he will try to say afterwards.

In short, skill at finding and *reading only the important parts* is the most valuable in any endeavor to *get more per hour* in reading. It is far more accurate than *skimming*. It is used where we cannot *locate the part to read* because we do not have any particular question to answer. But we must repeat the cautions we have already given about "getting more per hour." This kind of speeding up presumes, *first,* that we will be satisfied with less than we would get by other kinds of reading, and *second,* that the material is familiar enough to permit the speeding up.

More Adequate Reading or Getting More Per Page

Most readers who are not satisfied with "ordinary reading," which means moving the eyes steadily ahead and getting just enough to satisfy, wish to get more out of the material than they get by ordinary reading. They are not trying to lessen the time of reading. In fact, they know they will have to take more time. But they want to get more ideas, thoughts, feelings, than they get by just ordinary reading. They desire *more adequate* reading.

Fast Reading or Slow Reading?

Here we have the old question, Who gets more out of reading, the fast reader or the slow reader? Our *first* answer would be that if by fast reader you mean the person with the higher I. Q., then of course the higher I. Q. gets more than the lower I. Q. in practically any kind of reading. Unfortunately, many persons do not see this I. Q. factor. They see fast readers with high I. Q.'s getting more than slow readers with low I. Q.'s. They then urge the slow reader to read faster, as if that would put him on a par with the more gifted fast reader.

Our *second* answer to the question presupposes that we are talking about a fast reader and a slow reader with the same native ability. We must also suppose that the two are equally motivated; each to get *all he can*. Then, the fast reader covers more ground than the slow reader. Suppose the fast reader reads a page in one minute; the slow reader reads it in two. Reading is a thought process. It is obvious then that the fast reader in one minute cannot think as much as the *equally capable* slower one can think in two minutes. Therefore the fast reader *cannot get as much per page* as the slow reader of *the same ability and motivation*.

But you will say that while the slow reader was covering one page, the fast reader was covering two. So we have to compare the fast reader's partial comprehension of two pages with the slow reader's more complete comprehension of one. Now there is no longer a comparison between two readers but between two kinds of reading. Is partial comprehension of two pages "better" than more complete comprehension of one page? Our answer will all depend on what we mean by "better." If a "survey" is all we want, then the fast reading is better. If complete understanding is what we want, then the slower reading is better. We are saying, "Which is better, getting more per hour or getting more per page?"

Teachers who assign reading should weigh carefully whether they want their students to work for more per hour or more per page. In the assignment the teacher should make it very clear what degree or kind of comprehension he expects. He can usually indicate this by telling what he wants the class to show as a result of their reading. What kind of questions will he ask? How full understanding will he expect them to show? What kind of a report are they to make? If an instructor is not skilful at explaining his wants to a class, they have to watch what he does for a week or two in order to find out. It were better if he knew exactly what kind of reading he expected and told them so.

More Adequate Reading in Terms of the Definition of Reading

In all our thinking of variations in the reading process, we should always refer back to our definition to see what it tells us. What does the definition of reading tell us about the problems of more adequate reading?

We have defined reading as *imagining, thinking and feeling about ideas and thoughts made from past experience suggested by perception of printed words.*" How can that process be made more satisfying or adequate? Obviously, it may be more adequate at any or all of three points. *First,* the *perception* process may, be more adequate. More adequate perception would give more meaning to the words perceived. *Second,* the process may be more adequate in *suggestion* of past experience. More and more appropriate past experiences may be suggested. *Third,* the process may be more adequate in the *imagining, thinking and feeling* done.

More adequate reading has a somewhat different meaning depending on the type of discourse one is reading, whether narration, description, explanation or argument. Narration and description deal with picturing of events. Explanation and argument may be based upon the picturing of events, or may deal only with the logic of ideas. In any case, these two processes go beyond narration and description into the world of abstractions. In considering more adequate reading, let us first consider the problems of narration and description.

Visualizing

The chief way in which we can "get more" than we do in ordinary reading of story material is to slow down to get the visual images the author intends us to get from description. We say "slow down" because drawing or painting a picture in the mind is somewhat comparable to making a picture on a canvas. If we are to put on the canvas a bush-bordered stream winding through meadows in the foreground, a hill to the right with a white house upon it, framed in tall elm trees, a view to the left up a small valley filled with apple orchards in bloom, with puffs of white cloud over all, each thing we put into the picture takes some time. It also takes some time to put each item into the mental picture. Did it not take time to draw the picture we gave you of the white farmhouse and its surroundings?

We do, it is true, get fleeting glimpses of pictures as we go steadily ahead in ordinary reading. Even at 300 words per minute, which means about two words per glance, with each glance lasting only about two-fifths of a second, we can get *some* visual images. It can easily be shown, however, that these are very poor pictures, vague and lacking in detail. All one has to do is to ask anyone who has been reading a story at the rate of 300 words per minute to describe the characters and the setting. Usually he will have very little to say. He may tell us "a girl met a tough character on a dark street and was rescued by a young man who stopped his car and jumped out just in time." If we say, tell what the three characters looked like, describe the street and car, etc., we get little or nothing. There was not enough visualizing to be described.

Part of the problem about lack of visualizing in reading is the present day use of *"incidental description."* Authors no longer stop and draw a word picture of a character as they did in many of the classics. Instead, they insert descriptive words while telling the story, expecting the reader to catch

the details as he goes on. In the case mentioned
above, the author might have inserted at one place
or another to give a picture of the street the adjectives "ill-paved," "crooked," "cavernous," and
the like. He might have added "scattered spots of
light from the few lamps," and "reflections from
puddles of water," and other items that should be
put into the picture. If these details are seen and
used, the picture will be built up. Unfortunately,
most untrained readers miss these touches of description altogether and so get no mental pictures,
or get only such as are supplied by their imaginations, not by the author. But we find that, if we are
to train readers to notice these touches of description, we must teach them to slow down and take time
to realize what the descriptive words mean and to
make a picture of them.

In school books also there is much description that
should be taken seriously. The historian who tells
about the landing at Jamestown intends the reader
to see the low wooded shores, the small landing
beach, the thickness of the forest all about. The scientist who tells how to determine specific gravity
wants the reader to see the vessel of water, the object hanging above it that is first weighed above the
water and then under the water. The geographer
who tells about life in Switzerland wants the reader
to see the narrow valley, with the steep slopes rising
high all about it, the small fields of green, the sturdy
low house with rocks on the roof to keep the shin-

gles from being blown away. All these things are
to be visualized, not skimmed over at 300 words per
minute. Painting mental pictures takes time; the
better they are painted, the more time they take.

We must realize of course that many writers use
mere word-ideas and readers often use mere word
ideas and are not aware that they should be doing
anything else. Many teachers have studied about
the countries and cities of the world and have a set
of adjectives for each. They think they know the
cities because the adjectives do have some meaning.
The teachers describe the cities and countries with
their sets of adjectives and the children hear and
remember them. Then when the child uses the right
adjectives, the teacher concludes the child knows the
right thing.

For instance, the teacher may read that Paris
is a very beautiful city, and the children may repeat that Paris is a beautiful city, and all conclude
that they know that Paris is a beautiful city. But
if you ask what Paris looks like, they have no idea.
They have not a single mental picture of Paris. Now
obviously really to *know* that Paris is a beautiful
city, you have to have some mental pictures of Paris
and those mental pictures must be beautiful. If the
teacher should read how Paris has miles of well-kept
stone houses of fine design standing close together
in a continuous row along wide boulevards that are
lined with trees, with many spacious open places and
parks, she might visualize Paris as a beautiful city.

If she conveyed something of this picture of Paris to her children, they could see it and see that it is beautiful. Instead, the word "beautiful" is tacked on to the word "Paris" and the result is called knowledge.

Pictures in the book are sometimes supposed to take the place of this visualizing from words. The comics do not describe anything. Everything is pictures, the people, the places, the action, and all. The picture magazines that are so popular give most of the space to pictures, with just a little reading matter beneath. We have encyclopædias that boast they give the world in pictures. There is a movement to put more and better pictures into textbooks in geography and history and science. We even have the visual education movement trying to supply us with slides and movies to illustrate everything to be learned about in school.

A moment's thought will, however, show that the pictures we give children are but a beginning. If we have in the book a beautiful picture of Columbus landing on the shore of the New World, we still have to imagine him getting from the ship to the shore, bargaining with the natives afterwards, getting back to the ship, sailing away, and so on. Even in science, if a picture gives us one illustration of a law we have to imagine all the other illustrations. In history, if we have a picture of what happened on one day in 1066, we still have to imagine what happened on all the other 364 days. So pictures are not a substitute for visualizing. They only give material *to be used* in the necessary visualizing. The more pictures we have, the better we can visualize, but we will still have to visualize most of life, both present, past and future.

If literary art is defined as giving us vicarious living, then the measure of literary art is how far it causes us to live the imagined experience, and that means to visualize the described experience and as a result to feel what the characters feel. We all know the reality of a good movie, and how we are right "in the picture" with the characters and how we live and feel with them. The good writer intended us to have the very same experience when we read his book. It is truly a "picture," and we are to see it just as we see the movie and live in and with it. When we see the movie we use the eyes of the body; with the literary work, we use the eye of the mind. Without visualizing, we do not experience literature. And if we do not experience it, it is not literature for us.

Visualizing and Meaning

Everyone is familiar with the principle that meaning comes from experience. We must add that it also comes from imagined experience. If all meaning had to come from actual first-hand experience, we would have few meanings indeed. Landsmen would know nothing of the sea, plainsmen nothing of the mountains. The poor could never understand the rich, nor the rich the poor. Men and women would be forever divided on many meanings. The young could not possibly understand the problems of the old until they themselves were old. People of different countries would be hopelessly divided in meanings. And no one could understand the meanings of ancient or mediæval times. If real experience alone gave meanings, each would live as it were on a little island by himself.

But imagined experience bridges the gulf between all the islands. We can read the work of the skilled author and become rich or poor, young or old, man or woman. We can live in imagination in any country or time. We can be of any class or profession or occupation. Obviously, imagined experience, though made up out of real experience in the last analysis, can go far beyond that experience and does go beyond it. It has been said that the truly educated man is a citizen of every country or time, and this is true through imagined experience, chiefly based on visualizing as he read. Visualizing puts the reader into a new place or condition, and the other elements of experience, such as thinking and feeling, follow.

Time to Visualize

We now return to the point stated earlier, that visualizing takes time. To show this more clearly, we quote below some well known passages. Let the

reader note that he can go through these passages
at 300 words a minute if he wishes. But he will not
get a very good picture if he does. We suggest that
the reader go through these as rapidly as he can or
as he usually reads. Then let him go back and read
slowly, putting every element of the picture in its
place. Then let him close the book and look at that
picture in his mind's eye. Let him test it for detail
and completeness. Does he have his characters accurately dressed? Does he have his scenes complete
with foreground, middle ground and background?
Has he visualized as well as he thought he did?

"The night had already fallen, and the moon was shin-
ing between the rifts of ragged, drifting clouds, before
Alleyne found himself in front of the forest inn. The
building was long and low, standing back a little from the
road, with two flambeaux blazing on either side of the
door as a welcome to the traveler. As Alleyne walked up
to it, he perceived that it was rudely fashioned out of
beams of wood, with twinkling lights all over where the
glow from within shone through the chinks. By the door
a horse stood tethered, the ruddy glow beating strongly
upon his brown head and patient eyes, while his body
stood back in the shadow."
(From The White Company, by A. Conan Doyle, Ginn & Co., Boston.)

"I turned my attention to the island we were approaching. It was low, and covered with thick vegetation, chiefly
of the inevitable palm tree. From one point a thin white
thread of vapour rose slantingly to an immense height, and
then frayed out like a down feather. We were now within
the embrace of a broad bay flanked on either hand by a
low promontory. The beach was of a dull grey sand, and
sloped steeply to a ridge perhaps sixty or seventy feet

above the sea-level, and irregularly set with trees and undergrowth. Halfway up was a square stone enclosure. Two thatched roofs peeped from within this enclosure.''

(From The Island of Dr. Moreau, by H. G. Wells, by permission of the executors.)

More Careful Reading

It is a matter of common experience for everyone that *when he wishes to get more* from reading, to get a more adequate comprehension, *he reads more carefully*. This is just one instance of the general human tendency to do with caution what is important. When we have important things to say, we speak more carefully and cautiously. When we have important things to do, we go about them with caution and care. So with reading. We read carefully any important directions. We read examinations with care. We read contracts with care. If any reading is important, it would be foolish not to give it careful attention.

Careful reading is used with narration and description as we have just seen in the care taken to visualize the scenes in stories and the people involved. But *careful reading is especially employed with explanation and argument*. With a story, we may skim over it and get the plot. But if we go too hastily over an explanation or argument there is danger we will get nothing. Explanation and argument is likely to be a closely knit chain of ideas, and if one link in the chain is missed, perhaps the whole will mean little. So care is much more necessary in reading explanation of ideas or discussion of ideas. Typically, school textbooks are explanation. That is why it is usually necessary to read textbooks with care.

More Careful Reading Is Usually Slower Reading

There is a general tendency, when we perform any act with more care, for us to perform it more slowly. Doing anything with care actually means paying more attention to how we do it and to the results we get. If we walk with more care, we usually walk more slowly. If we speak with more care, we tend to speak more slowly. Whatever we do with more care, we tend to do more slowly.

It is true that when we are under pressure we can pay much more attention to what we are doing and yet not do it more slowly. We may have a habit of doing any act, such as sewing, or painting, or washing dishes, or driving a car, and may be told to "be careful" for some reason or other. Immediately we may take much more care in what we are doing without apparently changing our habit of doing it. We all know, however, that we go on performing under a sort of tension. As a result, we soon become fatigued. After awhile, we find difficulty in going on with the normal habitual way of doing things.

It is much the same with reading. Our usual reading is a rather relaxed performance. We get enough to satisfy us. Suppose we want to get more and therefore read with more care, but try to continue our normal reading speed. We soon become fatigued. It is unnatural to read at the same speed but with more attention than normal. Soon we find ourselves either fatigued or slowing up in our reading rate to get relief.

More Careful, Slow Reading Gives More Meaning

If we slow up the reading process with added attention to it, we tend to get more meaning in three ways. The *first* way is that the words seem to have more meaning, individually and in their logical groupings. This indicates more meaning in the "perception of words," which is a part of our definition of meaning. We may perceive the words themselves as rapidly as ever but there seems to be between them a sort of "time to sink in," as it were. We know this in our giving directions to children; we speak slowly, with pauses between ideas, to give the child time to get our meaning. Orators and preachers know this fact, and they speak slowly when they wish their words to carry much weight. Business men read contracts slowly so that they will get their full force. Engineers read specifications slowly, to be sure to get the meaning. If we will try this out in reading, we find the same thing. To get the full meaning of the Gettysburg Address one must read it slowly, to give the meaning time to sink in. Certainly the time element seems to increase the meaning through the process of *fuller perception* of the meaning which the words carry.

In the *second* way, slower reading, with the greater attention it permits, increases meaning by giving more time for the "suggesting of past experience" which is part of our definition of reading. We all know that as we listen to a good speaker, many past experiences come into our minds which illustrate or modify what we hear him say. We think of our experiences "in between" the ideas expressed by the speaker. This is possible just because the speaker is going ahead at speaking speed, which is about 120 words a minute. We are thinking at least twice as fast. That is why we can "think in between." The same sort of thing occurs when we slow down in reading, while keeping our full attention on the material. As we take in the author's own ideas slowly, we have many ideas of our own too. So slow reading quite naturally provides for more meaning through more suggesting of past experience.

The *third* way in which more careful and slower reading increases meaning is through increasing "imagining, thinking and feeling" about the ideas and thoughts suggested. Imagining, thinking and feeling take time. In fact, the phrase "time to think" is common in our everyday speech. We can see the importance of "time to think" in reading if we realize that any time we devote to a book is inevitably divided between the author's ideas and our own. We must be thinking his ideas or our ideas. If we are reading very fast we must be spending most of the time with the author's ideas only. If we slow down, we get a chance to get in some ideas of our own. The slower we go, if we still concentrate on the subject, the more of our own ideas we can have in mind.

This emphasis on having time to imagine, think and feel about the ideas suggested by the reading matter brings up the possibility of mental digressions or "side trips." We all know that at times something we read sends us off on a tangent of thought. We may go away for minutes or longer on a train of thought that started with the reading matter. When we are doing this, are we still reading? Surely at some point we stop reading and are just thinking our own thoughts. How should we draw the line between thinking about what we read and "mental side trips," as we might call them? Perhaps one possible distinction might be that as long as we are looking at the page and continuing the succession of phrases and sentences, we are still reading, even though we are inserting our own ideas in between. Just as soon as we stop following the author, we have stopped reading and are just thinking. Of course it would be very hard to draw this line very definitely. There is no reason for doing so. It is much more profitable to include a great deal of this "suggested thinking" as reading, since it illumines the reading and gives greater understanding of it.

Reading as a Conversation

The emphasis on reading as a part of language has raised the question of whether reading is not in fact a conversation between the writer and the reader. If the reading matter were in fact read to an audience, we would find it has many characteristics of a conversation. The speaker (reading his address) actually looks at his audience and addresses them. He asks questions, pauses for the audience to think the answer, and then gives his own answer. If he thinks it is different from the answer his listeners gave, he explains why he thinks his answer is the better one. He makes statements and waits to see signs of the approval or disapproval of the listeners. He seems to hear objections from his audience, and he answers those objections. All in all, a good lecture is certainly a case of conversation or two-way communication between speaker and audience. If a lecture is not a good one, there is not this back and forth relationship, and the audience goes off to think its own thoughts about other things.

The situation we have described with a good speaker and audience is also true of a good writer and his audience. The writer speaks directly to certain persons he has in mind who will be reading his words. He anticipates their approval or disapproval, their questions and objections. He "feels" their reply, and their reaction. He seems to hear them "talking back." The good reader, likewise, actually does talk back to the writer. He may even do it aloud if he is interested and excited. Of course this is just a case of active "thinking and feeling" as we have already discussed. But the whole situation is illuminated and clarified if we think of reading as a two-way communication between writer and reader.

Are Thinking and Feeling Necessary to Reading?

Here we must admit that some schools of thought exclude thinking and feeling altogether from reading. They believe that reading is perceiving and accepting. They are usually of the authoritarian philosophy which demands that the newer generation accept the conclusions of the former generation. To them, reading is merely "knowing what is in the book." Unfortunately, there are still many schools which have this authoritarian point of view and many teachers in all schools which hold to it. Children under their charge grow up with the belief that learning and repeating what is in the book is reading.

Modern schools, which are concerned with developing personality and citizenship, do not, however, admit such a view. They insist upon "imagining, thinking and feeling" as part of reading. To encourage this thinking, they deliberately include, as text or library books, books which contradict one another. They encourage questioning in reading as well as elsewhere. They insist it is the duty of the intelligent man and the intelligent reader to know both sides to every question and to think about opposing arguments. Such is the democratic view toward thinking, discussion, and reading. And such a view calls for careful reading of worthwhile material.

Naturally some judgment must be used as to which books or what kind of reading matter deserves slow and careful reading. Long ago Sir Francis Bacon said, "Some books are to be tasted, some are to be chewed and digested." It would be folly to use methods of careful reading on every kind of reading matter. No such plan is suggested. Schools must therefore present to children and to older students many kinds of reading matter which deserve different kinds of treatment. Normally, recreational reading does not deserve slow and careful reading, but there are worthwhile novels which deserve time and thought. Factual material may be given slight attention if it is on unimportant matters, or if it is biased and obviously misinformed. But when we find factual material that is well done, and on matters of importance, surely we should take time to "think and feel" about the ideas suggested. This discrimination both in the field of fiction and of fact should become a matter of habit for all of later life. Therefore we must try to teach this discrimination by our work in school. Discrimination is learned by discriminating, not by merely accepting the ideas of others.

The Ideal of Complete Comprehension

It will be of interest and value to ask ourselves at this point what we really mean by "understanding fully" or by "complete comprehension." These phrases are often used or other phrases, such as 100% comprehension, that mean the same. We have been talking of the cursory comprehension of ordinary reading, and the better comprehension of slow and careful reading. What would *complete comprehension* be?

Everything in this world is defined or explained in terms of its relationship to other things. To know one relationship means to know something; to know more relationships means to know more. Therefore we may say with complete logic that to understand anything fully would be to know all its possible relations to all other things in the world. In fact, we can say that understanding can extend in three directions. *First,* we can see more relationships in the present, with other things and people and with events that are going on at the same time. *Second,* understanding can extend backward into the past, asking what causes or events preceded, and what are all the relationships that have gone before.

Third, understanding can be increased by looking ahead into the future, asking what relationships there will be or may be with what will follow or result. Thus to see all possible relationships in all three of these directions would be to understand fully. Obviously, such complete understanding of anything will always be impossible. All understanding will be partial. But we can work in school and outside to make understandings, for our students, ever more nearly complete, as well as to get them to see that ever fuller understanding will require a lifetime of growth.

To illustrate these generalizations, we can take anything you wish. Suppose we take the word *mother*. The small child hears *mother* and attaches the word to a certain person. For a long time *mother* means "feed and take care of me." When the child begins to get around, the word takes on more relationships. He soon finds in the word *mother* the new relationships "restrict and punish." He also finds "satisfies curiosity and helps" as added relationships. So on and on the child finds that the person he calls *mother* is the center of ever-increasing and expanding relationships. Soon he discovers that other children also have *mothers*. School brings to the child ever differing relationships between his *mother* and the rest of the world. If he has brothers and sisters, still new relationships attach to *mother*. So it goes on all through life. If the child is a boy, he marries and shortly finds new relationships in the word *mother*. As his own children grow up, *mother* keeps on adding relationships with more people and things and events and crises. The study of biology and evolution would add still other relationships about the concept of *mother*. No one living has ever exhausted the meaning of *mother*, because life keeps

showing everyone more and more relationships between the idea of *mother* and the rest of the world.
It even takes a war to make some of these relationships clear.

We might do the same with any other idea. Everything is known in terms of its relationships with
everything else, and therefore complete understanding seems to be an ideal toward which we always
move but which we never attain. Meantime, we must
think of understanding as "adequate under the circumstances" or "not adequate under the circumstances." When we send a boy out into life with
an understanding of *number,* we mean an understanding that is adequate for his possible life needs.
If he were going to become an engineer, then a much
fuller understanding would be needed. Similarly, to
say a girl should "understand" cooking, means one
thing if she is to be a housewife and another if she
is to be a dietitian. Understanding will always be
relative, and that means relative to the needs of the
person and society.

"Ordinary reading," as explained, does give certain understandings. For school use, however, we
usually desire more understanding, and therefore
school demands more careful reading. The student
in any area or the specialist will desire much more
complete understanding. He will not only read carefully, but he will "study." That implies *searching*
for meaning. The philosopher searches for meaning.
So does the researcher in any field. And the re-

searcher is just the one who knows he will never have complete understanding, but only *more nearly* complete understanding.

The Author's Purpose or the Reader's Own Purpose?

The problems involved in getting more per hour or getting more per page can be looked at from another angle. What is the purpose of the reader? Is he trying to find the message which the author tried to convey, or is he trying to find something to satisfy his own mental needs? That is, if he is reading an article on Medicine as a Profession, is he trying to find out what the author has to say about medicine as a profession, or is he trying to find out whether he personally would be suited to become a doctor? If he is reading for this purpose of his own, he will probably skip the historical part of the article. He may skim over the statistics. He will read carefully the parts that appeal to him or that seem to suit his needs. If he is cautious, he will also read carefully concerning the drawbacks to the profession; if he is very self-confident, he will skim or skip over those, feeling sure they do not apply to him. A student reading in this way may be able to tell you what *he* got out of the article, but he will perhaps not be able to present to you a balanced outline of what the author tried to say. He was not interested in the article as the work of doctor so-and-so: He was interested in it only as a possible answer to his own questions.

Our own experience tells us that in practice we usually combine these two purposes. Even when we are looking for the author's message, we are still inserting into the reading our own purposes and needs. As a result we are slighting some parts that we are not especially interested in, concentrating on other parts which appeal to us, or even going off on mental excursions at times according to our own desires. In contrast, when we are looking up something entirely for our own needs, we sometimes get interested in what the author is presenting and follow him for a time. If he becomes less interesting, or if our own needs assert themselves, we may cease to follow him and go on our own way. Nevertheless, though we do combine them, it is useful to distinguish between these two purposes in reading, (1) *getting the author's message* and (2) *finding what we want,* so that we may use the appropriate method of reading at the time and expect the results that will come from the particular purpose.

Should we teach students to read for their own purposes or to read to get the message that the author intended to give? As the school now manages the work, we often do not make it clear to students which way they should read. Therefore some students learn how to read for their own purposes, while others think all reading should be to report the author's message. Obviously, students should do both things at different times and for different reasons. We can make this clear by reviewing the different study methods we have discussed.

Skimming (discussed on page 363) may be done either to discover the author's message or to find something to suit the reader's purpose. We may skim for the author's outline, for his main point, or for his train of thought. We may also skim to find out whether the material interests us or will answer some question we have.

Locating the part to read or looking with a clue in mind (see pp. 366-8) is usually done to suit our own purposes, and that purpose is usually to answer some question, whether our own or the teacher's. Whenever the teacher gives study questions, the reader will look for the part to read to answer those questions. Whenever a student goes to a reference book to find material for a talk, a paper, or a project of some kind, he is locating the part to read for his own purpose. He ignores everything else.

Reading only the important parts (see pp. 368 to 372) usually means reading the parts that the author thinks important. For that reason we look where we think the author placed his important ideas. We try to follow the author's outline and to place its parts in proper coordination and subordination. This technique is the one best suited to following the author's purpose.

Visualizing (see pp. 375-382) is usually an attempt to get more of what the author intended to give. We

believe that he has described things we want to see
or should see, and we try to "see" them. Of course
the reader often applies his own purpose too and
therefore skims or skips descriptions. In that case,
the reader has decided he wants less than the author
wished to give. So the reader follows the author as
far as the story is concerned but refuses to follow
him in detail. A further extension of the same con-
flict is shown when the reader starts to skip through
the story or even turns to the end to see how the
story ends. The author certainly never intended his
carefully planned suspense to be destroyed in that
way.

Slow and Careful Reading (pp. 383 to 387) of a
whole chapter or article is certainly a following of
the author. It is accepting his plan of writing, his
detail, his illustration, his explanation. It is a con-
scientious following of the author's thought in every
detail. This does not mean acceptance. We can read
carefully in order to disagree more completely and
successfully. But we are surely following the author
when we read by this slow and careful method.

Remembering and Study

It is doubtful whether remembering is any important part of study as done in real life. When one
studies directions so as to understand them, there
is no need to remember, for the directions will always be at hand when needed. The cook need not

remember the recipe; she always has the recipe book when she needs it. Even the lawyer need not always remember, for he can make notes and have the notes before him. Undoubtedly in any field of interest or work, the great need is for comprehension. Of course there are persons who try to store their memories with facts so that they may display those facts at times, but such persons are few. In nearly every case, the book in which the facts were read is there to supply the information or to answer any questions. A history professor once said, "My memory is on the shelves of the library," and he was just stating what is the case with most of us.

How Much Remembering Should We Expect?

There are good grounds for telling children, "If you can't tell what you have read, you just haven't read." This means that any true comprehension makes some definite impression on the mind, and the reader should be able to tell that impression. But what and how much should the reader be able to tell?

In the case of narration and description, we have said that the reader should visualize the story, with the people, the places, and the events. Surely then the person who has understood the story can tell us something about the people, the places, and the events. How fully should the reader be able to describe what he has read about? Here it is generally a question of *the amount read* and *how soon it is told about. If the child reads a short section of a story,* say six to eight lines, *and tells of it immediately, he should be able to give almost every detail.* This is because not too many details were gone over and the recall is immediate.

If instead the reader covers a whole page, we cannot expect every detail. In the first place, a whole page would contain a number of descriptions or events, and as each new one was added, the memory of the previous ones would be blurred. So perhaps the reader could give us details about what was described at the bottom of the page, but not about what began the page. Usually, the more that is read at one time, before the retelling, the less detail we would expect just because of the nature of remembering and forgetting.

Great variation should be expected, depending on the person doing the reading. After all, the reader is retelling what made an impression upon him. Different things make impressions on different people. So in the case of story reading, one person will give much detail about one person or place or happening, and another person will give more detail about different things. In any imaginative reading material, the purpose of the writer is to fire the imagination of the reader. His success depends, however, on what that particular reader's background is. So our rule that *the longer the selection read, the less detail will be remembered* has to be modified for particular readers and things read about. If the retelling is done some time later, there will be still further variation. We all know how, as time passes, some things stick in the mind and others do not.

In the reading of explanation or argument, the same principle holds true, that after reading six to ten lines the reader should be able to give almost complete details, but that after reading a longer amount, such as several pages, less complete detail should be expected. If the explanation involves visualizing, there is of course the same problem as in visualizing of stories, that with a larger amount of reading, less description will remain, and that with different persons we expect a great difference in details.

However, whether the explanation causes visualizing or not, there is a difference between explanation and story material. Explanation and argument are built upon logic. The sequence of ideas is logical, and the inclusion of details is logical rather than imaginative. So we can expect more logical remembering in the case of explanation and argument. This means that main ideas and more weighty ideas are to be remembered rather than incidental and less weighty ones. In short, if a short selection should leave a memory of all details *the long selection should leave a logical outline.*

"Pumping" the Reader With Questions

Very false notions prevail as to what children remember of what they have read because of the unfortunate custom of "pumping" the reader with questions. In many classes, the pupils go over the material with more or less attention, close the book, and wait to be asked a question. The question then stirs up some recollection or sounds more or less familiar, and the pupil "thinks up" or guesses what the answer ought to be.

We say that the pupil "guesses" advisedly because the question always gives half the answer and often more. If the students read about China and the teacher asks about the rivers of China, her question tells the students they have read about rivers. They may not have remembered that unless reminded. If the question asks if the rivers are long or short, the class is reminded of what was said about length of the rivers. Without the question they may not have recalled anything about length of rivers. So the "recitation" goes on, question by question. Each question gives something that was in the text. Each question prods the memory. With this prodding, something comes back to the reader, and he frames an answer. With this method of pumping for information, the teacher keeps the class going, and gets some information out of students. Unfortunately, she then assumes that the class knew what they gave in answer to questions. But real knowing means knowing without suggestion or aid.

The only fair test of remembering what is read is to ask one question only, "Tell what you have read." After years of being pumped for information, a large proportion of students in upper grades and high school simply cannot tell a thing they have read without the aid of questions. Fortunately, with very little practice, the situation can be changed. Have the class read a paragraph, close the book, and then ask individuals to tell what they have read. They may fail miserably. But they should then be told to open the book and read it again. Then have them close the book and tell. They will do better, but may have to open the book and reread the second time before they can give a good performance.

Just a little practice will give children the idea that "If you cannot tell what you have read, you haven't read." Very soon it will be found that the children actually can tell what they have read after they have read it. This means just a change of habit. Formerly they had the habit of "go over it and wait for a question." Now they have the habit of "go over it and remember what it says." That is the habit needed for intelligent reading in school.

WHY THE SCHOOL EMPHASIZES MEMORIZING

One may well wonder about the tremendous emphasis on remembering in the schools. Why are the students memorizing so strenuously and continuously? *First,* perhaps there is the tradition of schools that learning is memorizing and that the learned person is the person with a well-stocked memory. Such a concept may have been valid when the knowledge in any field could be compassed within the pages of a book or two. Then one could have the facts in his field "at his fingertips," as they used to say. But now the knowledge in any field is included in veritable libraries. It is nonsense to try to "know all about" matters in any field. The concept of the stored memory which furnished all information is ridiculous in the present state of human knowledge.

A *second* reason for the emphasis on memory is perhaps our desire to catch the students who neglect their work. We want to make sure they read the assignment they were told to read. So we quiz them on it to see if they know what the assignment contained. Now we must admit that there are plenty of students, trying to slight their work, who will read their assignments hastily or not at all. It may be our duty to catch and eliminate from school persons of such character. But it is a pity if our whole concept of study should be warped by this one desire to find out who has read the lesson and who has not.

A *third* reason for having material memorized is the delusion that what is remembered for a day or week or month is permanently a part of the mental equipment. Students repeat their lessons glibly day by day, and often as a result are excused from final examinations. But does that mean they can also repeat those lessons at the end of a month or semester? Experience shows the contrary. And even if they could repeat their lessons at the end of the semester, how about at the end of ten years? Is

not education for life? And life after school is a
matter of forty or fifty years. Is this school memorizing to last that long? If it is not, of what value
is it?

The alternative to testing by remembering is testing by application or explanation. If a student can
use a piece of knowledge, he is showing he understands that knowledge. Explanation is another kind
of use, since it is use in a mental situation. Good
teachers are always striving to secure use of knowledge rather than mere repetition of it. Textbooks
sometimes help the teacher by suggesting uses for
the information given in the chapters. Teachers'
manuals sometimes help. But unfortunately, most of
the questions supplied to teachers are still "repeat"
questions, and the teacher is so busy that she per-
force uses them for lack of time to devise "use
questions" of her own. Let us hope that there will
be more and more testing by use and less and less
testing by repetition from memory.

TEACHING HOW TO REMEMBER

If remembering is going to be part of school study
for a long time to come, we should teach the children
how to remember. If we give them no instruction,
they will use *visualizing the page*. When asked a
question, they will stare off into space and try to
see the part of the page and the exact words of the
book. Many children can do this, and many more try
to. It is natural that they should. We remember

people and things by using a memory image; why not remember a definition or a vocabulary that way? Of course the answer is that words look too much alike to be remembered by memory image and also that the memory image is only temporary. It will not last for days or weeks or years. This last is no argument for the typical student, of course, because he wants to remember only for the recitation or the examination. But for most students, visualizing the page just does not work.

The second way of remembering is *by rote,* that is, by repeating over and over until the tongue seems to know the answer automatically. This is an easy method in the sense that all one has to do is to repeat and repeat and repeat. It is a most unintelligent method, but it does work in many cases. If the teacher has given questions that have definite answers, the student can read the answers over and over until they seem to come to him unconsciously. Of course there may be little if any meaning, but the student will be confident because he "has the right answer." If the teacher is so inconsiderate as to ask for explanation of the answers, there will be failure, but many teachers do not ask for explanations.

The third way of remembering is *logical remembering,* and it is the only intelligent method. It has the maximum meaning; it has the maximum use in life; and it lasts the longest. In fact, all through life we often say, "I have forgotten that, but if you give me time, I think I can figure it out.'' We are saying, ''My visual or rote memory has failed me, but I think I have a logical memory of it.'' The only trouble with logical remembering is that it takes effort and time. One has to think, and one has to take time to think.

Two study methods that we have emphasized result in logical remembering. The first is ''reading only the important parts.'' That method picks out the thought structure of the author and shows the relationship of one thought to another. Of course one may read the entire section but he should then go back and ''read the important parts'' over again so as to see the relationships more clearly. Sometimes the student underlines the important parts, or numbers them in outline form, or copies them into a notebook, and then instead of studying the logic of the ideas tries to visualize the notebook page or the underlined sentences to aid his remembering. Or he may repeat the outline to himself in order to use rote memory. Such methods should not be necessary if there is real understanding of the important parts. The other method of getting remembering by understanding is slow and careful reading. If the meaning ''sinks in'' sufficiently, if enough past experiences are suggested, and if there is enough thinking about the material, there will be logical remembering.

Of course the teacher who wants to get logical remembering by the class must not ask questions that require the other kinds of remembering. If the exact words or statements in the books are called for, of course they can be remembered only by visualizing or rote. Logic will give the ideas but not the exact words. Likewise, the teacher who wishes logical remembering must ask for explanations that will naturally call up the material so remembered. In life, the situation suggests the needed knowledge. So in school, the situations or questions must logically suggest the remembered knowledge.

To summarize, study in life implies understanding but not necessarily remembering, since the book or whatever is read can always be consulted again. But in school we ask for remembering. If we do, we should see that it is the best and most permanent kind of remembering, logical association. And we must ask for use of reading in such a way as to make logical remembering possible.

Testing Reading

"Ordinary Reading" is tested by having children read as they ordinarily do and give us a report on that reading as they ordinarily do. Teachers are testing ordinary reading when they have the children read books of their own choosing and then tell what they wish to tell about what they have read. The reading speeds given in Chapter VI are for such ordinary reading.

ORAL READING TESTS

The several Oral Reading Tests probably get "ordinary oral reading." The child knows he is being tested, and he may know that there will be some questions or reproduction, but he still tends to read orally as he always reads orally. The performance with the voice tends to be the same and so perhaps the comprehension is also the same as usual with oral reading.

SPEED OF READING TESTS

None of the other standardized reading tests measure ordinary reading, however. Every one checks on comprehension, and even though this check is very slight, the reader changes his process of reading. For instance, some such tests include somewhere a word which "does not belong," and the reader soon discovers that the problem is to find and cross out that word. He therefore ceased to comprehend in the usual way. Instead, he changes to "looking for the word which does not belong," ignoring everything else. Some tests ask but a single question after the reading and that question calls for only a slight reaction by the reader, but the demand for that slight reaction makes a great change in the method of reading. For instance, a well-known speed of reading test asks only for the underlining of one word in answer to one simple question. The answer is at all times obvious. But note the speeds of reading shown by the norms on this reading test.

TABLE V

Speeds on a Standard Speed of Reading Test

These norms secured by counting the words read up to the point in
the test that the child of each grade is supposed to reach,
and dividing by the time allowed.

Grade	Words per Minute
III	56
IV	78
V	108
VI	123
VII	145
VIII	167

By comparing these speeds with those on Table IV,
page 331, it will be seen that they are approximately *half the speed of ordinary reading.* That is
to say, even the underlining of one word in a very
easy question causes the children to slow down very
much below their "ordinary" speed of reading.

TESTS OF STUDY READING

All other reading tests, except those for oral reading or mere speed of reading, test study reading.
Speeds are much slower than those given above for
the above test. Questions are always asked, often
very hard questions. The only difficulty with these
study tests is that we cannot tell very well *what kind
of study reading* is being tested. The tests are of two
types; one may be called the "short response" type,
in which after a paragraph of reading, only one or
two questions are asked. The other may be called

the "long response" type, in which after a paragraph is read a good many questions are to be answered. What does the child do when doing these tests?

In the "short response" type, there are three possibilities. The child may (1) read carefully and then answer the question; (2) he may read hastily and still be able to answer the question because the question suggests the answer; and (3) he may read the question first and then locate the answer by skimming for a clue word. These three kinds of study are very different things, and one cannot tell which the child taking the test is doing. Perhaps he does part of one, and part of another. At any rate, the score on the test does not tell us what kind of study reading the child is good or poor at. Therefore, we do not know what kind of teaching he needs.

In the case of the "long response" test, the problem is even more complicated. Here there are usually five questions on a paragraph of five to eight sentences. We have first the three possibilities of the short response test: (1) careful reading first, (2) hasty reading first, and (3) reading the question first. Then we have the possibility (4) of rereading because there are so many questions that the material is forgotten or confused. Many persons taking these tests report that they can answer the first two or three questions from one reading but that they have to go back and reread to answer the fourth and fifth questions. We also have the problem of (5) "thinking apart from reading" caused by such questions as "Which is the best title for the paragraph?" Many other possibilities are caused by the great variety of questions asked by the long response kind of test. Obviously, the score on such a test means the child is good or poor in something, but we do not know just what. Again, we do not know what kind of teaching we should now give him to help him become a better study reader.

Summary

"Ordinary reading" is very important because it is the kind most persons will do for most of their lives. It means that the eyes jump rhythmically across the page, stopping at regular intervals, taking in whatever part of the line is seen, the reader getting enough comprehension to satisfy him.

The kind of reading that gets more than one does from ordinary reading can well be called study reading. Getting more from reading may mean getting more for the time put in, that is, getting more per hour. This may mean (1) *skimming,* for general impression, which means fewer fixations and shorter ones as the eyes go across the page. We do not know what to think of this kind of skimming because, we do not know what the reader gets from it. We do know it requires a familiarity with the material.

(2) *Skimming with a clue in mind* is done by looking down the page for either a word clue or an idea

clue. When the word or idea is met with, the reader begins to read that part. (3) *Reading only the important parts* means that we read prefaces, tables of contents, introductions, summaries, paragraph beginnings, and the like so as to get the gist without reading everything.

Getting more from reading may mean *getting more per page,* or more adequate reading. More adequate reading may result from *visualizing,* which gives us the pictures the author intended us to have, and therefore gives us more meaning. *More Careful Reading* involves visualizing in description but in explanation and argument usually means slower reading. It gives more meaning by giving time for meaning to arise in the mind, by giving time for suggesting of past experience, and by permitting more imagining, thinking and feeling.

Reading can well be thought of as a conversation in which the reader talks back to the writer. Modern philosophy of education demands this talking back or reacting.

Complete comprehension is an ideal that we should keep before us. It would mean seeing all relationships, present, past and future, and is therefore forever impossible. Instead, we should strive for "adequate comprehension under the circumstances."

In reading, we may seek to discover what the author tried to convey, or we may seek to discover what suits our own purposes. In practice, the two often mingle, but we should make clear to the student which one he is expected to do. Skimming may be done for either purpose. Locating the part to be read is usually done for our own purposes. Reading only the important parts seeks to find out what the author thinks is important. Visualizing also follows the author's purpose. Slow and careful reading is the method best suited to find out all that the author intended.

Study implies remembering, but how much remembering should we expect? If the child reads only a short paragraph and tells immediately what he has read, he should be able to give every detail. If a longer selection is read, less detail should be expected. Only a logical outline should be remembered. "Pumping the student with questions" is no test of remembering because the questions supply information and make suggestions. Children should be asked to "Tell what you have read." Schools emphasize memorizing because of tradition, because they want to catch the students who slight their work, and because they think the material remembered will last for life, which it obviously cannot. The test of reading should be application, not remembering.

If any material should be remembered, it should not be retained by visualizing the page, nor by rote repetition, but by logical understanding. Such understanding results from reading or rereading only the important parts and also from slow and careful reading.

Standardized tests are not very good tests of reading. The oral reading tests do give an ordinary reading performance. But the other tests are study tests because the student does not "read" as he does under ordinary circumstances. But even agreeing that they are study tests, we do not know what kind of study is being used, since the tests may be done in a great variety of ways.

CHAPTER XII

Studying a Topic

We have defined "ordinary reading" as the kind we do when we run the eyes steadily across the line, without stopping or hesitating, all the while getting enough ideas or thoughts to satisfy us and keep us going. We have called this "ordinary reading" because it is just what we do most of the time when we say we are reading, and what we do unless there is some special reason for doing something else. We have then defined "study reading" as other kinds of reading with different purposes and therefore using different methods. The one who, in studying, is satisfied to get less per paragraph than he would get by ordinary reading, goes faster. He goes slower when he wishes to get more from each paragraph than he would get by the method of ordinary reading.

We now wish to consider how the different kinds of reading that may be called "study reading" are involved in the work of the school, and how we can train children in those different kinds of reading. We wish the children to recognize that, when they study, their goals *are* different from when they "just read," and we wish them to know how those different goals should cause a different method to be used. We shall treat these differences under two different

415

headings, to suit two different plans of study used in the schools. This chapter deals with "studying a topic."

Reasons for Study by Topics

In modern education, study by *topics* is becoming more and more popular. Topics may be studied either by a group or by an individual. At many grade levels, *the entire room, or a committee* of the children in the room, study some such topic as Safety, or Blackbirds, or the United Nations, or Charles Dickens, or Australia, or any other topic from the many subjects taken up in school. The topic studied may be one of a number of *Units* chosen beforehand, or it may be a special topic taken up for a special reason, as the result of the reading of the newspaper or as part of Current Events, or of Nature Study, or of any of the regular or occasional subjects included in the work of the school.

There are several good reasons for an increase in study by topics. *First* of all, we are becoming more and more convinced that children learn best when they are strongly motivated, and we find that in special topics we often find excellent motivation. When a topic is being discussed by the newspapers or by parents and over the radio, it is only natural that certain grades should be encouraged or permitted to choose those topics for special study. *Second,* the mere choice of a special topic "centers" all the school work and coordinates or integrates all the usual school subjects. With a topic before them, the children can read about it, discuss it, write about it, spell words connected with it, use numbers concerning it, use art work based upon it, and in every way integrate or combine all their work about that center. In this way much more practical learning can be secured in all fields.

Third, we are coming to feel that the content of the curriculum should be as far as possible suited to each individual school, and therefore we cannot use the same textbooks or curriculum outline in schools with different backgrounds and community settings. So each school should more or less discover the topics which its own children should study, and should find out just at what level each topic properly belongs. In this way, the school tries out various topics or centers of interest and finds from experience which ones are most profitable and at what level they work best. So over a period of time, each school makes its own curriculum. It can do this if the material is thought of in topical form. Then the topics or units can be tried out and evaluated and shifted as seems best.

Fourth, with the increase of materials in the educational field, both in books and magazines, much material is becoming available. The single textbook no longer seems, to many people, at all adequate for the needs of the school. In other words, people are beginning to think in terms of libraries instead of in terms of a single book. When a single topic is thought of, it is found that many books and pamphlets and magazine articles can be found on that topic. Many books have sections on the topic, and all these sections taken together are much more ample than the part of a single book. So there is an enrichment that was not possible in former times when there was not much material or much money to buy such material.

Finally, it is felt that the "library method," as this may be called, permits provision for individual differences in two ways. First, materials can be found on many levels of reading difficulty, so children at different reading levels can all find material suited to them, and from which they can get interest and profit. Second, this reading by different children of different things permits social participation by all. All can "share" or give something to the group. With our greater emphasis on social learning and on the social adjustment of children, this method provides a splendid opportunity to adapt to individuals by providing different materials, making different assignments, and expecting different results from each one.

In all these ways, topics are studied by groups. But in all schools, either using units or using uniform textbooks, according to the older plan, there is much chance for *individual study of topics.* The teacher may regard the textbook assignment as a minimum of common learnings. She may then expect the children individually to branch out on their

interests and to find out more about some aspects of
the subject. If a period of history is studied, different children may individually choose different characters to find out about and report on to the class.
If a section of geography is being studied, many
aspects of the special section of the country or of
the world can suggest individual study. The children can investigate particular cities, particular
industries, and the like to find out things they are
interested in.

This use of individual study of topics or "research" as it is sometimes called, is also used in
the field of composition. Children write about topics
of their interest, and they are expected to work on
their individual topics by study reading before they
write. This practice continues all the way up through
high school. We even find teachers of physical education having the students investigate or study different special topics and make reports to the class.
Naturally, all these reports may be oral instead of
written, or they may be given orally first and then
put into writing. But the principle is the same. The
individual student develops a special interest, he
chooses a topic on that special interest for study,
he does study reading on it, and he then makes some
kind of a report.

Reading Is Just One Source of Information

Since at this point we are considering the use of
books in the study of topics, we shall be dealing al-

most exclusively with books and reading as a source
of information. The practical teacher will remember, however, the other sources of information and
use them as occasion permits. She should discuss
these other sources with the children so that all can
find things out in as many ways as possible.

The *first* and most obvious way to learn anything
is to *go and find out for yourself*. For children this
may mean observing things about them, as in study
of trees or birds. It may mean going places and seeing, as in watching whether people obey safety
rules. It may mean experimenting, as in finding out
differences between hard woods and soft woods. The
school has not done nearly enough to make children
observers of the world about them. So let us not
forget this possibility in the study of the many topics the school takes up.

Second, children can *ask people* in order to find
things out. On many topics they can ask their
parents. Other questions they can ask of business
men or other workers. There is much important
knowledge that is not in books but that is known by
the people we meet every day. Of course, children
need to be taught courtesy and diplomacy in making
this kind of inquiry, but such inquiry should be encouraged as a means of getting a practical education about life.

Third, audio-visual aids may be available in the
school or from the central office which may greatly
help in the study of a topic. In fact, when the topical

approach is used, schools usually build up audio-visual aids on those topics. Film libraries specialize in supplying material on the often-studied topics in the curriculum. This is a most important source of information.

Fourth, children can read to find things out. This study-reading is the subject of this chapter, and will naturally be taken up at length. But the other three ways of learning should not be forgotten in connection with any study project a class or individual may have.

Motivation Is Crucial

Whether the study of a particular topic is to be done by a class, a committee, or an individual, motivation is crucial. Unless there is an eagerness to find out, nothing much of benefit will happen. Teachers have discovered this long ago. If a group or an individual is not eager to attack a topic, there will be no real attack. There will be a listless going to the sources the teacher assigned or pointed out. There will be a listless and unintelligent copying. There will be half-hearted writing up or other presentation. All this is strictly according to human nature. Study involves effort and work. And the drive to work must be a desire to attain a goal of some kind. What goals can we hold before children to get them to attack topical study with enthusiasm?

As we have already suggested, *the most effective driving force for study is curiosity*. The individual

has the desire for a solution of some problem that
teases his mind. He goes after the solution and
works tirelessly until he is satisfied, or until he finds
he cannot be satisfied. We find this drive of curiosity in many children but often about subjects that
are not part of the immediate classroom situation.
Some boys are eager to learn about radio, and they
work at it in and out of school. Some boys or girls
are so eager to learn about acting and the theatre
that they spend countless hours in rehearsal or work
about the school stage. Teachers are often able to
secure some of this same driving curiosity about
topics in history or science or literature or other
fields. Usually, of course, we can arouse only a
milder form of curiosity and therefore expect a
milder form of effort to satisfy it. But it can be
agreed that curiosity is the best motivation for study
and we shall continue to strive for it in all subjects.

A much more common goal for the effort of study
of a topic is *securing the approval of the class*. The
individual will work hard at a project in order to
make an acceptable or outstanding presentation to
the class. A committee will also work hard on a topic
in order to make a good report. Similarly, the whole
class will work hard on a study project in order to
present a program to the school, or to another room,
or to a group of parents. Here we have a use of the
social nature of children, and a perfectly proper use.

The drive of curiosity is usually combined with
this drive for social approval, and it is hard to dis-

tinguish between the two. It is not really necessary to distinguish in most cases, unless the teacher wishes to be sure to develop curiosity. The drive of curiosity will continue after the report to the class and after the social approval situation is over. Likewise, curiosity will secure effort in many fields and on many projects where social approval will not operate very strongly.

In very many cases the drive behind study of a project is the natural desire of the children to *please their friend, the teacher.* We do wish to please our friends and win their approval. If the teacher is such a friend, and if she represents adult approval as well, children will be impelled to work for her on any project she suggests. If the teacher is skilfull in choosing such projects, the children will develop curiosity about the topics, and they will find social approval in work on them.

If, however, the teacher is not so understanding of children and their needs and suggests the wrong topics, the children will begin to do minimum work; and the habit of doing a minimum job is one that we certainly wish to avoid if at all possible. Unfortunately, this is just the habit that so many children get from their years of school, and it is a habit that their later employers loudly denounce. It tends always to become the habit when the work is done *just* to please the teacher. For this reason, good teachers try to avoid assigning of projects and instead try to cause such attractive projects to be "discovered" that the class and individuals in the class will choose them and attack them without her urging. She will use her personal influence only when it becomes absolutely necessary.

Finally, there are children who study faithfully and well because of their *ideal of themselves* as persons who always do a good job. These children are few, and are usually the ones who are more mature than usual for their age. We are glad for these children, but we cannot expect the great majority of children to be like them.

Habits to Develop in Study of Topics

After strong motives for study are developed, proper habits must follow. Study is after all an activity, and an activity is learned by taking part in the activity, as in the case of swimming, singing, reading, modeling, drawing, or any other. Attempts have been made at various times to teach information about "how to study" before the activity of study was engaged in. Practical teachers have always found, however, that knowledge about study is best learned as needed. We shall therefore deal with the habits to be learned during the study of topics, and will necessarily bring in references to knowledge as it is needed. In a later section, information about study aids is more specifically taken up.

1. The Habit of Covering the Field

There is a strong tendency on the part of school children, as on the part of the average person, to "look something up" in a reference book, to find some information on the subject, to copy it down and then to present it as the answer. That kind of "amateur research" is very common at all levels, but it need not be. It is very easy for a teacher, no matter what the topic or what the grade level, to ask, "Have you looked at all possible sources?", "Have you covered the field?" The teacher will naturally also enlist the aid of the librarian, either in school or public library, in helping at this point. The librarian can point out all possible sources of information, and then the teacher can ask if all were looked into.

To initiate this habit the teacher can well emphasize this point in the first activities in which a class engages. She can have all possible sources listed. She can then have the work divided, and have different committees or individuals look up every one of the possible sources. She can make the chief point the fact that "we have covered the field" and have all the information that is available. Just a few projects in which this complete covering of the field is emphasized will impress the idea of this type of thoroughness, and from then on, the idea can be mentioned and recalled so that in time there may develop a habit of covering the field in any investigation. Then we will not find a child saying, "I have found something," and being satisfied with that.

2. THE HABIT OF EVALUATING SOURCES

Unfortunately there is a common feeling among those of limited educational experience that whatever is in a book is so. Perhaps teachers have had a good deal to do with the building up of this feeling or idea since they constantly quote books as authority for their own statements or send people to books to find answers. But if we are to put books into their proper relation to life we must somehow lead children and therefore the future adults to evaluate what they find in books.

The first thing we need to impress upon children is that *every book was written by a man*. The man sat at a table with a pen or at a typewriter and he wrote the book word by word. If this be so, then we have several questions to ask about that man. These questions are valuable for discussion of radio broadcasts, of newspaper articles or of any other kinds of materials heard or read.

1. *How did the author learn about the subject?* That is, is the author telling us in the book something he found out himself or something he has read in another book? What were his sources? Did he see some events or persons or places himself? Did he get original papers? Did he have the opportunity of knowing the facts or of knowing all the facts? Often we can look up an author in *Who's Who?*

or other reference book and find out something about
him and what he has done. Reviews of a book will
often tell us about the author and what he knew
about the thing he was writing about.

2. *Does the author give us the whole story?* A
book often leaves out very important things. It fails
to tell us what happened before a certain time or
after a certain time. It sometimes leaves out facts
about people and events that we very much want to
know. It is very important in reading any material
or hearing any talk to ask if we are getting the whole
story or just a part of it. Of course, a book is limited for space. It has to leave out a great deal. But
did it leave out some essential facts?

3. *Does the author tell the story fairly?* Even if
a man tells the whole story he may present it in a
prejudiced way. Are there signs of any prejudice
in the book? One way to tell this is to catch the man
in some statement that we know something about
ourselves and which we therefore know to be
"slanted" or twisted. Here we are in the field of
prejudice and we must be careful. It is easy for a
prejudiced person to accuse another of being prejudiced. An entirely impartial and fair person will
often be called prejudiced by all other persons because he does not fit into their prejudices. But in
evaluating reading materials we cannot avoid the
question of whether we are given the story in a perfectly fair and balanced way.

Part of this evaluating process includes looking at the dates when things were written. An account that was considered perfectly complete and fair in its time may now be so out of date as to be largely false. So much is learned year by year that often only up-to-date materials can be trusted.

4. *Does the author reason logically?* Much of what we read may not be a statement of facts but may instead be logical reasoning. Is the author's reasoning truly logical? To discover lack of logic in a writer or book does much to weaken our trust in it.

We have made a rather full discussion of evaluation but we do not infer that all this process should be gone through at all grade levels with all topics studied. We must begin evaluating gradually and build it up as time goes on. But the habit of evaluating sources is very important for all of present-day learning and thinking. The teacher or school which attempts to have children learn by study of topics cannot overlook evaluation of materials read.

3. THE HABIT OF SKIMMING AND THE HABIT OF READING IMPORTANT PARTS

The actual nature and development of habits of skimming or of reading parts has been explained and discussed in the previous chapter. Skimming with a clue in mind, implying as it does "looking for something," running the eyes over material with a word or idea clue in mind, has wide usefulness in this kind of study since we are looking for *material related to a topic.* The habit of *reading of parts* is also likely to suit the needs of topical study since it enables one both quickly to locate something that fits the topic and also to cover material on a topic quickly to see if it should be studied more carefully.

4. THE HABIT OF USING REFERENCE AIDS

The person skilled in reference study goes immediately to the suitable reference aids when a subject of study is suggested. He may look in the dictionary for a definition of the topic, he may then go to the encyclopædias to find what they have, he then goes to the library and consults the card index, he gets the books mentioned and looks in the table of contents or index of each. Thus he habitually uses the series of reference aids. After one had thus used reference aids frequently one may be said to have the habit of using them. We shall discuss those aids later under "knowledge of reference aids."

5. THE HABIT OF NOTE TAKING

The average person does not take notes and then is sorry he did not when his memory fails him or is not accurate. We need to impress upon children either by advice or by their own experience that notes are necessary if one is to read a number of sources and then know where he got his information and just what that information was.

We cannot be too sure of what system of taking notes we should develop. Usually we are advised to have notes on cards so that they can be shuffled, though some persons find a notebook just as useful. We are urged to quote figures and definite facts, giving the volume and the page where we found them. But there is also a need for making notes of one's own ideas and thoughts in order to catch them so that they will not disappear in the daily course of thinking. For children, specific directions for taking notes are advisable, though we may expect that the individual will develop his own system as time goes on. But the habit of having notes of some kind is very important if in school we are to have clear cut reports and if a useful foundation for study in later years is to be built.

6. The Habit of Organizing Ideas

In much of the reference reading that is done in school all that is wanted is just a summary of a certain book or article. In that case, the problem of organizing ideas does not arise. Since the student is just following one author, that author has already done the organizing. The extract or summary just follows the plan of the original. This use of one book only is not the kind of study of a topic with which we are here concerned.

Genuine work on study of a topic means the collecting of facts or opinions about that topic from a number of sources. The result may be several pages in a notebook or a stack of cards containing notes. These notes have in themselves no organization except that they are on a single topic or phases of a single topic. The work of the group or individual is then to arrange the notes or facts or opinions in some suitable order so that they can be told or written with interest and profit to the audience. This means a job of organizing ideas.

Organizing of ideas must always be done in terms of a purpose and that purpose is nearly always the presenting of the ideas to a certain audience. The class or individual making the study needs to think of the audience to which they wish to present their study. A class can assume the report is to be presented to the principal or to another class or to their parents or to the class that will follow them, or to any individual or group. The important thing is to have an audience in order to organize to suit that audience.

Usually the thought of the audience will clarify the plan or organization. Sometimes it will appear necessary to interest the audience first; sometimes that interest is assumed. Sometimes the report is historical in plan, putting things in order of time; at other times it will progress from an overview to details. It is not possible to make general rules for the presentation of materials of every kind whatever. The children will usually sense the suitable order or they will discover it after trying to outline the material in various ways.

Later, on pages 457 to 468, we shall discuss more fully the problems of outlining as they deal with the analysis of textbook material. At this point, we are dealing with the outlining of original writing material. It has been found that students can learn from the outlines of others how to outline themselves. Therefore, outlining of textbooks can help in the outlining of reports. However, in order not to repeat, we shall leave the major discussion for the later section. Of course, it is understood that the outlines used by the class or by individuals reporting the study of a topic will be quite simple most of the time and perhaps all the time. The point we are making is only that there must be developed the idea that there should be an outline before there is reporting either orally or on paper and that this use of an outline should become in time a habit that is part of the plan for study of topics in school.

Knowledge Required for the Study of Topics

To the teacher, who has gone through college and taken many courses which required the use of the library and of reference books, it is often inconceivable that children are so ignorant of the mass of information that has been piled up for us by writers of the past and by makers of reference books. Many colleges and universities require of every student a course in library and library materials and methods, just so that the students can use the library for their courses during training. If one has not had such a course, the next best thing is to have worked in a library for even a short time and thus discovered the resources of libraries and of books.

If the teacher herself has had none of these experiences, she can go to a library and ask questions of the reference librarian, especially about how her students would go about finding information in the library. Reference librarians are glad to take time to explain all the materials and methods, especially to teachers. Then the teacher will be armed with a wealth of information to pass on to her classes.

We shall review the knowledge that students should have if they are properly to use the vast resources of information stored up in books and libraries. We shall follow a certain order, but that does not mean this is necessarily the order to use in teaching. The children will use the resources that suit the topic and that are most directly available to them. The teacher will teach what is needed. The order we shall follow is from the simpler sources to the more complex sources, and is adopted just for a logical sequence.

GLOSSARIES

Many books, even at the fourth grade level, have glossaries in the back to tell the pronunciation of words and their meaning. Such glossaries are necessarily very incomplete. They seldom give all the words the children need, and they usually give just the meaning needed in the particular context in

which the word is used in the book. But a special
point should be made of exploring the glossary, running through it for interesting words, seeing if some
of the words are already known, and, in fact, arousing interest in the glossary. Care must be taken not
to make use of the glossary a disliked task. It must
always be fun to find out about words; otherwise
children will not want to find out about them. Children may notice the incompleteness of the glossary;
that is, that some words have other meanings than
given in the glossary. In that case, the natural thing
is to go to the dictionary.

The Dictionary

Children should know that there are many different dictionaries. They should know that the big dictionary has up to 600,000 words, that the college dictionary may have up to 100,000 words, or only about
one-sixth as many, that the high school dictionary
may have 50,000 words, or half as many as the college dictionary, and that the grade school dictionary
may have only 25,000 words, or half again. Children
should know that the difference in size of dictionaries is only partly in the number of words included.
Part of the difference is also in information it gives
on the individual words. The children should compare the treatment of the same word in different
dictionaries. They will find that there are differences
in the guide to pronunciation, in the number of
meanings, in giving of synonyms, in fullness of indi-

vidual definitions, in giving derivations, and in giving sentences to illustrate usage. All these facts help to make for an interest in the dictionary and they also make for an understanding of just what the dictionary does or does not do.

The teacher who wishes to get children interested in using the dictionary should write to all the companies which publish dictionaries and ask for booklets of information about dictionaries. If the teacher has a great amount of this interesting information, and passes it on to her classes, she will find that they will have much more respect for dictionaries and more desire to use them.

The children should be shown the other information contained in dictionaries. Most dictionaries include material on the names of places in geography, and often they include material on famous names in history or literature. Such material is sometimes in the single alphabet and sometimes in the back of the book in separate sections. Many dictionaries include other interesting information in special sections, such as lists of foreign words which may be met with in English. In short, the dictionary has many resources that are little known by our students.

The use of pictures in the dictionary should be understood. They are not put there just to make the book attractive, but to explain things which are not easily explained in words. For instance, it will be found that most plants and animals are explained by pictures, and often so are mechanical devices, such as screws. If one tries to explain these things, he will discover that words will not suffice. The trouble with the pictures is that they are so small and that they do not tell relative size. Most dictionaries try to overcome this by putting beside the picture little figures, such as "1/16th natural size" or the like.

Encyclopaedias

Children are much impressed if they are told some facts about the encyclopædia. They should be told how many men it takes to make such a book, and this fact is usually told in the preface by the publisher. They should also know how many years it takes, and how much money. The encyclopædia publishers will furnish all this information in attractive form if the teacher will ask for it. Then the students should have a clear cut idea of the difference between the dictionary and the encyclopædia. Dictionaries are supposed to be "wordbooks," though they usually include much information that is of an encyclopædic nature. The encyclopædia is an "information book," which is supposed to include a summary of all the facts known to humanity at the time of its writing.

Encyclopædias have a section or introduction in which the fields of knowledge included are given in logical outline order. Children should see such sec-

tions to understand that encyclopædias are logically
built, and are not just miscellaneous gatherings of
knowledge. All knowledge in the world has been divided by experts into various "fields" of knowledge.
In each field there are experts. The makers of the
encyclopædia hired a great crew of experts, each in
a separate field, and these experts assembled the
knowledge, or got others to assemble it for them.
Finally, of course, the articles are put into alphabetical order, but that is just for the convenience
of the one using the work.

An important idea for anyone using an encyclopædia is "cross reference." Very often at the end
of an article, or even at the beginning, will be found
a note such as "see biochemistry," or some other
section. This means that much knowledge seems to
fit into more than one field, and therefore the experts in two or more fields included some information about the same thing. That is why the cross reference is given. You look up your topic under one
field, and then they will tell you to look it up under
another and perhaps still another. Very many people never get the idea of the importance of cross references; they imagine that a single section covers
all of a topic. This is seldom true, because of the
way human knowledge is interwoven in many ways.

An important point to make about the study of
some topics is that knowledge changes and increases.
Therefore, one should always look at the date of the

reference work. In many fields of science, the last few years have changed the outlook very much, and new information of great value has just come to light. This may also be true of history, where recent research or study has changed the views formerly held. In fact, it is always well to try to find the latest information, and this applies also to use of encyclopædias. Unfortunately, many schools invest once and for all in an encyclopædia and the children keep on using the same one for many years. In many fields, this is not good study or good teaching. We should try to keep up with the making of encyclopædias. The old ones can be used, but when there is a point at issue, we should check with the latest work.

Special Encyclopaedias, Gazetteers, Etc.

Few persons own special encyclopædias or other special reference books, but a large library will have a good many. There will be an encyclopædia of architecture, another of anatomy, and so on through many of the special subjects. A book which includes knowledge of geography is usually called a gazeteer. A book which includes men's names and careers will be called a dictionary of biography. Children may not need to learn these special names, but they need to know that there are special reference books on many special topics, which may be used in addition to the general encyclopædia.

The Library Card Index

Children should be given some information about the card index they will find in every library. For instance, they need to know that it is usually three indexes in one. One may be the *author index,* listing all books under the author. The second may be the *title index,* in which all books are listed again under the first word of the title. And third, there may be a *topical index,* which gives the names of books under the topic. Some libraries have a shelf list, in which the books are represented by cards, and the cards are arranged just as the books are on the shelf.

Children will be interested if shown the Dewey classification, or whatever classification is used in the local library. They will be intrigued by the idea that the number on every card and on every book tells so much about it. If they understand that the books are standing in the stacks exactly in the order that is given them by the numbers, they will be less likely, if allowed in the stacks, to put a book back just anywhere. They will be interested to know that in all libraries books are "lost" every day because they are put in the wrong place and just cannot be found. Someone has to "read" the stacks every so often to find those lost books.

An interesting plan is to have the children in any room make a card index of the books in their own library. They will be fascinated by the work, and they will get a new respect for books and a new understanding of classification of content. Any librarian will give suggestions on just how to do this.

THE READER'S GUIDE

Children will be much impressed if they can be taken to a large library and shown the bound volumes of periodicals. They will be astonished to see what a huge pile of volumes a single familiar, paper-bound magazine will make. If they can be allowed to leaf through the bound volumes of magazines, they will be struck by the immense amount of interesting material of all kinds which they run across. But how is one to find anything in that forest of volumes? The answer is a simple one: by using the Reader's Guide. If children can just run through the Reader's Guide, they will find a variety of material that is hardly conceivable. The guide gives references on everything one can imagine. And each reference is to a certain series of bound volumes, and to just one of those volumes, and to certain pages in that one volume. The whole situation of being able to get so easily so much knowledge is astonishing, and leads many children just to look up certain things they have often wondered about.

The use of the Reader's Guide is limited, of course, to the magazines available in the particular library the teacher can use. Often there are few bound magazines. In that case, the Guide cannot be used a very great deal. It is better to teach the use of the indexes to the volumes of the magazines which are available. Then the children would not be frustrated by failure to locate desired articles.

In large libraries, there are other published indexes, such as the Education Index, and others. The teacher who knows about such resources should suggest them in particular cases, but it is confusing to children to be told of too much that they have no use for. Let Guides and indexes be learned through use.

BOOK INDEXES AND TABLES OF CONTENTS

Our reference to knowledge about book indexes and tables of contents is put last because in using a library, one has to locate the book first before one can locate what is in the book. However, in the usual course of teaching, the children are ordinarily introduced to the table of contents very early in the grades, even in the first grade, when they wish to locate a certain story by looking at the table of contents. The use of an index is often taught with the first technical book, such as a geography. So by the time that use of reference books is taken up, the children understand fully about using tables of contents and indexes in books.

One feature of indexes often neglected is the use of the cross references. Anyone who has tried to make an index has found how impossible it often is to include some material under one topic only. He has the choice of repeating his reference under several topics or of putting it under one and then giving a cross reference under the others such as "see Remedial Reading" or the like. Cross references are common in indexes and children should have experience in using them.

Summary

Study implies different purposes from ordinary reading and therefore different methods. We shall see how these different purposes and methods are involved in school work. This chapter deals with "studying a topic."

School study of topics is becoming common for many reasons. *First,* topical study gets interest. *Second,* topical study integrates learnings. *Third,* topical study enables each school to make a curriculum best suited to its pupils. *Fourth,* much miscellaneous material on important topics is now available. *Finally,* topical study permits the best adaptation to individual differences. Groups may study topics under the newer plan of learning, or individuals may study topics under either that plan or the more traditional textbook one.

Teachers should not restrict all topical study to reading, since children may also learn by finding things out for themselves, by asking others, and by audio-visual aids.

Motivation is crucial for topical study. The usual motives we try to arouse are *curiosity, desire for approval of the group, desire to satisfy the teacher's expectations,* or *desire to live up to a self-ideal.*

In the study of topics, certain habits should be developed: (1) *The habit of covering the field,* and not just gathering bits of information. (2) *The habit of evaluating sources,* and not believing that everything in a book is necessarily true. (3) *The habit of using rapid reading methods* such as the habit of Skimming or the habit of Reading Parts, whichever suits the purpose best. (4) *The habit of using reference aids,* such as are found in books and libraries. (5) *The habit of note taking* so that material may be quoted correctly, and (6) *the habit of organizing ideas collected* to make a good report.

For the study of topics, children need to have knowledge concerning *glossaries, the dictionary, the encyclopædia, special encyclopædias, The Reader's Guide,* and *book indexes* and *tables of contents.*

CHAPTER XIII

Studying a Textbook

We have discussed first the study of a topic because that is the method toward which school practice is tending. However, most schools are as yet unprepared to adopt that plan of learning for their students. Most schools continue the customary practice of adopting for each subject, at any level, a single textbook, and studying that textbook. We shall therefore discuss the problems involved in teaching children how to study a textbook under this usual system.

The Textbook Just One Source of Information

As already suggested on page 419, we should impress upon our students that there are many ways of learning about any subject. In addition to our intensive study of any textbook, these other ways can be used. First, in connection with many textbook topics, children can find things out for themselves by observation or experiment. This is especially true in the field of everyday science. Second, in connection with some topics, the children can inquire of their parents or others. This will be true in some science work, and also in courses in health. It is true in social science work which brings up problems of community life and government. Third, there may be audio-visual aids, such as exhibits, pictures, films, and the like which can be added to the textbook work for interest and added information.

Fourth, no matter what the subject or the textbook, there are always supplementary books and magazines. Schools vary a great deal in the number of such resources in addition to the text. Some schools provide supplementary books in the classroom; most provide supplementary books in the library. Some schools provide magazines of all kinds that can supplement the text. But teachers vary even more in the extent to which they like to use supplementary materials. Some practically ignore supplementary sources, sticking closely to the text. Others use supplementary materials widely and constantly. In all our discussion of use of a text, it will be remembered that there may be in addition these four other sources of interest and information.

Complete Comprehension of the Textbook

We have pointed out that in the study of a topic, when many sources are being used and when much material is to be gone over, various kinds of rapid reading and skimming are possible, and often necessary. Therefore in such study, partial comprehension is often to be assumed. However, the textbook used in a school course is *not* to be partially comprehended. There is nothing in it which is to be skimmed or skipped. No relatively useless or unnecessary material is presumed to be included. Everything in the text was put in there for the purpose of registering in some definite way with the student. Everything is to be comprehended. That is to say, *100% comprehension is expected* (see Chapter XI, page 391 to page 393 for explanation that since ultimate, complete comprehension is never possible, 100% comprehension here means "complete under the circumstances").

We know that complete comprehension of the textbook is not universal. *First,* such large textbooks are often adopted that there is not time in the year for complete comprehension. Skimming or reading of parts may have to be resorted to. *Second,* the material in the textbook may be so far from the experience of much of the class that very many are totally unable to comprehend fully without teacher help. *Third,* teachers do not take time, or think they do not have the time to help with comprehension.

Fourth, some teachers are not interested in full comprehension because they want to dwell only upon part of the text. *Fifth,* teachers help students so much by the questions they ask that answers can be given without complete comprehension. This is especially true if questions are so asked that the exact words of the book can be used in answer. Thus the student is given a direct cue, and he can give back the words that are expected even if he does not understand what they mean. For these and other reasons, it is undoubtedly a fact that complete comprehension is not very general in many schools or in many subjects.

If less than complete comprehension is desired by the teacher, that fact should be made very clear to the student, and he should be told just what degree or kind of comprehension is expected. He should not be left to guess at what is wanted or to adopt his own choice of how much is to be comprehended or what is to be comprehended. If the teacher wishes to omit certain parts of the text, she can make this clear in two ways. She can point out what is to be skipped, so that it may be definitely passed over and not merely neglected. Or she can give study questions, so that the material that answers them can be learned and everything else passed over as less important or unimportant.

As a matter of personality training, as well as efficiency in learning, it is desirable that we let the children know just what is expected and then see that they do just what is expected. To appear to expect a good job and to accept a poor job is bad training for all concerned. Let us not so manage the class as to seem to encourage or to accept slipshod work. Let us make the job definite and then have that job done honestly.

READING ABILITY BEFORE STUDY

All through the school system we are constantly making the mistake of asking children to study material that they cannot read. Thus learning is blocked and repeated frustration set up. The children must learn to read before they can learn to study. Reading means instant sight vocabulary habits of word attack, and general meaning vocabulary. Development of these is needed before study becomes profitable. The primary grades are largely devoted to the teaching of reading. If the reading skills are not developed before the middle grades, then the middle grades must make the teaching of reading their first concern parallel with the teaching of study. Children cannot study if they cannot read.

For this reason, study of content subjects is much facilitated if the reading matter in those subjects is made easy reading. That is, reading difficulty should not stand in the way of learning the content. Authors of content books are realizing this fact and are making easier and easier books in their fields. In consequence, children are learning more and more from studying such books.[1]

Habits in Study of Textbooks

The usual thing is to emphasize that certain skills must be learned for use in the study of the textbook. It is true that we want the student to acquire certain skills, but it is much better for the teacher to think of teaching *habits*. If the habit is secured, the skill will follow, whereas if the emphasis is on skill, the necessary steps for habit formation may be neglected.

---

[1] See pages 352 to 356 in Teaching Primary Reading, Garrard Press, Champaign, Ill.

Habits Always Begin With Attitudes

As already emphasized elsewhere, only those who want to acquire a habit do acquire it. The first step in habit formation is the desire to get the habit. In the case of study, we may as well admit that if a child does not want to learn how to study he is never going to become a student. We may drive him to go through the motions, but if he does not want to make those motions, he will stop making them as soon as we stop driving. It is so very easy for adults, and especially teachers, to forget this simple psychological fact. It would seem that we would have it forced upon our notice by all our experience with children. How many of the things we "make" children do, do they continue to do when we stop "making" them?

Let us look at the matter in another way. Think of all the things that *we* have been "made to do" that we stopped doing immediately when the force was removed. We can think of all the subjects we were forced to study that we quit studying instantly when we were forced to study them no longer. We can list all the "good habits" our parents and teachers forced upon us that we did not want to learn. We do have some good habits, it is true, but they are ones we want to have, not the ones others wanted us to have. If anyone will honestly examine his own life, and honestly think of what children in school do in school and out, he will be forced to admit the truth of the statement, "Only those who want to acquire a habit ever acquire it."

This consideration brings us back again to the central principle of all education, "Motivation is the most important step." We must motivate study. The three motives already discussed in Chapter XII must always be remembered. Children will study out of *curiosity*. Children will study out of desire *to keep up with the group*. Children will study *to please the teacher* they like. Children will study because of a *self-ideal* that pictures them to themselves as the kind of people who study or who do the job assigned. We must use any or all of these motives, or any others that apply in the individual case. We will then develop the desire to learn how to study. And with increased habits of study, there will come increased success in study, which is again a strong motive force. And after habits are established we can get a good deal of practice in study. As a result of this practice, skill will gradually develop.

TEACHING ATTITUDES AND HABITS REQUIRES STUDY ALONG WITH THE CLASS

The only way a teacher can actually develop the right attitudes and be sure the right habits are learned is to begin the course by studying the assignment right along with the class. The assignment is made, the teacher and class open books, and all together they start to study. The teacher begins the motivation by thus showing that she is willing to help and to go along with the group. Her spirit of cooperation builds up cooperation from the others. Then as she and the class study the words, the sentences, and the paragraphs or larger units, she shows her own interest in the material and the others catch some of that interest from her. In addition, she continually injects into the discussion interesting information from her own large store of experiences. The material which at first may have seemed strange and lifeless takes on vividness and therefore interest. The teacher helps give it more meaning, and with meaning comes interest also. She shows the many associations of the new with the old, of the strange with the familiar. All this is in a sort of running comment along with the study and not as a lecture.

After motivation, the teacher must see that the methods we shall explain in this chapter are followed, and followed so constantly and consistently that they become habits. This is only possible if she studies with the class. She keeps asking those questions that the students should ultimately ask themselves. She keeps calling attention to those things that they must finally pay attention to without her. She keeps seeing that the right procedures are followed, and finally, those procedures may become habit. In some subjects, this studying with the class may take a week, with others a month or more. But it has been found that the practice results in vastly more learning in the long run. Of course, when the teacher no longer actually studies with the class, she will make such assignments as will remind them just what to do and how to do it.

What Habits Shall We Teach?

1. THE HABIT OF LEARNING THE MEANING OF EVERY WORD

An essential requirement for complete comprehension in study is *knowledge of every word meaning.* In ordinary reading this may not be necessary; one can get a story even if some words are blanks as to meaning. In extensive study, this may not be necessary, since the student may get the main idea or may get the desired information even if many words are unknown. But the intensive study of a text, with the purpose of 100% comprehension, demands that the meaning of every word be known.

When the teacher is studying with the class, she will question every word which she thinks some students may not fully understand. She will find that many are sure they know certain words when they do not. There is much "misknowledge" current about word meanings. But by questioning and having class contributions as to word meanings, the teacher will uncover differences of opinion about words and lead to a certain doubt in the children's minds which will make them less certain of their word knowledge in future study and cause them to be more willing to study words. She will emphasize use of context especially, but also the use of familiar parts of the words which suggest meaning from known words. She will have the dictionary used as a final authority as to meaning, and this will give her the opportunity of calling attention to the various different meanings the dictionary may give for one word. Here the class will have to refer back to the context to see which meaning is intended.

All of this study of words for meaning should be a sort of mental game. It must be pleasant or the teacher can never expect children to do any of it when she is not watching them. She must develop a feeling in the class that word meanings are fun, and also that they are important. There is fun in discriminating between synonyms, between "close meanings" which are not exactly alike. There is fun in deciding why the author used a certain word instead of another like it. This may lead to some understanding of the skill of the good writer in using the most suitable and most powerful word.

Many teachers will say there is not time for this study. There *has to be* time for it if we ever expect children to learn how to study. And if they do not learn how to study, the years ahead in high school and college may be largely wasted. It is a truth we must admit that, in any field, a small amount of knowledge, thoroughly understood and therefore well remembered, is vastly better than a large amount imperfectly understood and therefore quickly forgotten. If we completely understand, we "learn for keeps."

2. The Habit of Understanding Every Sentence

Teachers have such extensive language ability that they often do not realize how a sentence of even two lines in length will confuse children. Any teacher can look ahead through an assignment and find sentences of three, four, or five lines in length. In every such case, we may well be very suspicious of whether many of the children will actually understand what those sentences say.

Long sentences are usually signs either of poor thinking on the part of the writer, or, if the thinking is good, of the practice of "packing" a sentence. Many writers try very hard to pack into every sentence a great deal of meaning. They will work out a sentence like an elaborate design. They will put in the main idea, preceding it perhaps by several qualifications, modifying every word to be sure to give the exact phase of meaning they intend, adding adverbial phrases and clauses to build up their thought, stringing two or three adjectives to every noun to give more force or grace, doing all this slowly and carefully as if they were molding a work of art. (The sentence you have just read is intended as a sample of the kind of sentence we refer to.) Such writing used to be thought a literary accomplishment. Nowadays, however, we want simple,

straightforward statements. Children are accustomed to such statements in most of what they read.
When, therefore, they are given a text with the old
style "built up" or "packed" sentences, they are
often completely lost.

Our only recourse is to pick out such sentences
and ask the class to tell in their own words what
they say. What usually happens is that the class will
repeat the ideas of the long sentences in three or
four different sentences of their own. Such practice,
while the teacher is studying with the class, leads
the students to see that there is no real mystery
about those difficult sentences. They need just to be
taken piece by piece and "translated" into our own
thinking.

After the teacher has shown this fact, she
still has the problem of getting the children to work
on these long sentences after she no longer leads
them but merely assigns the lesson. One device here
is for her, during the assignment, to call attention
to the "first sentence on page 47," and the "next
to last sentence on page 48" or something of the
kind, and say that she will want to know what those
sentences say. Then the students will attack the difficult sentences and discover what they mean. To
build up the habit of trying to understand the individual sentences is very difficult, it takes time, and
it never will be done by many children. Yet we must
work toward this end if we want 100% comprehension in textbook study.

3. The Habit of Understanding the Thought Structure

Children need to learn that in every piece of writing there is a structure, a kind of skeleton of thoughts, which the writer built up before he began to do any writing at all. They need to know that this skeleton of thought was built first and was then "clothed" with other thoughts and ideas to make the article or chapter or book. The problem of the reader is to discover, in the pages and pages of words, sentences, and paragraphs, just what is this original skeleton of thought.

Children may discover this idea of the "skeleton of thought" or the idea of "thought structure" through trying to do pieces of writing themselves. This is not usually done, however, because the writing done by children is so simple as to demand no very elaborate or extended structure or outline. We usually find that the reading matter that children meet with has a much more elaborate structure than any they themselves would devise; therefore we have to get them to see the structure in the work of others first. This is not to discount our efforts to have the children outline or plan their talks made to the class or their pieces of writing. We should emphasize thought structure as much as possible. But the demands of this writing will never equal the demands of their reading.

We should also call attention to the fact that good writers try to show the reader the thought structure by many devices, most of which we shall refer to in a moment. However, some writers think it a mark of good writing to conceal the evidences of structure. They try to make transitions so smooth that the average reader does not see them and so does not know that a transition from one point to another has been made.

Still other writers are so unskilled that they give us textbooks and articles which defy our efforts to find thought structure in them. That is, there are a host of textbooks which simply cannot be outlined even by an expert, just because there is no outline in them. They are just ideas strung together without system or with a system that does not appear to the reader. It is in fact about time publicly to admit that much of the difficulty children have in reading textbooks is in the poor writing of those textbooks. It has been proposed that every textbook have as co-author an expert writer who will put the specialist's material into readable form; but this proposal has not been adopted.

Outlining

The habit of understanding the thought structure actually means the habit of outlining what you read. This means *discovering* the outline, *not* making a new outline. We have mentioned (page 430) that in extensive study of a topic, much material is gathered from many sources, and the student must do his own outlining of the material. But when a text is being studied, the text is already outlined. The reader does not organize the ideas; he just finds out what the organization is. There has been much confusion on this point, and some students try to take a book and rearrange it into their own outline. This is not the kind of textbook study we are here dealing with.

We should emphasize, therefore, that we are here concerned strictly with "following the author." The outline we shall speak of is the author's outline. The important things we refer to are the ones that the author thinks are important. The main points or minor points are the ones the author designates as major or minor. *We are entirely concerned with taking the text as it is and understanding it in terms of what the author put into it.* Any independent arrangement or evaluation is a part of study of topics instead of study of a single book, and is treated in the preceding chapter.

WORKING UP FROM PARAGRAPHS OR DOWN FROM MAIN POINT

There are two different methods which may be followed in working out the outline or thought structure of a piece of writing. One may be called the "working up" method, meaning that we begin with the paragraphs and work up to the structure from them. According to this plan, we would take each paragraph, one at a time, and discover its topic or central thought. If there were fifty paragraphs in the chapter or selection, we would thus arrive at fifty topic or paragraph statements. We would list these fifty from the first to the last. Then we would go over them and decide which ones go together, in this way arriving at larger topics or thought divisions. We would then consider these larger divisions and see if they could be grouped into still larger divisions. In this way the progression would be from the minor points, to the more major points, then to the chief points of the whole discussion, and finally to the central topic or thought of the whole.

This progression from the paragraph, or the "working up" method, is the one usually followed in books on teaching outlining or the discovery of thought structure. It has the virtue of seeming to go from the simple to the complex, from the part to the whole. It does begin with small, manageable units. It introduces the student to the idea of what a paragraph is for and how a paragraph should be read. One of the techniques of teaching how to study any subject should be beginning with the reading of paragraphs and telling what the paragraph is about.

We must be aware, however, that this "working up" method is not the one used by the mature adult reader. He will not use so laborious a method. Instead, he goes *first* to the point of the whole chapter or article. The adult reader discovers that point from the title, from the beginning statement, from a skimming of the whole, or he builds it up as he reads.

His chief interest is in the main point and that is why he seeks for it first. *Second,* the adult reader looks for the main divisions of the whole discussion. He does this by noticing the author's suggestions of his main points, which are often given at some point in the article. The adult reader wants these main points because if he is to remember anything about the discussion, it is the main points he wants to remember. *Finally,* if at all, the mature reader pays attention to the minor points or ideas which may be represented by single paragraphs.

That this "working down" from the central topic or thought is very different from "working up" from the paragraphs is seen if we consider the case of the chapter with fifty paragraphs we have just mentioned. The mature reader does not pay much attention to the points of the individual paragraphs. He does not want fifty points. He wants the main one and he wants three or five or six main divisions. Obviously, the main ideas of certain of the fifty paragraphs are some of the points he is looking for, but most of them are not. He may notice paragraph ideas as he goes along, but he immediately discards any which he sees are minor points. He seizes on those which he sees are major ideas. This means he may note especially the point of paragraph two, the point of paragraph 18, the point of paragraph 27, the point of paragraph 42 and the point of paragraph 48. All the others he passes over immediately.

How does the mature reader pick out these points, without first assembling 50 different paragraph statements? He does this in two ways. The *first* way is by noticing the "signals" that the writer gives him as he goes along, which signals we shall discuss later. The *second* way is by noticing the logic of the thought as he goes along. He may get this logic by "skimming for general impression," as explained in the previous chapter.

We have said that paragraphs should be studied as part of study of any subject matter. We must at once say that as soon as possible, the attention should go from paragraphs to the main topic and main divisions of a subject. This means that, at first, the study will be by paragraphs, but that soon the student will be asked to read the whole assignment and to think of it first as a whole, and then to break it down into divisions.

When can this be done? We do not have facts at this point, and the teacher must decide which way to direct the study of her class. She will consider (1) the maturity of the class, (2) their interest in the subject, and (3) the kind of book they are studying. These three conditions, or any one of them, may cause her to delay transfer to the study of the whole assignment, or may cause her to hasten the change from paragraph study to study of the whole. Of course the two methods are not mutually exclusive. While the whole assignment is being surveyed for main point and main divisions, there may also be study of individual paragraphs to discover the author's message in them. The two methods supplement each other.

KINDS OF PARAGRAPHS

A stumbling block to the study of paragraphs is the fact that a paragraph is a division of written material that is often made for other reasons than strict logic. Readers are repelled by too long paragraphs. They feel that the beginning of a new paragraph gives them a sort of new "mental breath." So writers often make paragraphs at somewhat illogical places just so as to cut the material into "easy-looking" paragraphs.

Even when paragraphs are made logically, *there are three distinct kinds of paragraphs*. The one teachers refer to most often are the *"statement" paragraphs,* which are really a sentence-statement expanded by adding other facts or ideas. The author who uses statement paragraphs usually begins with a sentence outline. Then he expands each sentence into a paragraph. The reader can then reverse the process and find the statements with which the author began and thus find his thought structure.

Statement paragraphs are not as common as they should be just because writers do not work out their thinking into sentence outlines as often as they should. They are most common in articles which are really arguments. In such cases, there is likely to be a list of arguments or reasons, each of which is a statement. Usually the statement paragraph begins with the topic statement, though sometimes the paragraph begins with a transition, leading from the former paragraph to the new one. Sometimes, of course, there is reason for placing the topic statement at the end of the paragraph. The usual reason is that the writer is afraid the statement will not be accepted if placed first. So he gives the reasons for or the explanation of the statement first and then gives the statement which he wishes to make. Statement paragraphs are usually logically built up, since the initial structure is logical. The topic statement is usually quite apparent.

A much more common type of paragraph is the *"basket" paragraph,* which does not make a statement but which is all about a certain topic or subject. Such a paragraph can easily be conceived of as a sort of "mental basket" into which all the things that are related to one topic are put. The paragraph may contain a great many statements, no one of which is the topic statement of the paragraph. Instead, all of the statements *concern* a central topic. Very often students think every paragraph must make a single statement or have a topic statement, and they therefore try to make one of the statements in a "basket paragraph" parade as the topic statement of the whole. The way to avoid this is first to ask what the paragraph is "about." Then ask whether it says a single thing about that topic. If it says, in effect, a single thing, then it is a statement paragraph. If it says many things about that topic, then it has a topic only, and is a "basket" paragraph.

The *third* type of paragraph is the most common one used in stories. A story is a continuous string of narrative, each part following the part before. It will be found that a narrative can be divided into paragraphs in many ways. There are many "joints" to the story, and a new paragraph can be begun at any of these joints. For easy reading, the modern policy is to paragraph often, and hence to have short paragraphs. But the same material can be logically paragraphed in many ways, just because the story is in effect a "train of thought" and this train of thought can be divided at many points.

The *"train of thought" paragraph* has a sequence from the beginning to the end, but it may or may not be on a single topic. It certainly does not have a topic statement. It will be found that many explanatory articles use train of thought paragraphs. The explanation goes on according to some natural sequence, and the writer paragraphs at a point which gives ease of reading or emphasis. Within the paragraph the ideas follow one another but may go from one topic to another. Many books on all subjects contain "train of thought" paragraphs. The writer just writes on and on, each thought following the one before, and he paragraphs every so often chiefly for looks. The student trying to find topics or topic statements in such paragraphs is bound to be disappointed.

A "divided long paragraph" is also a common occurrence in writing. The writer sees that his discussion of a topic is going to take more than the usual paragraph length. So he makes a cut at a convenient place and just goes on with the same topic. A good place to make such a cut in a long paragraph is between the statement of the point and the illustration of the point. That is why so many paragraphs begin with the words, "For instance." This means they are an appendage to the paragraph that went before. Some such paragraphs may be seen in this book.

There are other *special kinds of paragraphs* that we must recognize if we are skilfully to discover the thought structure used by an author. One of these, the *transitional paragraph,* is usually easily recognized. In the first place, it is usually shorter than other paragraphs. Second, it usually definitely states that it is closing one part of the discussion and beginning another. Often it merely closes, leaving the beginning of the next topic to the paragraph that follows. Others kinds of paragraphs that appear are *introductory and concluding paragraphs.* These might be called "basket" paragraphs because in making a beginning the writer often has to put in a number of things that precede his discussion but which he merely states and does not develop. Likewise, in closing, the author may wish to make some statements that he throws together in a kind of final leave-taking. Often, of course, the conclusion is made with a *summary paragraph* which is easily recognized because it lists the points made or repeats the main points of the article.

It is the existence of these special kinds of paragraphs, *introductory, transitional, concluding* and *summary* that enable the skilled reader to get the thought structure rapidly and make him able to "work down" from the main point to the chief divisions. If students are to study an article as a whole, they should receive early training in noting these special kinds of paragraphs.

"Signals" of Structure

A study of "signals" by which an author guides the reader to his thought structure has been made by Rachel Salisbury, author of "Making Sense" (Scott Foresman and Co.). Miss Salisbury divides "signals" into "full signals" and "half signals." The full signals are the uses of numbers or letters during the discussion to point out ideas. The author may say "first," "second" and so on, or he may use the numbers 1), 2), 3) and the rest in the series. He may also use the letters A, B, C, etc. or a, b, c, and so on.

The reader should immediately notice any such signals and watch for the rest of any series which is begun. The reader also needs to watch for the shift from the numbering of main ideas to the numbering or lettering of minor ones. For instance, under the discussion of *"first,* the climate of the country," the author may take up *"a),* the rainfall," and later after discussing *b)* and *c)* he will go back to *"second,* the soil," and so on. The careful author can use these full signals to give the reader a complete outline if he wishes.

Many authors are afraid of appearing mechanical by use of numbers or letters and instead use certain words which Salisbury calls "half signals." Some of these words are *on the one hand, on the other hand, some* and *others, in the beginning, later on, this* and *that, still another, finally,* and many other words which point out without actually numbering. Here, as with the full signals, there is the need for watching shifts from main points to minor points, because the words used do not in themselves show the order of importance.

DEALING WITH POOR WRITING

Here we must repeat that much of the material we give to school children is poorly written. It does not have a clear thought structure. It does not have definite thought divisions. This is very natural since very many of the persons who write books are not trained writers. Writing factual material is just as much an art as writing fiction. There is great skill required in taking masses of ideas, all interrelated in many ways, and straightening them out into a clear, logical structure. There is still another art

in presenting those ideas clearly, one at a time and
one after the other as they have to be presented in
printed matter. To present ideas coherently in the
best order, to show that order, and to make the
whole smooth reading, is an art which is not very
common.

When the writer's thought is not logical and his
arrangement is not clear, the teacher must help the
class. One way is to point out the main idea if that
is not clear. Or the teacher may then have to point
out the main divisions. In other words, the teacher
must give some of the structure which will not be
evident to the children. If the writing is quite hope-
less, all the teacher can do is to give the class a list
of study questions, leaving it to them to find the
answers. They can do this by use of word or idea
clues, without having to work out the writer's
thought structure.

Other Habits in Study of Textbooks

Our discussion of the *habit of understanding the
thought structure* of the text led us necessarily into
a lengthy discussion of *outlining*. We now return to
our listing of the habits needed for effective study
of textbooks.

4. The Habit of Self Testing

It is very common for a student, when asked, "Do
you know your lesson," to answer, "I don't know."

He means just what he says, because he will not know until someone questions him on the lesson. He has read it, perhaps more than once, but he does not know how much he has understood or retained. He may even have studied it logically, but he still does not know if he can explain it, or if he can remember it. He just "does not know."

The student who is most successful will have discovered that he can be sure that he knows if he will test himself. One way to test himself is to tell what he has learned to someone else, a roommate or a brother or sister, or his mother or father. If he can tell it and explain it, then he knows he understands and remembers. Lacking someone else to whom to tell the lesson, the student can tell it to himself. He can close the book, and either aloud or under his breath state and explain the points he has learned. If he can do this after study, the chances are he can do it in class. In fact, telling is the very best way of imprinting the material strongly on the memory. So a good student not only uses his habits of study, but he develops that habit of self-testing to be sure of understanding and remembering.

5. The Habit of Reacting

We are here putting near the end of our discussion a habit of comprehension which should more properly be first of all. However, we have wished to clear the ground of various more technical matters before taking up this basic and fundamental habit of the student, whether he be a student in school or a student during all the years of after school life.

One reads with the mind. One learns to read better by bringing more and more of the mind to bear on the reading material. One does this by calling up more and more of related past experience, and by doing more and more with that past experience. As the student's definition states, "Reading is imagining, thinking and feeling about ideas and thoughts made from past experience suggested by the perception of printed materials." If reading is thinking and feeling, the more thinking and feeling, the more reading.

Reacting to reading material is based on original nature but in school such reacting bacomes a habit. In the primary grades, the habit is quite common. The stories given the children are about other children doing the things that the little readers would like to do. The children of the primary grades usually react so definitely and unanimously that the teacher has difficulty keeping them from blurting out their remarks or from all talking at once. But beginning with the middle grades, the study material rapidly goes away from child experience. It goes to far corners of the world and to strange places and activities that are often not made real to the children. Reading may become reading words instead of reading thoughts. The reaction that would otherwise be natural is usually impossible. So the *habit of reading without reaction* sets in. This habit may continue all the way through high school and college. In fact, a major objection of college professors to their students is that they read and repeat but do not react with thoughts and feelings of their own.

One may say, of course, that children continue in the habit of reacting to things they read outside of school, to the comics and the like. There is considerable truth to this, since interest is itself a reaction and immediately tends to bring about other reactions of agreement or disagreement or associated ideas, and so on. Therefore if we maintain, grade by grade, interest in the reading done, we will maintain in school as well as outside this habit of reacting in reading.

But in school we want more reaction than just the natural spontaneous one to the stories read. The discussion of stories read in school is intended to make the natural reaction deeper and more profound, and to cause it to spread to more than just the action of the story. We want the children to react to the characters and to the setting, and to the plot, rather than just to the excitement and suspense. Here is where we want to develop and spread the habit of reacting.

We can say also that we have to develop *a habit of reaction to factual material,* especially to material that is not of the exciting kind. We have given a whole series of reactions that children should habitually make to any factual material they read, such as "Who wrote it?" How did he know about it? Does he give the whole story? Does he give it fairly and impartially? All these questions will not naturally arise in most children. But when we bring them up ourselves, children begin to find a certain excitement and thrill in asking such questions, and they may after a time *get the habit* of having these critical reactions to reading matter.

To get in children the habit of reacting, our *first* problem is the *choice of material.* The teacher can be sure of getting reaction to some stories or books or articles and can be pretty sure of having trouble getting reaction to others. *Second,* the teacher must sense how far to go in encouraging reaction. If she pushes the matter too far, she gets the opposite result from what she wishes. Children are easily repelled. Many teachers by using too much pressure get only one reaction, the desire to stop reading. So one must gauge wisely what questions to ask, and how many to ask, and when to go on. *Third,* there must be a slight but continual suggestion that reaction is expected and will be approved. A constant encouragement of comment and other reaction is what will produce a habit, not an occasional heavy siege of inquiry and discussion. Habits take time.

Study Workbooks

There are at present, and there always will be, a large number of study workbooks available to the teacher of any grade. Should she use them? Which should she use? How much? And how?

One is forced to believe that the makers of some of these study workbooks had no definite ideas of what study was. They seem just to have got some reading matter, put it in a book, and then asked about it any questions that occurred to them. Such workbooks may interest. Such workbooks may cause a general attention to the thought in reading. Such workbooks may impress the idea that you are supposed to know what you have read after you have read it. Such workbooks may give miscellaneous practice in many study habits.

On the other hand, many if not most of these miscellaneous study workbooks are uninteresting and bore the teacher and the child. In that case, they are definitely bad. No possible gain from reading and marking or filling in the blanks can compensate for the unfavorable attitudes produced. It is better to use no workbook than an uninteresting one.

There is another kind of study workbook. In this kind, the author does have a definite philosophy of study. He does know the definite habits he wants the children to learn. Then he makes the workbook to fit his specifications. Should teachers use this kind of a study workbook?

If the kinds of study emphasized in this "types of study" workbook are the kinds the teacher believes in or which she wishes to emphasize at the moment, then she will get good results from its use. There are several dangers, however. *One* is that the teacher will impose this same kind of workbook on a class or a group for too long a time and thus bore them because of the lack of variety that sets in. Loss of interest will definitely lessen or cancel results. *Second,* the teacher may get such good results in terms of filling in blanks and getting certain kinds of answers that she will think she has the study problem solved. She will have a false sense of success.

Actual study by children varies (1) with the child, (2) with his abilities and interests, (3) with the kind of material he is reading, and (4) with the kind of thing that will please his teacher. Kinds of study are infinite because every kind varies in many ways. Teaching of study therefore must be flexible. It cannot follow rigid lines, as a workbook may.

For workbook study to help classroom study and classroom success the teacher must get a "transfer" of attitudes, habits and skills. Some children will apply to their textbook study the workbook practice, but very many never will do it of themselves. They "succeed" with the workbook but are no better in class. The school that uses "types of study" books must take care that its thinking about study does not become rigid and unrealistic. It is study of the textbook that counts. Is it benefited by the workbook study? How?

Special Study Habits for Special Subjects

So far, we have been discussing *general study habits* which apply more or less to all subjects regardless of their own special nature. But general study habits have to be adapted to the special subjects. In addition, special subjects have their own special study habits.

If we begin to think of the special subjects taken up in school we at once see the presence of such special study habits. In arithmetic, for instance, there is the study of problems that requires the very special habit of visualizing the situation so that the problem is real, so that we see just what the people in the problem are doing, and what they are trying to find out. This is an application of the general habit of visualizing any situation read about but it involves the visualizing of the numbers, and sizes or prices of things as well as the general set-up.

In history, we have another special application of the general habit of visualizing, but we also have the problem of understanding time. For instance, a date by itself has no meaning. The date 1092 has no meaning until we begin to relate it to something. Every date may be understood in several ways. One way is to relate it to some century or to some historical "movement." Another way to understand 1092 would be to say it is 26 years after the Norman Conquest. In fact, this last method of understanding dates, that is, relating them to certain "guideposts of history" is most profitable for children. Thus dates around 1492 become "so many years before or after the discovery of America." The student of history has a string of these guideposts down the centuries and can use them in this way to "understand dates." This use is a special study habit for history.

In science, isolated facts can be understood and remembered by the study habit of locating each one as the illustration of some law, such as thinking that the skidding of an automobile is an illustration of the law of inertia that a moving object tends to continue to move in the same direction unless stopped or redirected by some force.

In art, what we have called study habits are divided into "understanding habits" and into "appreciation habits." We understand a picture, we say, if we know who painted it, what his special interests and techniques were, what his place was in the development of painting, what kinds of technical composition, color scheme, etc., etc. it represents. The art teacher emphasizes these things as "understanding habits" in art. But she also should emphasize "appreciation habits," since study of art should develop appreciation. One of the appreciation habits is to catch the "first impression" a work has upon you. What is that first impression? Then we watch the "continued effect" upon us. De we remain interested, or do we tire of the work? Does our interest change, or does the appeal of the picture shift? We must give the picture time in two ways: we must regard it carefully at a sitting, and we must come back to it again and again and see what happens. These are the habits of the art critic and the art connoisseur. Children should be aware that they exist and should try them out on such works as are available; for instance, on pictures hanging in the corridor of their school.

A special but important application of the general habits of understanding and appreciation is in the study of works of literature, such as poetry. Here the habits of understanding are often emphasized by English teachers, with attention to the author, historical setting, qualities, and so on. We also need to emphasize the special habit of "giving the poem a chance" by hearing it read aloud, by reading it aloud, by hearing it read by various persons in different ways. We also need to point out that time is a factor in appreciation of poetry also. We should read the poem weeks later to see if anything has happened to our feelings about it.

Teachers of the special subjects could help us all by bringing to our attention the special study habits that are useful and appropriate to their own subjects. General study habits will help us, but special study habits can carry us much farther into effective learning in all the many fields in which educated persons wish to develop themselves.

Summary

In our emphasis upon the textbook as the object of our study, we must not forget all the other sources of interest and information which may supplement the textbook.

For textbook study we must have the ideal of complete comprehension. Other types of study and use of other materials may permit partial comprehension, but the textbook was made and is used with the expectation of 100% comprehension.

The best approach to skill in use of the textbook is in terms of the habits that must be formed. But habits must begin with attitudes, since one does not acquire a habit that he does not want to acquire. The teacher may secure the desired attitudes toward study only by studying with the class at the beginning of the term. She also sees that the following habits are used as she studies with them so that those same habits will operate when she puts the class on its own for study.

What Habits Shall We Teach?

1. *The Habit of Learning the Meaning of Every Word.*

2. *The Habit of Understanding Every Sentence.*

3. *The Habit of Understanding the Thought Structure.*

For an understanding of the thought structure of a chapter or an article, *outlining* is necessary. This may be done by beginning with the topics or statements of paragraphs and working up through the minor and major points to the topic or point of the whole. That is called the "working up method" and is commonly taught. However, the practiced reader uses the "working down" method, beginning with the main point, and going down to minor points as far as he is interested in doing so. Outlining is complicated by the three kinds of paragraphs, the "topic statement" paragraph, the "basket" paragraph, and the "train of thought" paragraph, each of which has its use in writing. The skilled reader also learns to know special kinds of paragraphs—transition, introduction, conclusion and summary. He finds the main point and main divisions by attention to "signals" of structure given by numbers or letters or by special words.

Poor writing is a special problem, and when the text is not well organized or outlined, the teacher must help the class by giving part of the structure or by resorting to study questions.

Other Habits in Study of Textbooks are:

4. *The Habit of Self-testing,* by which the student can measure his own understanding and remembering, and

5. *The Habit of Reacting,* which is fundamental to all reading with understanding.

Study Workbooks are of two kinds. The kind which includes miscellaneous material and asks rather random questions may interest but cannot help much. The "Types of Study" workbook is useful if it does not cause the teacher to neglect real study of the textbook, which cannot follow the rigid form of the workbook.

Special study habits are needed for all the special subjects, such as arithmetic, history, science, and so on.

CHAPTER XIV

A Lifetime Reading Habit

Beginning with the conditions of Readiness, we have traced the development of the reading process through Building Sight Vocabulary, Developing Independent Word Attack, Increasing Meaning Vocabulary, Securing Fluency, and Getting More Out of Reading Through Study. The culmination of the whole process, if it is to be of real value to the individual and to the society of which he is a part, must be a Lifetime Reading Habit.

School Is for Life

Strangely enough, we who live with children in schools must constantly remind ourselves that school is for life. There is the ever-present pressure to get through the day, the week, the month, or the semester. We have always before us immediate goals. In reading we have a lesson or a book to get through. We have certain words to teach. We have a step in sounding to explain. The children are living in the present, without thought of distant futures. We are tempted to follow their example, and forget the long years ahead.

One way to make the problem concrete and vivid is to think of each individual's life as being in three parts. The first part, the one usually thought of as preparation, ends with the young man's getting married and getting a job. Now he is a member of the adult community, carrying the responsibilities of such a member. Up to that time, until around twenty-five years of age, he was something of a parasite, unsettled, wavering between one plan or another.

The second part of the individual's life is usually spent in raising a family. Here the man is establishing himself financially, and both man and woman are caring for children, looking after their health, their adjustment, their happiness. The second part of life comes to a close after the children in turn grow up, go away, marry and set up households. This second part of the individual's life usually ends somewhere around fifty years of age.

Then for most people there begins the third part of life. The responsibilities of family are largely over. Financial stability has usually been achieved either through collection of money or by establishment in some line of work. There is much leisure time after work, and there is much need to occupy that time pleasantly and profitably.

The development of reading ability comes, obviously, in the first part of this three-part story. It comes usually before the age of fifteen. But why do we develop this reading ability? Obviously so that it can be used during all the other stages of life. With the present steady increase in length of human life, this reading ability which we develop so early should last and be of continued value and profit for fifty to sixty years of living. It functions in choosing of an occupation and of a life-partner. It functions in raising a family and doing a job. And it functions most definitely in the years of leisure that come to old age.

In short, any development of reading, to be of any real value, must include a lifetime reading habit that goes on and on for a very long time. Our problem then becomes, How can we best develop such a Lifetime Reading Habit?

Real Education Demands a Lifetime of Reading

Viewed in the large perspective just described, school is obviously just the "introduction" to an education. School gives a little taste of this and a little taste of that. What we call the curriculum is just a sampling. School geography, for example, is a rapid superficial survey of the world. No single country, not even our own, is treated in adequate detail. A few individuals take college courses in geography and get a more adequate idea of some parts of the world. But, for most, the slight acquaintance given in the elementary school is all they get unless they are interested enough to get more through a lifetime of reading. This does not mean necessarily the reading of books on geography, but the noticing of items on geography in the daily paper, reading all or part of the many articles on geography in the magazines, and so on. The small taste given in the school is just the beginning of knowledge in this enormous field.

Similarly in every other curriculum area, the school material is just an "introduction" to start a lifetime of reading in the field. There are two very good reasons why this must be so. *First,* children cannot do more than get a vague, superficial idea of any great field of knowledge. They begin with what they know and go a short distance further. But they are children, preoccupied with their immediate living conditions and needs. They are not students who delve into a subject deeply. *Second,* there is not time for anything more than a slight, superficial treatment of any subject.

For instance, during school years we say something to children about volcanoes. We give a rough idea of the causes and the effects. That is all we have time for. But the study of volcanic action throughout the world and what it has done in formation of land masses, change of land levels, formation of rocks and soils, and so on is something of great interest that adults should learn about as time goes on. They do this as a result of reading about the relation of diamond mines to volcanic cones, the presence of such cones in many parts of the United States, the relation of old lava flows to the Columbia River valley and others in this country, the effect of volcanic ash on soils in many places, the location of chains of mountains throughout the world, the various kinds of building stones and their volcanic origin, and many other items that come up in newspapers, magazines, books, and even conversation as one lives on through life.

In contrast to this fact, that school is just a beginning, many children have the very queer impression that they get away from education when they get through school. They feel that their education is finished when they graduate. They feel there will be no more "need" to learn. As a result, a vast number of individuals "stand still" in education at the same level they had reached with their last year of school. If the teachers had pushed them along to grade VIII, they remain Eighth Graders in knowledge and thinking for the rest of their lives. If, instead, the teachers had prodded them along through high school they remain high school graduates the rest of their lives, actually twelfth graders in most lines of knowledge and thought.

The moral of this sad situation is certainly that in all such cases, the school has failed to give an understanding that the individual is educated, not by eight or twelve years in school, but by a lifetime of reading. Of course many of the individuals who celebrate an end to learning will, as a matter of fact, keep on reading and will thus keep on educating themselves then though they have never planned on doing so. They may have a reading habit that they have never associated with continuation of education. But with all too many, however, there is no reading habit and no intention of continuing education. Then the individual will probably remain largely at the level he had attained when leaving school. We should try to avoid such an ending of education if at all possible. And the surest way is to direct our efforts consciously toward developing a lifetime reading habit in all children.

"Better Types" of Reading Matter

READING FOR MORE ENJOYMENT

First of all, most reading will always be done "for the fun of it." The teacher's serious purposes must not lead her to forget that fact. Animal stories, for instance, will always pass our time with pleasant imaginings, though they may not teach "lessons" and thus may leave us no better citizens or human beings. Similarly, adventure stories, when innocent of false values and sheer misinformation, may properly be read "for fun" by children of all ages. *In this field of out-and-out recreational reading, "better type" means stories which are more enjoyable.* This means they are better done and, therefore, give us more good fun for the time or money we invest. From this point of view we can distinguish only two grades, the less and the more entertaining. It is most important that whatever other characteristics the books that the teacher suggests may have, they should at least belong to the *more entertaining* class. And this means she will tell the children of books that will prove more interesting *to them,* not to an adult like herself.

READING FOR "EDIFICATION"

A second meaning for "better type" of reading matter is books *which are calculated to improve the character of the reader*. Parents are especially interested in the selection of books of this kind, and the schools are giving the matter more and more attention. In fact, a national competition was once held for plans by which reading could be caused to develop character, and the result was a list of books containing the literature which may be read to or by children, with an analysis of each book for the character influence it may be expected to have.

There is not the least doubt that the books children read influence their character profoundly. We know how quickly a child's ideals and habits can be altered by imitation of some much admired playmate. We try to select teachers whose character children can and will imitate. In the same way, children will admire and imitate the people that books create in their imagination. We tell tales of national heroes with this purpose in view, but probably more effective are the tales children read about others of their own age. The Boy Scout Association of America is well aware of this, and is trying through its library committee to get its members to read stories about boys of sterling character. In fact, all persons who have thought about the question at all are sure that edification or its opposite through reading is an undisputed fact with which we must actively deal.

We should here make the proviso that the example in a book is many times weaker than an example in real life. A second fact we must remember is that children do not imagine all the good or all the evil they read about. They read of robbers on the highroad, but they do not imagine at all the mental attitude which makes a man demand another's money at the point of a revolver. The same is true of examples of self-denial, heroism, and the like. Imagination requires experience, and lack of experience protects children from the harmful aspects of much of what they read in adult books and magazines, and at the same time makes them miss the moral lessons that many authors try to convey.

Unfortunately both children and adults have a great prejudice against reading for edification. One cause is that "good" books about "good" people are often stupid tales about nonentities. This is a result of the notion that a person can be good just by not being bad, and this negative attitude produces a proper rebellion on the part of normal live people. Another cause is that to be told one needs to be edified amounts to a definite reflection upon one's character, and this we naturally resent.

The answer to both these difficulties is that teachers need to recommend stories about real or imagined persons who have all the dynamic qualities and yet whose characters can be freely imitated. The most striking illustration of this method is our universal recommending of tales of noble knights. The

rather violent deeds of these persons appeal to basic
inborn tendencies, and yet they encourage cultiva-
tion of bravery, honor, courtesy, and many other
desirable traits. In modern stories the problem is
not so easy because at first glance the bad people
seem to monopolize the action and romance. More
and more, however, we are getting modern writers
who can present good people attractively. For instance, defenders of law and order have stories as
romantic as those of thieves. There is as much appeal to stories of worthy success in school, in business, in love, or what not, as there is to tales of
wrongdoing in all these spheres. In the past many
dynamic personalities had tended to "go to the bad"
because the world did not provide enough room for
them in constructive work. More and more, however,
we are getting away from such a situation, and it is
more easy to get both interest and edification.
Finally, let it be remembered that the character improvement must be entirely incidental. Do not tell
a child that a book will make him better, or you will
rouse a not unwarranted resentment. In fact, many
children are convinced that elders always recommend books that are "good for them" and consequently prefer to take the advice of other children
as to what are good books.

Reading for Learning

A third meaning of "better type" of books is
those *which increase the reader's useful informa-*

tion. Children can early realize that they may learn something from books. If they have found out that it is fun to learn things, this gives books an added appeal. Unfortunately many children are slow to realize this fact, and some never do. Consequently the teacher cannot emphasize at the start the profit to be got from reading. Instead she can recommend books for the excitement of their action or the strangeness of their setting, being sure that learning will result. Geography tales in the early grades are recommended because they give interesting adventures of other boys and girls in strange places. It would be useless to say, "This is a good way to learn a lot of geography," but the geography is learned nevertheless.

With older children we should definitely set forth the principle that reading should be worth while as well as entertaining. This very idea is becoming rather common with regard to moving pictures. Adults and children know that entertainment is provided every evening at the picture show, but intelligent people, young and old, wait for "good" pictures. By this they mean pictures which not only give a lot of entertainment but also leave the solid satisfaction which comes when something new has been learned or thought about as the result of the time and money spent. The same mental situation appears with regard to books. Most intelligent people feel that they are wasting their time if they read books which are *merely* entertaining. A book must be interesting, but they want the added satisfaction of feeling when they are through that they "got something."

Combination of Types

It goes without saying that many books may be better along a number of the lines enumerated. We need only insist that they consistently be better in the first way—in giving more entertainment. So many books do one good or teach or stimulate thought but become dull in doing so. Adults may possibly continue reading under such circumstances, but not children, who demand a life of active enjoyment, whether in reality or imagination. "More fun" must, therefore, be insisted upon, and the other appeals should be added as may be possible.

What Makes Up a Lifetime Reading Habit

It must be understood, of course, that there will not be and cannot be any lifetime reading habit unless there is fluency at some useful level, as emphasized in Chapter X. There must be some level of reading material which the individual can attack with ease and confidence. That level may be the level of the pulp magazine, but at that level there is a never-ending supply of material of many kinds; and the one who can read easily at the pulp level need never be without something to read. Or the level may be that of most of the paperback books, which is a bit higher perhaps than that of the pulp magazines because the subject matter may be much more diverse and cover a wider vocabulary. The reading level of the newspaper can hardly be identified because every sort of material is in the newspaper, and readers of the news choose the headlines that interest them and thus make a selection from the whole.

Granted fluency at some useful level, what makes some persons "readers" and others not readers? Again we must make allowances for persons of different dominant interests as described when we were pointing out that some children are "thing-minded," some are "people-minded," and some are "word-minded." Obviously, even adults differ in these ways, some being inclined to spend their spare time with tools, some with people, and some with books.

Most persons are not dominantly of any one of these types, but include all these tendencies in varying degree. That is, a man may have tools, and he may have friends, and he may have magazines or books. At one time he may be more interested in one than in the others. If he gets a furniture building project in mind, he may spend all his time with his tools. If he has an interesting new neighbor, he may spend all his spare time chatting with him. But such interests change from time to time, and the man's leisure is usually divided between several activities. How much of a share in those activities will reading have?

Fundamentally, *what causes an individual to read during all of his life is the knowledge that reading is the open door to more living, and to deeply satisfying living.* Every person has a thirst to live more fully, and the reader knows that through reading he can do so. He may actually get little reading done because of the press of other affairs, but he is still a reader. He knows that when he can get his hands on reading matter, and get a moment or two to himself, he will read. College students loaded with studies still may have the hunger for reading, though they may do none of it outside of their studies for months. Mothers of families, rushed from morning to night with many duties, look forward to the day when their burdens will be lighter and they can read. Men in a rush of business still subscribe to magazines, and look longingly at them as they pile up, hoping that by some chance they can get at them and do some reading. The reader is the one who wants to read and keeps on wanting to read. And he wants to do so because to him reading is the door to wider, fuller living.

How Does One "Get That Way"?

People who read very little or not at all constantly wonder at "readers." They see other people buried in a book or magazine. They see these "readers" in a hotel lobby, when the "normal person," as they would say, watches the people. They see these "readers" on buses or trains, when other people are looking out of the window or conversing. They see these "readers" sitting beside a reading light in the evening when other people are just talking with company or are playing cards. They see these "readers" in offices, filling in a lunch hour with a magazine or book. They ask wonderingly, "How does one get that way?"

Two reasons perhaps explain why some persons are readers, leaving out any inborn tendencies or influence. *One* reason is the *imitation of others.* Undoubtedly there is much of imitation about the origin of the lifetime reading habit. Children who come from a family of readers naturally consider that reading is a normal activity that all persons should indulge in. They consider that books and magazines are a normal part of home surroundings. They assume that a magazine table and a bookcase are parts of the furniture of all homes. Likewise, children so raised constantly see their parents immersed in books. The parents are obviously enjoying themselves with reading. So the child assumes that a lifetime reading habit is normal. The child expects to be a reader himself when he grows up.

Teachers and librarians work on this tendency to imitate. The teacher has books and magazines on her desk. She often speaks of her reading. She assumes that "one reads," and she lets the children know about her habits and feelings about books. If the school has a good library and an active librarian, more imitation takes place. Any child who goes into the library and meets a pleasant person there, surrounded with books, is bound to feel that it is natural to have books around and to read them. Seeing other children at the library tables "buried" in books has the same effect. Of course "one reads."

Much more powerful, however, is the *second* reason for becoming a reader, that is, *one's own personal experience with reading*. Here there are two factors, one's experience with learning how to read, and one's experiences with reading materials. If a child has difficulty learning how to read, that difficulty casts an unfavorable light on all reading. That is why we must be more successful than we have been in teaching reading. The second factor, reading materials, is perhaps more important. Does the material a child reads make him feel that books and reading open the way to new and interesting and exciting experiences?

Basic reading series have done a great deal to give children reading that will make them think of books as the way to interesting experiences. Experts in child development guide the making of those books. Those experts are most successful, so far, in the making of the primary books. The readers for the first three years seem to thrill children. The stories appeal to the children's imaginations and they open up excited discussion and thinking about new things to do and new places to go. Thus the primary books can be said to be good instruments to begin the lifetime reading habit.

We cannot say we are so successful, however, with materials for the middle and upper grades. We do try in those grades to stay close to child interest and to make reading remain a thrilling experience as it was to the younger children. But tradition brings in much material that is not suited and brings in school subjects which are not adapted as they might be to children's experiences. Our better readers tackle all this material with enthusiasm and success. Our average readers have their enthusiasm dampened. Our poor readers are definitely repelled.

We have elsewhere emphasized that one solution is to maintain all through these difficult years a "rapid reading period" when each child reads "on his interests at his level." Only such a period will carry many children through the middle and upper grades with the conviction that reading is a gateway into an exciting and interesting world. We have explained the whole situation on pages 355 and 356, but here we must reiterate that this "rapid reading period" is with many children an absolutely essential link in building a lifetime reading habit. And without that habit, the lifetime education of these children will not go on.

A final area of reading experience that may make the individual a lifetime reader is the entry into adult reading that comes in the high school years. That is the time to introduce each one to the reading resources of the adult world. We have emphasized the need of teaching how to read the newspaper so that the children may become aware of its stores of interest. We have pointed out the need to introduce children to the enormous number of magazines on all subjects and interests. We have urged that the choices of the book clubs be discussed, that the currently popular authors be made known to them.

In short, we have tried to impress that the school must orient the child to the reading world of adults. Unfortunately, it often does not do this. To many children, all the "good books" are old uninteresting books, and they think that all modern books are frowned on by the teachers and the school. They think that the interesting magazines are all comics, and that all the other magazines are dull stuff. They have not invested a lot of money in buying the magazines and therefore they have no way of knowing anything about them except the pictures on their covers. In short, the school reading world has not interested them, and the adult reading world they have never met. What condition could be more unfortunate for forming a good life reading habit?

Kinds of Life Reading Habits

Not all "habitual readers" read the same things. Not all adults look upon the same books and magazines as doorways to desired experiences. Here there are many differences and the school should have something to do with making or guiding these differences.

Escape Reading

Most of the lifetime reading that is done by most people is "escape reading." That is, they read to "get away from" the drab realities of life, to get away from the worries of the day, to get away from the disappointments of their individual existences. They use reading to get away into a more exciting world, a world that satisfies their unfulfilled longings, a world that is "closer to their heart's desire."

Some serious people condemn escape reading. They say it is a childish thing to dream of a more satisfying life, of being a more glamorous person, of succeeding in the imagination, and so on. They say "escape reading" is a drug. They think we should read to improve ourselves, to grapple with reality, to become wiser and better. Unfortunately, some of these persons are teachers, and they express to young people their condemnation of "mere" escape reading.

Wiser persons, however, including many psychologists, recommend escape reading as one of the ways to happiness. They point out that life can never fulfill the desires of most persons' inner being. Life is full of disappointments. Life is full of vexations and worries. How is this burden of disappointment, frustration, anxiety to be lifted? How, except by escape reading?

Of course, as always, there is a middle ground. If escape reading takes up all the time and prevents all other reading, it may become to that degree

harmful. There should be a place for serious reading. But this adjustment is one that depends on the
person and upon that person's life at the moment.
Many persons, when under stress and strain, have
to escape by the lightest and frothiest of reading.
These same persons, under happier circumstances,
do go to more serious material. Some individuals
especially need escape reading because of their temperament; other persons do not have the *same need
or do not have it in the same degree.* Before one
could give reading advice to anyone, he would need
to know about those two circumstances; first, the
temperament of the person he is advising, and second, the life circumstances of that person at the
time.

No particular guidance is needed for escape reading. If the individual has fluency at the proper level,
and if he wishes to find escape material, he will have
it all about him. It is on the magazine stands; it is
on the racks of pocket books; it is on the shelves of
the bookstores and libraries. There is plenty of it
of all kinds to suit every taste. The reader needs
only the time and the eyesight to pursue his escape
as far as he wishes.

Self-Discovery Reading

Much of what is called escape reading may also
be self-discovery reading. After all, reading is about
people. No matter what the story, it is about the
doings of men and women. And in those doings, the

drives and the needs of men and women appear, and their ways of fulfilling those drives and needs. All kinds of men and women appear in the stories, some of them like ourselves and some of them different. We are bound to identify ourselves more or less with the people in the stories, and in doing so, we learn something about our own drives and needs and motives. In fact, all reading which is about human beings and that is more or less true to human nature is also self-discovery reading.

A better kind of self-discovery reading is provided by the serious novels and stories of authors who are trying to find out and to tell us what men and women are really like. We do not mean "psychological novels" but novels with good psychology. Such novels are written, of course, by our better novelists, since only a sensitive, thoughtful author can show us human nature as it is.

In the school, the teacher can help direct children toward self-discovery reading by frankly showing how we learn about ourselves by reading about others. The books used in school are usually good for such purposes. The teacher can have the class discuss whether the people in the book are "real people" and if they represent the people we know. Then it is natural to discuss how the people in the book feel and why they do what they do, and say what they say. Thus we build up interest in human motives and actions. This interest will later on show itself in the life reading of the children. They may become interested in novels which tell more of human nature and tell it more truly. They will be set on the road to a habit of self-discovery reading.

SOCIAL CONSCIOUSNESS READING

A great deal of all the reading matter presented to adults, in books or magazines, deals with social problems, such as poverty, class distinctions, education, religion, and many others. Many adult readers definitely have the habit of choosing such reading matter. They find great stimulation in reading of the way the different authors attack such social problems, and they like to think of these problems and talk about them to their friends. They have a definite kind of life-reading habit.

So far, the school has had little to do with building up this life reading habit on social problem material. Perhaps this has been because teachers have not been too much interested in this kind of reading. Perhaps it has been that teachers have felt children were not interested in it. Perhaps the school has been restricted in its reading on social problems. Whatever the cause, the reading matter of the school has not so far been very social in its emphasis.

It is to be hoped, however, that as time goes on, the school may do more to develop social consciousness, especially through reading. Surely there are social problem books which can be read without arousing undesirable controversy. Some of these books are ones dealing with social problems of former generations, and these may lead to interest in social problems of the present. Some books can be read in some schools where they would not be accepted in others. At any rate, here is an area of lifetime reading interest that needs more attention if we wish to develop this interest in more people as time goes on.

World Discovery Reading

International affairs are driving home to all of us the importance of understanding of the world we live in. UNESCO and other agencies are trying to stimulate reading of all kinds of material dealing with world problems. These materials are, first, purely *descriptive*, telling us what other countries and their people are like. They are also *comparative*, showing the contrasts between life and peoples in different countries and regions. They are then *analytic* or *philosophic*, trying to find ways of getting all peoples together, to get over prejudices, to cause better understanding. All of these materials are appearing in all forms, in pamphlets, in magazines, in books.

Surely the school can do something to promote a lifetime reading habit of world-discovery. In the field of world problems, we are not in the controversial area of social domestic problems. We can get together better on what is to be read, and what we are to think about it. The first beginning perhaps is through the school newspapers for upper grades and high school which specialize in current events. These are full of world problems. They lead naturally to the reading of the newspaper, with its reports on the United Nations and other world efforts. Pamphlets are also available for school use on these subjects. The books are as yet on too difficult a level for children, but there is enough other material.

Development in this field is rapid, and shortly there will be some arrangement for special school time for world affairs. We can then secure more materials and devote more time to reading them and to discussing them. Teachers are being taken on international trips and thus being better prepared to lead such discussions. The plan of teacher exchanges has the same result. In fact, prospects are bright for securing a lifetime reading habit of world discovery.

SCIENCE LIFE READING HABIT

Great efforts are being put forth from many sources to develop in children and adults a science life reading habit. The schools begin by having science readers from the first grade on. The school newspapers feature science material, year after year. In high school, general science is being made a more and more attractive course. The fields of agriculture and of home economics are showing how science is applied to daily life. Science museums are publishing easy reading magazines for school children. All the world knows that the yearly advances of science are stupendous. Yet there does not seem to be much of a science life reading habit in the adult world.

This limitation of science life reading habit is shown by a survey of a magazine rack in any news-stand. Where is science? There is very little of it. There is a little of mechanics and mechanical work. There is more of aviation, which is a branch of applied science. There is something of farming, which is an applied science. But there is not much else. The same is true if one looks over the new books in a bookstore. There is very little on science as such. This in spite of the ever-recurring attempts to "popularize" science by special works on the subject. Perhaps we should be encouraged by the popularity of science fiction, but let us hope that such fiction leads to a reading of non-fiction in this field also.

Perhaps the problem in science reading is the overwhelming diversity and amount of material in the field. Perhaps the problem is the inevitable technicality of science. It may be that science reading requires just too much knowledge and study. At any rate, we do not seem to have the lifetime reading habit in science that we have in other fields. Perhaps the situation will change. Perhaps the school will give a better background for such reading. Let us hope so, if adults are to have a lifetime reading habit in science.

Reading for All, on Many Subjects, at Many Levels

In conclusion, let us repeat that the future of our people is essentially their educational future, and their educational future lies largely in their reading. Making all due allowances for radio, for television, for movies, for traveling, or what not, the chief educational possibility is in the reading of the millions of magazines and the thousands of books that are printed and put on the newsstands and in the bookstores and libraries each year.

All of these possibilities are possibilities only for those who are lifetime readers. Those with a lifetime reading habit will avail themselves of some of these reading and educational opportunities. They will inevitably grow in some way as a result. They will develop in understanding, in appreciations, and in personal worth.

The school should consider as one of its major duties and opportunities the development of a lifetime reading habit in every child. This may not mean the same kind of a lifetime reading habit, since children are different. But every child should think of some kind of reading matter as a doorway to new and interesting experience. We make him think this both by our example and by the experiences we cause him to have during the school years.

Summary

The culmination of reading development is a lifetime reading habit. The reading that we teach during the early years is to serve for all of the rest of life. During all of one's lifetime, reading is the most educative force. In fact, without it, no one can become fully educated.

What causes the individual to read during all of his life is the knowledge that reading is the open door to more living, and to more deeply satisfying living. Individuals become readers as a result, first, of imitation of others, and second, by having satisfying experiences with reading. This means a satisfying experience in the primary grades, through the middle and upper grades, and in high school, where the introduction to adult reading should be made.

A lifetime reading habit may be of various kinds. There is *escape reading,* to get away from the frustrations of daily life. There is *self-discovery* reading, to learn more of one's own desires and needs. There is *social-consciousness* reading, to become more familiar with the problems of our social life. There is *world discovery reading,* to become acquainted with the peoples of the world and their problems. There is *science reading,* to keep up with the developments of science in the world. But the important thing is that there must be reading for all, on many subjects, at many levels, so that through reading all can continue their education throughout life.

APPENDIX A

THE BASIC SIGHT VOCABULARY OF 220 WORDS
IN A SINGLE ALPHABET

a	can	go	laugh
about	carry	goes	let
after	clean	going	light
again	cold	good	like
all	come	got	little
always	could	green	live
am	cut	grow	long
an			look
and	did		
any	do	had	made
are	does	has	make
around	done	have	many
as	don't	he	may
ask	down	help	me
at	draw	her	much
ate	drink	here	must
away		him	my
	eat	his	myself
be	eight	hold	
because	every	hot	never
been		how	new
before	fall	hurt	no
best	far		not
better	fast	I	now
big	find	if	of
black	first	in	off
blue	five	into	old
both	fly	is	on
bring	for	it	once
brown	found	its	one
but	four		only
buy	from	jump	open
by	full	just	or
	funny		our
	gave	keep	out
call	get	kind	over
came	give	know	own

pick	sing	think	wash
play	sit	this	we
please	six	those	well
pretty	sleep	three	went
pull	small	to	were
put	so	today	what
	some	together	when
ran	soon	too	where
read	start	try	which
red	stop	two	white
ride			who
right	take	under	why
round	tell	up	will
run	ten	upon	wish
	thank	us	with
said	that	use	work
saw	the		would
say	their	very	write
see	them		
seven	then	walk	yellow
shall	there	want	yes
she	these	warm	you
show	they	was	your

These basic service words may be taught with the Basic Sight Vocabulary Cards or with the Group Word Teaching Game (both published by the Garrard Press, Champaign, Ill.; the cards for 50c and the game for 75c).

INDEX